K

Governance, Administration and Development

Also by Mark Turner and David Hulme

SOCIOLOGY AND DEVELOPMENT: Theory, Policy and Practice
(*D. Hulme and M. M. Turner*)

PAPUA NEW GUINEA: The Challenge of Independence
(*M. Turner*)

PROFILES OF GOVERNMENT ADMINISTRATION IN ASIA
(*M. Turner and J. Halligan*)

MINDANAO: Land of Unfulfilled Promise
(*M. Turner with R. J. May and L. R. Turner*)

REGIME CHANGE IN THE PHILIPPINES
(*M. Turner*)

MAKING A DIFFERENCE: NGOs and Development
(*D. Hulme and M. Edwards*)

NGO PERFORMANCE AND ACCOUNTABILITY: Beyond the Magic Bullet
(*D. Hulme and M. Edwards*)

NGOs, STATES AND DONORS: Too Close for Comfort?
(*D. Hulme and M. Edwards*)

FINANCE AGAINST POVERTY: Volumes 1 and 2
(*D. Hulme and P. Mosley*)

Governance, Administration and Development

Making the State Work

Mark Turner
University of Canberra

and

David Hulme
University of Manchester

First published 1997 by
MACMILLAN PRESS LTD
Houndmills, Basingstoke, Hampshire RG21 6XS
and London
Companies and representatives
throughout the world

ISBN 0–333–56752–8 hardcover
ISBN 0–333–56753–6 paperback

A catalogue record for this book is available
from the British Library.

10 9 8 7 6 5 4 3 2 1
06 05 04 03 02 01 00 99 98 97

Copy-edited and typeset by Povey–Edmondson
Tavistock and Rochdale, England

Printed in Hong Kong

Contents

v

List of Boxes and Tables

Boxes

ix

Tables

Preface

The idea for this book arose over the breakfast table in Canberra in 1990. At that time both of us had deep concerns about the ways in which the public sector in developing countries operates. However, we had even deeper concerns about the dominant policy agenda of that period, which focused on minimizing the role of the public sector, rolling back the state until it almost disappeared and which had just begun to naively decree 'good government' for all.

From our years working together at the Administrative College of Papua New Guinea – reinforced by research and consultancy in Asia, Africa and Latin America – we were well aware of just how difficult it is to improve the performance of bureaucracies. However, we were convinced, and remain convinced, that public sector activity can make a major contribution to the achievement of developmental goals and the creation of reasonably stable societies that can meet the material, social and, perhaps, spiritual needs of the bulk of their populaces. In part this was an analytical conclusion of our readings of East and Southeast Asian development and of the history of Western Europe. It was also grounded in our personal experiences – two Liverpudlians who had benefited from high-quality state education, a national health service free at the point of delivery and the knowledge that a public social security net underpinned our efforts to secure livelihoods and careers.

While elements of ideology no doubt support our belief that the public sector has a major role to play in development, neither of us are ideologues. The claims of the far left ('the state must do every-thing') and the far right ('the market can do everything') have always appeared fallacious to us. The 'either . . . or' analyses of most of the twentieth century must be replaced by 'both . . . and' in coming years. The big question is not 'public or private': rather it is, how do we get 'public and private' to most effectively meet social needs.

This book has been a long time in the writing, but fortunately as the decade has rolled on we have found that the simplistic 'private–good, public–bad' propositions that we heard in 1990 have been largely discredited. Policy debate about 'governance' still remains in its infancy, though, and none of the major international development agencies have yet found a way of relating their normative political models to the complex and very varied societies of the developing world.

Everything has a history, and many of the ideas and issues that we explore here were part of the debate about 'development administration' in the 1960s. From these roots the reader will find that s/he has a vast interdisciplinary range of concepts and analytical frameworks to explore. On one side is the development studies literature, with its web of economic, sociological and political ideas. On the other is the literature of management, grounded in organization sociology, psychology and business studies. We have tried to relate and bridge these literatures throughout the volume, and hope that we have achieved some success in this endeavour.

No book of this sort could be produced without the help and assistance of many other people. We name only a few here but our sincere thanks to all who have indirectly helped us in our task. First mention must go to our long-suffering publisher, Steven Kennedy. We have missed final deadline after final deadline, but never once has he let this spoil his good humour – sincere apologies Steven! In Canberra, our thanks to Sheila Wood for applying her multiple skills and technological expertise to the production of the manuscript. In Manchester our thanks to Debra Whitehead for processing the manuscript and Jayne Hindle for managing the lines of communication between Manchester and Canberra (and Dhaka and Nairobi, and Manila and Vientiane amongst others). Thanks also to Paul Mosley, now at the University of Reading, for tutoring David Hulme in the gentle art of academic overcommitment and helping him develop the confidence and energy to handle several writing tasks at one and the same time.

Colleagues and students at the Universities of Canberra and Manchester have contributed greatly to the evolution of the book, as have contacts with public servants, NGO staff and aid agency personnel in the many countries we have worked during the 1990s.

And last, but never least, our thanks to Lulu, Georgina, Andrew, Edward, Jasmine and Saffron for tolerating our absences and our preoccupation with governance and administration, as we struggled to find the time to write this book. We have all learnt that lawns do not need cutting!

DAVID HULME
Manchester

MARK TURNER
Canberra

Acknowledgements

The authors and publishers wish to thank the following for permission to reproduce copyright material: Arrow Publications for permission to quote from E. Duncan (1989) *Breaking the Curfew: A Political Journey through Pakistan* (Box 4.7); AusAID for permission to reproduce their project cycle diagram (Box 6.4); *Canberra Times* for permission to quote from the issue of 13 October 1991; CIPFA, P. Dunleavy and C. Hood for permission to quote from 'From Old Public Administration to New Public Management' (1994) *Public Money and Management*, July/Sept, pp. 9–16 (Box 10.4); Earthscan for permission to quote from J. Clark (1991) *Democratising Development: The Role of Voluntary Organisations* (Box 9.1); Elsevier Science Ltd for permission to quote from D. D. Gow and E. R. Morss (1988) 'The Notorious Nine: Critical Problems in Project Implementation', *World Development*, vol. 16(12), pp. 1399–418 (Box 3.4), J. W. Thomas and M. S. Grindle (1990) 'After the Decision: Implementing Policy Reforms in Developing Countries', *World Development*, vol. 18(8), p. 1165 (Box 3.5) and p. 1167 (Box 3.6), and M. Nellis and S. Kikeri (1989) 'Public Enterprise Reform: Privatisation and the World Bank', *World Development*, vol. 17(5), pp. 659–72; EROPA for permission to quote from M. R. Hayllar (1991) 'Accountability: Ends, Means and Resources', *Asian Review of Public Administration*, vol. 3(2), pp. 10–22; Guardian & Observer News Services for permission to quote from W. Sachs (1992) 'Development: A Guide to the Ruins', *New Internationalist*, June, pp. 4–6 (Box 1.1); Addison Wesley Longman for permission to quote from R. Chambers (1983) *Rural Development: Putting the Last First* (Box 1.1); Marcel Dekker Publishers for permission to quote from A. Farazmand (1991) *Handbook of Comparative Development Administration* (Box 4.6); Monthly Review Foundation for permission to quote from H. Alavi and T. Shanin (1982) *Introduction to the Sociology of 'Developing' Societies* (Box 1.1); Oxford University Press for permission to quote from J. K. Nyerere (1966) *Freedom and Unity* (Box 1.1), G. M. Meier and D. Sears (1984) *Pioneers in Development* (Box 1.1), World

Bank (1993) *The East Asian Miracle: Economic Growth and Public Policy* (Box 3.3), World Bank (1995) *Bureaucrats in Business: The Economics and Politics of Government Ownership* (Boxes 8.1, 8.3, 8.4 and 8.8), World Bank (1994) *World Development Report 1994* (Box 8.5), and J. Boston, J. Martin, J. Pallot and P. Walsh (1996) *Public Management: The New Zealand Model* (Box 10.3); Penguin for permission to quote from A. G. Frank (1971) *Capitalism and Underdevelopment in Latin America* (Box 1.1), and W. Bello and S. Rosenfeld (1992) *Dragons in Distress: Asia's Miracle Economies in Crisis* (Box 3.2); Prentice-Hall for permission to quote from W. Moore (1963) *Social Change* (Box 1.1); Routledge for permission to quote from J. Farrington and A. Bebbington (1993) *Non-Governmental Organisations, the State and Sustainable Agricultural Development* (Boxes 9.3, 9.4 and 9.5), and D. A. Rondinelli (1993) *Development Projects vs Policy Experiments: An Adaptive Approach to Development Administration* (Table 6.1); Sage Publications for permission to quote from D. A. Rondinelli (1992) 'UNDP Assistance for Urban Development', *International Review of Administrative Sciences*, vol. 58(4), pp. 519–37, and W. E. Bjur and A. Zomorrodian (1986) 'Towards Indigenous Theories of Administration', *International Review of Administrative Sciences*, vol. 52(4), p. 406; The World Bank for permission to quote from B. Nunberg and J. Ellis (1990) 'Civil Service Reform and the World Bank', *Policy Research and External Affairs Working Paper* No. 422 (Box 5.3), J. van der Gaag (1995) *Private and Public Initiatives: Working Together for Health and Education* (Box 5.4), G. Lamb and R. Weaving (1992) *Managing Policy Reforms in the Real World* (Box 8.2), and International Finance Corporation (1995) *Privatisation: Principles and Practice*. Every effort has been made to contact all the copyright-holders, but if any have been inadvertently omitted the publishers will be pleased to make the necessary arrangement at the earliest opportunity.

To our wives and children –
for their tolerance and good
humour when we retreat to
our studies!

1

Development and its Administration

The decades since the end of World War Two have witnessed an unrivalled drive for economic and social development by the majority of the world's nations. The leaders of these countries (often referred to as the Third World) have exhorted their citizens to strive for development and have formulated policies and implemented programmes towards this end. However, the achievement of development goals in a short time has proved elusive for all except a small number of 'tigers' in East Asia. Many processes and factors have been identified as contributing to the differing levels of achievement, and prominent amongst these has been the argument that public sector organizations have often performed poorly. They have failed to provide politicians with sound advice on policy, have taken on inappropriate roles and have been both inefficient and corrupt. Less commonly heard but of equal significance is the argument that countries that have experienced rapid sustained development – South Korea, Taiwan, Singapore, Thailand and Malaysia – have had effective public sector organizations.

It seems that all are agreed on the proposition that the nature and performance of public sector organizations are critical elements in determining developmental success. It is this topic that is the focus of our present work. In this book we seek to:

• explore the complex and diverse context of development and public sector organizations both in terms of intellectual history and through more conventional environmental factors of an economic, social, demographic and political nature;

1

- analyse the ways in which public sector organizations influence development policies and programmes and the effects this has on results achieved;
- identify and discuss the appropriateness of approaches for improving the contribution that the public sector makes to development; and
- contest the dominant ideology of the last decade – 'public–bad, private–good' – that has argued for minimising the role of public sector organizations in development.

We do not claim that public sector organizations and processes are not in need of reform. Far from it – there is ample evidence of dysfunctional bureaucracies avidly devouring scarce resources but failing to produce anticipated outcomes. It is not difficult to find policies that serve to keep illegitimate governments in office rather than attending to the business of strengthening the economy and improving welfare for the poor. There has been considerable criticism of official aid agencies that give or lend money for projects that bring limited gains to target populations. There are instances where improvements have proved unsustainable due to lack of budgetary foresight, excessive reliance on footloose experts and preoccupation with prestige rather than with solid but unspectacular gains. Many initiatives have foundered on poor management, inappropriate planning and an unwillingness to involve the beneficiaries in the organization of changes that will affect their lives.

These negative views of development and its administration have become more common but there are positive experiences that give cause for cautious optimism in some contexts (for example, Caiden and Kim, 1991; Korten and Siy, 1988). These contrasting positions can be best appreciated with reference to several of this book's underlying assumptions and themes. First, the organizational aspects of development cannot be reduced to a technical fix. Metaphors which liken organizations to machines can be extremely misleading as they suggest that changing a spark plug or adding a transformer are somehow equivalent to selecting a new departmental secretary or re-orienting a staff development and training section. Management systems, administrative techniques and organizational designs are not neutral value-free phenomena. Thus, administrative reform and innovation are not simply a matter of installing some piece of managerial technology which has proved effective elsewhere. There are no universal principles of management and no universal management tool kits.

The second theme concerns the importance of organizational environments, that envelope of factors and forces in which organizations operate. Although the air-conditioned, high-rise accommodation of public service agencies in some developing countries may appear to divorce them from society, organizations are not closed technical systems. They are necessarily involved in multiple relationships with other organizations and individuals. Complex webs of relationships are thus woven and have profound effects on the operation of organizations. There are also social and economic forces which impact on organizational activity. For example, declining exchange rates and falling commodity prices will mean reduced government income and will exert severe pressure on public service budgets. National culture may be a key determinant of the way in which activities are conducted and may influence operational norms and practices as much as the public service manual of procedures. And the influence is unlikely to be one way. Organizations are not simply acted upon but can also influence their environments. The whole purpose of development, and organizations that are there to promote it, is in fact to alter environments in ways that are beneficial to target populations.

The third theme emphasizes one aspect of the administrative environment, that is the importance of political considerations in administrative analysis and practice. Organizational action takes place in political contexts. Power and authority permeate relationships between organizational members and between these persons and those in the external environment. The range of patterns and possibilities is enormous and is reflected in a wide diversity of practice. Technical rationality will frequently be a poor guide to decisions and behaviour. The explanations of particular policy choices, planning decisions, implementation difficulties, and un-learned lessons of evaluation will be found in political analysis. If, for example, we wish to comprehend why rural organizations for the poor have often failed we need to understand the political landscape in which those organizations attempt to operate. Society, state and organizations are enmeshed in political relationships. Competition over resource control and allocation is ubiquitous and for the analyst, practitioner and potential beneficiary alike the map of power and authority is an essential aid, more useful than the latest scientific planning tool.

The fourth theme flows from the environmental issues. It is that organizational improvement is not a panacea for development. Development is multi-faceted and success or failure are based on more than organizational design, administrative reform or human resource management. Such items have a strong bearing on whether developmental progress will occur but they are never the sole determinants. As Bernard Schaffer (1969, p. 202) observed more than two decades ago, 'The whole lesson is that development administration works only in conjunction with other factors of change'. Furthermore, public sector organizations can be utilized to oppress or to defend the privileges of certain classes and groups in society. They are not innately benign but must be directed towards the attainment of developmental goals. But what is development?

Development

Since the Second World War, development has been synonymous with economic, social and political change in the countries of Africa, Asia, Latin America, the Caribbean and the South Pacific. These countries have been variously labelled as underdeveloped, less-developed, developing, the Third World and the South. They are a diverse group but united in their commonly declared commitment to development. But there is no consensus about the meaning of development. It is a contested concept and there have been a number of battles to capture its meaning. In this section we review these ideological engagements (see Box 1.1 for a range of meanings – can you identify which meaning in the box belongs to which theoretical perspective outlined below?).

Until the end of the 1960s the modernization perspective on development held sway. Development was seen as an evolutionary process in which countries progressed through an identified series of stages to become modern. The form of the future did not require the imagination and speculation evident in earlier evolutionary theorists such as Marx, Durkheim and Weber. The future for the developing countries was already in existence and could be seen in the form of the advanced Western societies, most especially the USA (for example, Moore, 1963). The means of getting there was also clearly delineated. The tools of scientific planning would enable the 'underdeveloped' nations to escape from this undesirable status and become fully

BOX 1.1
Competing meanings of development

- 'Modernization is a "total" transformation of a traditional or pre-modern society into the types of technology and associated social organization that characterize the "advanced" economically prosperous and politically stable nations of the Western World.'   (Moore, 1963, p. 89)

- 'The questions to ask about a country's development are three: What has been happening to poverty? What has been happening to unemployment? What has been happening to inequality? If all three of these have declined from high levels, then beyond doubt this has been a period of development for the country concerned.'   (Seers, 1977, p. 3)

- '. . . these capitalist contradictions and the historical development of the capitalist system have generated underdevelopment in the peripheral satellites whose economic surplus was expropriated, while generating economic development in the metropolitan centres which appropriate that surplus – and, further, that this process still continues'.
                                            (Frank, 1971, p. 27)

- 'In much of the preceding discussion we have in fact referred to the struggle among three contending "fundamental classes," [indigenous bourgeoisie, metropolitan bourgeoisie and landowning classes] which seek various forms of representation in the state and vie with each other to direct the formulation and implementation of public policy along lines that serve their particular class interests.'   (Alavi, 1982, p. 305)

- 'We in Africa, have no more need of being "converted" to socialism than we have of being "taught" democracy. Both are rooted in our past – in the traditional society which produced us. Modern African socialism can draw from its traditional heritage, the recognition of "society" as an extension of the basic family unit.'   (Nyerere, 1966, p. 170)

- 'What happened [*i.e. economic development*] was in very large measure the result of the individual voluntary responses of millions of people to emerging or expanding opportunities created largely by external contacts and brought to their notice in a variety of ways, primarily through the operation of the market. These developments were made possible by firm but limited government, without large expenditures of public funds and without the receipt of large external subventions.'   (Bauer, 1984, p. 31)

- 'Rural development is a strategy to enable a specific group of people, poor rural women and men, to gain for themselves and their children more of what they want and need. It involves helping the poorest among those who seek a livelihood in the rural areas to demand and control more of the benefits of development.'   (Chambers, 1983, p. 147)

- 'Development always entails looking at other worlds in terms of what they lack, and obstructs the wealth of indigenous alternatives.'
                                            (Sachs, 1992, p. 6).

modern in a few decades. This faith in rational planning was exported to newly independent nations and eagerly absorbed and broadcast by élites and dominant classes.

This ideology of development was at once optimistic and ethnocentric. It was optimistic in assuming that the 'problems' of underdevelopment such as poverty, inadequate social services and low levels of industrial production were amenable to straightforward solution by the application of rational management techniques. It was ethnocentric in that modernity was perceived as being Western and that Western technology, institutions, modes of production and values were both superior and desirable.

The approach was also heavily oriented to economic growth as the driving force. Changes in social and political institutions would simultaneously contribute to economic growth and be inevitable companions to and outcomes of such growth. Results did not match expectations. By the late 1960s, there was increased poverty, growing indebtedness, political repression, economic stagnation and a host of other ills. Development needed rethinking, and it came both in liberal reformulations and in more dramatic form through various neo-Marxist interpretations.

The liberal reformulations questioned the meaning attached to development and proposed new definitions which lessened the role of economic growth. Authentic development was seen as progress towards a complex of welfare goals such as the elimination of poverty, the provision of employment, the reduction of inequality and the guarantee of human rights. The changed definition had practical implications summed up in slogans such as 'redistribution with growth', in policies such as 'the basic needs approach', and in planning packages such as 'integrated rural development'. As the biggest provider of developmental aid and as a leading think-tank on development practice, the World Bank was often viewed as the leading agency promoting such liberal reformulation. Its critics alleged it paid lip-service to the new objectives or that they were unattainable in the prevailing global context.

The neo-Marxists did not dispute the changed emphasis in the meaning of development. They disputed whether it could be achieved. Why had countries in the Third World largely failed to make the transition to fully developed capitalist economies? They rejected the modernization school's explanations concerning the tenacity of tradition and institutional shortcomings and looked to historically grounded analysis of political economy.

One group, called the dependency school, argued that the global economic structure was an exploitative system which generated and maintained 'the development of underdevelopment' in nations of the periphery (for example, Frank, 1971; Sweezy, 1982; Wallerstein, 1979; Amin, 1976). The nations of the core had since the advent of a world economy in the late fifteenth and early sixteenth centuries enforced a system of inequitable domination on the periphery through such techniques as conquest, threat, market restriction and industrial protection. Such tactics enabled strong states to perpetuate the weakness of the peripheral states. Development could only occur through radical solutions which altered relationships in the world economy. Suggested actions included development programmes which emphasized self-sufficiency, substantial even total de-linking from the world economy and socialist revolution. The meaning of development was not under challenge just the means. Indeed, many of the neo-Marxist writers were more production-oriented than their liberal counterparts.

Other neo-Marxists, while accepting the usefulness of the concept of the world capitalist system, were concerned about 'simple reductionism [that] can remove from history all its ambiguities, conjectures and surprises' (Cardoso, 1977, p. 21). They looked at the variety of experience – the rise of the newly-industrializing countries such as Singapore and South Korea compared with stagnant GNPs, political instability and immiseration in certain African nations. Could one overarching theory explain such massive differences? Such diversity demanded closer attention to detail, in-depth studies on a smaller scale with less theoretical ambition. In order to achieve this, many authors employed the notions of mode of production and social class as their major analytical tools. They selected particular countries or regions and looked at the specific ways in which different modes of production (for example, pre-capitalist and capitalist) were 'articulated' to make distinctive social formations. They traced the historical development of social classes. It was admitted that some development was possible in peripheral societies but the benefits were restricted to dominant classes and their allies. Nobody suggested any possibility for autonomous development in the prevailing world economy. The metropolitan bourgeoisie was always lurking in the background able to determine the structural constraints within which any development would take place and to whom the benefits would flow.

While obviously different in many respects, the modernization and neo-Marxist approaches to development do share some fundamental similarities. Harrison (1988, pp. 151–2) observes that both derive from European experience and have been formulated by intellectuals, planners and politicians who have been socialized into this tradition. Both have visions of before (traditional or pre-capitalist society) and after (the modern capitalist society or the idealized socialist society) with an intermediate stage which is what exists now. Finally, neither perspective has ascribed much importance to the 'views, wants, ambitions and wishes of those about to be developed'.

Such views are allegedly incorporated into neo-populist types of thinking although even here one can find evidence of populist ideology being imposed from above or from outside on people who are passively mobilized or who actively oppose their own mobilization. Neo-populists are the creators of 'alternative development strategies' which Kitching (1982, p. 98) characterizes as focusing on 'small-scale enterprises, on the retention of a peasant agriculture and of non-agricultural petty commodity production and on a world of villages and small towns rather than industrial cities'. Equity considerations are always prominent. The neo-populists thus perceive a different meaning to development than both modernization and neo-Marxist theorists, and in the new populist forms means and ends frequently overlap and are sometimes identical.

Julius Nyerere's attempt to establish a revitalized and improved authentic African socialism in Tanzania in the 1960s and 1970s is a good example of neo-populism in action. Nyerere believed that pre-colonial Africa was socialist with families living according to the basic principles of *ujamaa* – mutual respect, sharing of property and income, and the obligation to work. The colonial and post-colonial orders had distorted economy and society. What was needed, Nyerere argued, was a reactivation of these important *ujamaa* principles of socio-economic and political organization with a few modern improvements, such as attention to the subordinate position of women and the eradication of poverty. The new social order would be comprised of villages consuming and producing cooperatively, with any industrialization being labour-intensive, technologically appropriate and geographically dispersed. Increasing production was seen as important but was overshadowed by emphasis on equity in distribution. Unfortunately, the results were not as predicted by the theory. Economic growth was disappointing, the public sector expanded but gave poor service, and there was peasant opposition to forced 'villagization' and communal agriculture.

Other neo-populists could include E.F. Schumacher (1973) and his famous advocacy of 'small is beautiful', Michael Lipton (1977) and his critique of the urban bias in development or Bernard Narokobi (1983) and his rejection of Westernization and promotion of indigenous cultural values, 'the Melanesian Way', as the guide to true development for Papua New Guinea and other Pacific island peoples. There are ecodevelopers, so called because of their belief in 'an ecologically sound development' (Glaeser and Vyasulu, 1984, p. 23) necessary to save the planet and its people from impending, self-induced, environmental doom.

Much of today's attack on developmental orthodoxy derives from the neo-populist tradition. It is forcefully articulated by spokespersons for NGOs and others disenchanted with what they regard as the dismal record of development. They make direct links between the negative effects of so-called development and crises affecting the world, notably arms proliferation, environmental disaster, the persistence of poverty and the repression of human rights. They see previous explanations of both modernization and neo-Marxist variety as deficient and identify leading villains as the state, dominant social classes and the World Bank. Aided by allies in the economically prosperous countries, these villains are accused of peddling developmentalism, an ideology which 'defines the principal social objectives of all countries as consumption and accumulation' (Ekins, 1992, p. 205).

For Wolfgang Sachs (1992, p. 4), 'development stands like a ruin in the intellectual landscape . . . the outdated monument to an immodest era'. It has become a shapeless word denoting a concept of no content, which functions to legitimize planned interventions to solve the latest problem or crisis evident in the so-called developing world – and all in the name of a higher evolutionary goal. Similarly, Bayart (1991, p. 52) berates development as a 'disastrous notion', one built on colonial fantasy and possibly with roots in an even older philosophical tradition.

Such radical views of development have been supplemented by critiques from neo-classical economists who derive their intellectual inspiration from a very different source. They are hardly ideological bedfellows with the neo-populists but they do share a strong dislike of government intervention and past development strategies. Collectively identified as the 'counter-revolutionaries' by Toye (1987) the neo-classicists have advocated policies restricting state intervention in

the economy and society. They point to inefficiency and ineffectiveness in planned development and celebrate the optimal resource
allocation which reliance on the market allegedly provides. It is to
define the practice of development for which they have been compet-·
ing, and they have found a sympathetic audience in official multilateral and bilateral aid agencies. For some of the counter-
revolutionaries the Third World is in fact a creation of foreign aid
(Bauer, 1981, p. 87).

As our brief and selective survey of 'what is development?' has
shown, there has been considerable debate over the definition,
explanation and practice of development. This struggle over meaning
is intense today. It is not a discrete semantic debate conducted by
academics but has a direct impact on the lives of billions of people.
The struggle over meaning relates to critical policy matters such as
what actions will be taken to alleviate poverty, who will have access
to what resources, and who will be empowered? The intensity of the
debate reflects a widespread disillusionment with the results of
development after four decades of practice and can be seen as a
political battle to determine the nature of future practice.

We agree with Goulet (1992, p. 470) that development is 'a two-
edged sword which brings benefits, but also produces losses and
generates value conflicts'. In the benefit column Goulet lists clear
improvements in material well-being. Examination of the statistics in
the World Bank's annual *World Development Report* bears out this
assertion. He also notes technological gains which relieve people from
burdensome physical tasks, institutional specialization, increased
freedom of choice, a higher degree of tolerance and greater worldwide
interdependence. Such gains will be felt differentially according to
who you are and where you live, and according to the values one
places on the meaning of development you may not feel they are gains
at all.

There have been severe losses, misguided interventions and poor
results in development practice – and one does not have to be a neo-
classicist or radical neo-populist to appreciate this. It is unfortunately
easy to identify the persistence of poverty (over 1 billion according to
the World Bank in 1990), environmental crises, war and social
dislocation, and unequal relations between nations. Differential
developmental success between nations (compare the records of
Singapore and Taiwan with those of Malawi and the Philippines)
can hardly escape attention, and even within nations micro success
may contrast with macro failure and vice versa. Goulet's list of losses

is less conventional but equally important. He focuses on the destruction of culture and community and the rise of acquisitive personal orientations. There is pervasive social alienation produced in the turmoil of development and 'the meaning systems of numerous cultural communities are evacuated' (p. 471).

Development requires rethinking and renewal. It has been done before and should be a constant process. As critics point out, development has often degenerated into mere rhetoric in which admirable official goals, such as the satisfaction of basic needs, job provision and better social services, are supplanted by operational goals which focus on debt-servicing, crisis-management and defence of privilege. But this does not mean that the concept of development should be discarded, rather that it should be rejuvenated. It should be subject to critique and there should be efforts to make official and operational goals coincide. There should also be a clear appreciation that any definition will be value-laden, a product of personal preferences and that there will never be universal agreement on a single meaning and policy package. However, we believe that approaches such as the following do hold out hope for the future and capture the multi-dimensional nature of development and the importance of ethics and wisdom in determining what it should be (see Box 1.2).

BOX 1.2

Defining development today

The first 5 points of the following definition of what constitutes development were the outcome of a 1986 seminar at the Marga Institute, Colombo, Sri Lanka. The authors have added the last item, perhaps indicative of their values.

- An economic component dealing with the creation of wealth and improved conditions of material life, equitably distributed;
- A social ingredient measured as well-being in health, education, housing and employment;
- A political dimension including such values as human rights, political freedom, enfranchisement, and some form of democracy;
- A cultural dimension in recognition of the fact that cultures confer identity and self-worth to people;
- The full-life paradigm, which refers to meaning systems, symbols, and beliefs concerning the ultimate meaning of life and history; and
- A commitment to ecologically sound and sustainable development so that the present generation does not undermine the position of future generations.

Source: Modified from Goulet, D. (1992) 'Development: Creator and Destroyer of Values', *World Development*, vol. 20(3), pp. 467–75.

Development administration

With the invention of development by the Western nations in the immediate post-war period and its adoption as state ideology by the governments and emerging élites of the poorer nations, the question arose as to how the promised social transformation was to be achieved. 'The primary obstacles to development are administrative rather than economic', declared Donald Stone (1965, p. 53). Others agreed and development administration was created to play a major role in facilitating development.

Development administration represented the practical application of modernization theory. Its promoters saw it as 'a midwife for Western development – creating stable and orderly change' (Dwivedi and Nef, 1982, p. 62). It was a form of social engineering imported from the West and embodying faith in the application of rational scientific principles and the efficacy of Keynesian welfare economics. In its early days at least, it reflected the naive optimism and ethnocentricity of modernization theory, that there were straightforward technical solutions for underdevelopment and the West possessed them. It was also perceived by the US government and some of its practitioners as an integral element of the Cold War. Development administration would wage an unarmed managerial struggle against communism in the underdeveloped nations by engineering the transformation to capitalist modernity and the good life.

Development administration was a US-led movement with funds and personnel for its study and practice coming largely from US sources. Schaffer (1969, p. 179) reports some British suspicion, with people there perhaps seeing it as an attack on the colonial record or believing that it was something already familiar. But an international orthodoxy emerged that there were important differences between public administration in poor countries and in high-income countries. The distinguishing element was that in the developing countries there was 'that inconvenient combination: extensive needs, low capacities, severe obstacles' (*ibid.*, p. 184).

While the modernization perspective did not entail a monolithic approach to development administration several generalizations can be made. First, it was based on the notion of big government 'as the beneficent instrument of an expanding economy and an increasingly just society' (Esman, 1988, p. 125). Development administration was synonymous with public administration which itself was synonymous with bureaucracy. Second, there was an élitist bias. An enlightened minority, such as politicians and planners, would be committed to transforming their societies into replicas of the modern Western nation-state. They would establish themselves in urban centres and using bureaucracy as their principal instrumentality would spread the benefits to the rural areas. Third, development administration would tackle head on the 'lack [of] administrative capability for implementing plans and programmes [through] the transfer of administrative techniques to improve the central machinery of national government' (Stone, 1965, p. 53). Development administration was thus perceived as the transfer and application of a bag of tools. Fourth, foreign aid was the mechanism by which the missing tools of public administration would be transferred from the West to the developing countries. Fifth, culture was early recognized as an impediment to the smooth functioning of Western tools and dominant Weberian models of bureaucracy. Development administration had to overcome such cultural obstacles which were seen as the sources of bureaucratic dysfunctions.

The management theory which supported this approach was drawn from the Classical School (see Box 1.3 for a brief chronology of major approaches to management). This was the world of the 'scientific manager' (Taylor, 1911), of 'principles' of administration (Fayol, 1949) and the 'ideal-type' bureaucratic form of organization (Gerth and Mills, 1948). This approach to organizing public services retained its dominance in developing countries while being usurped or at least supplemented by newer theories in the West. For example, in the 1960s and 1970s the revitalization of the Human Relations school which stressed motivation, leadership and non-hierarchical forms had little effect on the bureaucratic model in developing countries (for example, Argyris, 1957; Bennis, 1966). Even participatory development initiatives, such as the community development movement, ended up being bureaucratized.

The attacks on modernization theory in the late 1960s and 1970s were parallelled by challenges to development administration. On the financial front, US funding for public administration projects declined rapidly and sharply after 1967 as did academic spending. The blame for poor developmental performance was in large part attributed to a failure of development administration, and development experts and institutions looked for new solutions. According to Siffin (1976, p. 66) there was a shift towards 'more complex and more economically oriented problem perspectives'. Also, people began to question the assumption that big government was the route to

---

BOX 1.3

A brief chronology of management thought

In contemporary development administration are found strands from many schools of management thought. Most approaches originated in the private sector and have been absorbed only slowly into the mainstream of development administration where, until recently, Classical theory and practice maintained a tenacious hold.

Approach	Date	Selected Features
Classical	1900	Organizations perceived as closed systems; stress on efficiency, control and the bureaucratic form
Behavioural/ Human Relations	1930	Emphasis on people rather than machines; close attention to factors such as group dynamics, communication, motivation leadership and participation
Quantitative	1940	Provision of quantitative tools to support managerial decision-making; found in management science, operational management and management information systems
Open Systems/ Contingency	1965	Organizations seen as systems of interrelated parts which relate to the environment; emphasis on 'fitting' organizational structure to the specific environment of the organization
Power/Politics	1965	Organizational decision-making is not guided by technical rationality but is determined by political processes; a dominant coalition will be the major locus of organizational power
Quality Movement	1955	Strongly pursued in Japanese postwar industrial development and much later adopted elsewhere; continuous improvement by working together and client focus; typified in total quality management, benchmarking, quality circles and ISO 9000
Managerialism	1980	Adoption by the public sector of private sector management practices; application of public choice theory and neo-classical economics to public sector management

---

development, a theme which gathered great momentum and power in the 1980s. In the West, this was the period which saw open systems and contingency theories of management become the dominant paradigm (for example, Lawrence and Lorsch, 1967). These theories argued that there were multiple ways of organizing and that the chosen option depended on the situation. The environment was elevated to an extremely important position in these theories and the principal task of managers was to fit organizational sub-systems to those of the environment. Despite these profound shifts in Western management theory, the closed systems of Classical Management theory still maintained strong practical support in developing countries.

Academics had entered a period of self-criticism, reflection and uncertainty about development administration. Schaffer (1969) pointed to a 'deadlock' in development administration and raised questions about whether bureaucracy could bring about societal transformation. Bureaucracy was, after all, dedicated to incrementalism and was characteristically inefficient. A symposium in *Public Administration Review* (1976) featured much criticism of previous ideas. Evolutionary models were discarded; the Western values imported with the administrative tools were exposed and judged inappropriate; and the nature of culture and its relation to administration was questioned. Siffin (1976) in reviewing development administration in the period 1955–75 wrote of a 'costly learning' experience both for recipients and disseminators. Among other things he noted that the administrative technology transfer had aimed more at 'maintenance' needs rather than 'developmental' needs; that mechanistic views of organizations focusing on technical expertise and 'purposive objectivity', although instrumentally important, were not the 'crucial creative levers of development'; and that public administration training and scholarship in developing countries had been emulative of the West rather than innovative.

Meanwhile the neo-Marxist assault on modernization theory identified development administration as a device to legitimate and promote the interests of the bureaucratic bourgeoisie (that is, top bureaucrats) and other dominant classes and/or élites. It was both an ideological prop and practical tool in perpetuating inequitable relations between classes. The technology of administration could not unilaterally promote the beneficial changes delineated in the meaning of development. Radical alterations in power structure were necessary before administration could be employed to such a purpose.

There was an obvious impasse for development administration in this thinking. Administration was not an independent variable. It could only be a facilitator of development under a radically different political order.

Class interests were an important explanatory variable for David Hirschmann (1981) in his commentary on the disappointing results of more than two decades of development administration in Africa. Like Schaffer, he also described a 'deadlock' but Hirschmann's deadlock moved beyond the inward-looking reflections of an intellectually unsure sub-discipline. He acknowledged that there had been many innovative and imaginative ideas in development administration but that they had been frequently ignored by leading African administrators. Why? The answer, said Hirschmann, was that bureaucrats focused on defending their class interests which put them in conflict with the majority of the population. Common development administration ideas such as less-stratified organizations with strong client orientation could be seen as revolutionary threats by the bureaucratic defenders of the status quo. Hirschmann was providing a social class version of the power-politics theories of management which had been advocated from the late 1960s onwards but surprisingly little used in development administration. These theories explained managerial decision-making in terms of the power of the 'dominant coalition' within organizations (Thompson, 1967) and argued that while organizational contingencies may constrain management decisions they did not determine them. In fact, managers had some latitude to make 'strategic choices' (Child, 1972).

Dwivedi and Nef (1982) went beyond 'deadlock' and asserted that development administration was in 'crisis'. Using a dependency-style framework they argued that development administration had been a 'dismal failure' responsible for 'anti-development', bureaucratic authoritarianism and seemingly everything that was wrong with development. While their case seems overstated and highly conspiratorial, they do raise a range of important and challenging issues. They claimed to move development administration well beyond its modernization origins and its focus on 'the manageability of the administrative structure' and face up directly to the 'incompatibility between bureaucracy, as a form of institutionalized social control, and development defined as quality of life for the population' (p. 65). However, Fred Riggs had been attempting to get a similar message accepted for almost two decades (Riggs, 1964) and, as we have already seen, environment-oriented open systems and contingency approaches had already become the dominant paradigm for general management in the West while power-politics models enjoyed growing support.

The environment in which administration is practised and the origins and maintenance of its ideological support are always in evidence in Dwivedi and Nef's article. These considerations had, by necessity, been creeping into work on development administration as the 'administration as neutral technology' paradigm had become increasingly discredited and the importance of politics in administrative analysis and action had become ever more obvious. The most important difference between administration in developing countries and in the West was being increasingly identified as that envelope of factors and forces which we collectively call the organizational environment. Whether it was the social class context, the influence of the World Bank, the type of regime, the nature of the policy-making process or simply the prevailing culture, the centrality of the environment for understanding administrative action and paralysis was becoming firmly established. There was, however, an obvious lag in development administration between the generation and dissemination of environmentally-oriented management theories and their widespread acceptance and application.

A second development forcefully advocated by Dwivedi and Nef (1982) was the search for alternative forms of organizational approach to development. Instead of simply criticising the failures, people began to look at the successes and innovations. What had the experience of indigenous experiments in China, Guinea-Bissau, Tanzania and Libya taught us? What had populist approaches to offer? Why had some organizations in Thailand, India, Sri Lanka and Bangladesh produced excellent development outcomes and considerable organizational growth (Korten, 1980) while others had not? Were these experiences replicable or were there principles of organizational design that could be easily modified according to changes in organizational environment? Rondinelli (1983) was keen to identify lessons from past experience that could enhance development administration in the future. His analysis indicated that the main reason for poor past performance in the public sector was the failure to cope with the complexity and uncertainty of organizational environments in developing countries. The remedy lay in changing structures and procedures so that experimentation and learning occurred. This creative hybrid comprises a human-relations type of management theory coupled with a contingency-style acknowledgment of highly variable environmental conditions, including the political environment.

The neo-classical economists had meanwhile gained considerable influence in policy circles and were also pointing to inefficiency and ineffectiveness in the public sector. While they agreed with Rondinelli's notion of experimentation they also recommended that the state should be 'rolled back'. Big government had not been effective government and it was time the principles of the market were allowed to operate. Reducing the size of the state and restricting the operations of the state would bring considerable savings. Programmes to increase bureaucratic capacity and efficiency and to encourage private sector growth through market mechanisms would then ensure that development would take place.

This radical and highly influential approach to administration and governance in developing countries was already in full swing in countries like the UK, Australia and the USA. Its intellectual origins lay in public choice theory (for example, Ostrom and Ostrom, 1971; Baker, 1976). In practical terms it encouraged 'managerialism' or the 'new public management' which drew heavily on the innovations and trends in private sector management (Pollitt, 1993; Zifcak, 1994). The old distinction between public sector and private sector management became blurred. The dissemination of this model to developing countries was undertaken by enthusiastic Western advocates and influential multilateral financial institutions such as the World Bank and IMF. In a remarkably short space of time it assumed orthodoxy in mainstream development administration although it is still tempered by the persistence of Classical Management orientations and critiques from those who have a more human-relations orientation to development.

Although there was some delay in the export of the new public management model to developing countries, subsequent efforts have ensured a rapid transfer once the process started. The lag which has characterized this transfer process until now has been greatly reduced and developing countries now have access to the latest ideas in management, most often drawn from the West or Japan (for example, the quality movement). Being up-to-date in global management trends has both advantages and pitfalls. It alerts people to the bewildering, exciting and potentially useful range of options available but it also opens up developing countries to experiments with techniques and practices which are totally inappropriate for their particular environments. The strongest voices are also often the richest and most powerful which means that South–South flows of ideas run the risk of being overwhelmed by North–South flows thus leading to the loss of some potentially valuable knowledge and experience.

Although the new public management did attempt to colonize development administration with a somewhat standardized approach, in the late 1980s development administration was emerging from self-criticism and doubt and was acquiring a new lease of life. The post-mortem on modernization approaches, the shock treatment of neo-Marxist theorizing, the appreciation of indigenous success stories and the neo-classical assault on big government had served to revitalize rather than destroy development administration. Even the World Bank recognized the importance of administration for development although not everyone agreed with the Bank prescriptions (Murray, 1983). Milton Esman (1988, p. 133) declared that 'development administration has not only survived the limitations of its founders, but it has successfully adapted to a much more realistic set of expectations about the process of development and the potentialities of the public sector'. Development administration, according to such writers, had matured but it was still dynamic.

So how do we characterize the contemporary practice of development administration? First, it is both an academic sub-field in the social sciences and a developmental practice. There is now a voluminous literature offering practical advice, analytic insight and descriptive accounts of administrative activities in development. It is a cumulative knowledge and wisdom which embodies lessons derived from modernization theory, liberal reformulations, neo-Marxist perspectives, neo-classical economics, public choice theory, neo-populist innovation and local experience. Unfortunately, we cannot assume that the lessons have been learned and built into current practice. Second, it is not a discipline in the sense of possessing a distinct body of theory. There is no paradigmatic consensus. Swerdlow (1975, p. 324) likened it to 'a subject matter in search of a discipline'. Development administration is built round a set of problems and can be viewed as an instrumentality of the development process. Third, development administration remains heavily but not exclusively focused on public administration. It is no longer premised on the notion of big government. This is in part due to disappointing results of official development interventions and to the shortage of financial resources. However, the identification of bureaucracy as problem rather than solution has been vigorously promoted by an 'improbable coalition':

Partners in this ideological marriage of convenience are business-oriented, low tax, anti-regulation advocates of the minimal state [*the neo-Classical counter-revolutionaries*] and the counterculture communitarians who regard government as the inherently exploitative instrument of a morally corrupt and violent capitalist establishment which is destroying the natural environment, promoting nuclear war, and encroaching on the rights of social minorities [*elements of the neo-populists*].

(Esman, 1988, p. 127. Italics added by the authors)

Issues such as privatization, the efficacy of the market, popular participation and the role of non-governmental organizations (NGOs) have forced their way onto the development administration agenda (see Box 1.4 for a selection of common themes in contemporary development administration). Bureaucracy is but one aspect, albeit a major one, of contemporary development administration. Even the term development administration is unfavoured in some quarters, perhaps because of its association with bureaucracy and with an earlier era of failed prescriptions and interventions, or perhaps because it does not convey the increased range of issues under consideration. Terms such as 'policy analysis' and 'management' are now often substituted for 'administration'.

BOX 1.4

Some contemporary themes in development administration

1. Governments are limited in their capacity, and these limitations should be incorporated into the design of public programmes.
2. Because governments cannot do it all, alternative and complementary channels need to be identified and fostered.
3. Programme designers recognize and capitalize on the pluralistic properties of public administration.
4. Participation is an important dimension in the administration of public services.
5. Societal contexts provide both specific opportunities and special constraints for development administration.
6. There is an enhanced appreciation of the uncertainties and contingencies inherent in deliberate efforts at developmental change.
7. There are renewed pressures on governments (a) to extract greater productivity from continuing expenditures and (b) to reorient government bureaucracies to serve large disadvantaged publics more responsively.

Source: Esman, M.J. (1988) 'The Maturing of Development Administration', *Public Administration and Development*, vol. 8(2), pp. 125–34.

'Public action' is a recent and popular concept which takes a wider perspective than public delivery and state initiative. It also incorporates 'participation by the public in the process of social change' (Drèze and Sen, 1989, p. 259). It represents a rediscovery of civil society and the role that institutions in that sphere can play in promoting collective private and public ends (Mackintosh, 1992, p. 5). The popular notion of 'governance' arises from a quite different analysis but in many respects follows a similar line (World Bank, 1992b; ODA, 1993). The relations between bureaucracies, politicians and the organizations which populate their environments is a recurrent theme of this book and of the current approaches to development administration.

Fourth, consideration of power and politics is central to an understanding of this mode of organizing. Organizations engaged in development activities are not exemplars of technical rationality acting under clear instructions from modernizing élites. Administration, management and policy-making are highly political activities which involve conflict, bargaining, coercion and coalition-building among groups and individuals both inside and outside the formal organization. Both macro and micro political processes are central concerns in the practice and analysis of development administration. Furthermore, as we have identified development administration as an instrumentality of development, its practitioners must be intimately concerned with the goals of development (see previous section). Whether in analysis or practice there is no value neutrality. All views and actions have some political meaning, especially if you believe that development should be oriented to the poor, mostly defined by the poor and incorporating a strong element of grassroots knowledge and wisdom.

Finally, it can be appreciated that development administration (or policy and management) applies to a huge number of people in a large number of countries. The countries vary enormously when measured by statistical indicators of development or in terms of culture and history. Even within nations, however small in population terms, there can be great regional differentiation. Collective titles such as Third World or the South give an impression of similarity to a disparate group of countries. Diversity is what development administration must address. We will examine this diversity in the next chapter.

2

Organizational Environments: Comparisons, Contrasts and Significance

All organizations exist in and relate to environments that affect their operations. The environments in which administrators and policy-makers operate in developing countries are both distinctive and diverse. They are distinct from those environments encountered by their counterparts in the rich countries of the Organisation for Economic Cooperation and Development (OECD), but between developing countries there are substantial differences. This means that management models which are successful in one place may be inappropriate in a different environment. Thus, the practices and prescriptions of administration in industrial countries may be parti-cularly prone to failure when transplanted to radically different developing country contexts. Even South–South transfers must be treated with great care and consideration.

The organizational environment is a vital element in influencing the nature of policy, administrative reform or any programme of planned change. Managers at all levels who have a good appreciation of the environment and express that in their decisions and actions have a far greater chance of success than those who choose to underestimate or ignore the significance of the environment.

In this chapter we will first explore the concept of environment and indicate some of the ways in which organizations interact with their environment. Then we will describe some of the components of the environment which have been identified as important by politicians, administrators, academics and other development professionals. Finally, we will draw some general conclusions about developing-country environments and what this means for policy-makers, administrators and development.

Making sense of the environment

To appreciate the vastness and complexity of the environment we can follow Robert Miles's instructions to 'take the universe, subtract from it the subset that represents the organization, and the remainder is environment' (Miles, 1980, p. 36). There are economic forces, social institutions, demographic patterns, other organization, international agencies and many additional elements which make up this general or macro environment. It may be too broad a definition of environment as, by incorporating everything, it fails to distinguish what is of immediate significance for the organization. To do this we can identify the 'specific' or 'task' environment as that part of the environment which is directly relevant to the organization in its specific work and in achieving its goals. For example, the constituencies which influence and interact with a Department of Health will show variation from those identified for a Department of Defence. Delineating the boundary between the general and task environments is obviously difficult but the broad distinction is still useful. Some management texts also identify an internal environment for organizations. This is comprised of culture, technology employed, work practices, intra-organizational politics and other elements found within organizations. We will not utilize this concept but the items which it embraces necessarily appear in other chapters of this book. In this chapter we are concerned only with the external environment.

While dividing the environment into different parts makes a useful start to our analysis, the critical questions from a management perspective focus on the degree of uncertainty and complexity in the environment. Some authors have suggested that for organizations to remain effective and efficient they must take steps to 'fit' their structures and strategies to the demands of the environment (Emery and Trist, 1965; Lawrence and Lorsch, 1967). Others have been less persuaded by such determinism and have employed the distinction between the 'influenceable' and 'appreciated' environments (Smith *et al.*, 1981). While managers will control certain decision areas in the organization (for example, deployment of staff, allocation of re- sources) they will not have such power outside. They may, however, be able to influence certain decisions by organizations and actors operating in the same or related areas. But there are other factors which are recognized and appreciated but which lie beyond the control of these managers. Such a view coincides with the 'resource dependence perspective' which gets away from notions of environ- mental determinism and identifies ways in which organizations can be proactive in influencing events and decisions in their environment (Pfeffer and Salancik, 1978).

Whether managers and policy-makers take a deterministic or proactive view of the environment they all need to engage in environmental scanning. This involves monitoring and evaluating changes in the environment so that appropriate actions can be made regarding organizational strategies and structures, and to national or local government policy. There is a huge range of scanning techni- ques, from informal but astute observation and analysis of current political trends to sophisticated data collection and computer analy- sis. They can adopt time frames which vary from long-term scenarios of 20 years or more to those which focus on next year only. Whatever the methods employed and whether the organization is in the public or private sector, it appears that organizations which pay attention to their environments have a much greater chance of performing well than those which ignore environmental scanning.

Furthermore, as developing-country environments are typically uncertain and growing in complexity the importance of environ- mental scanning as an input to public policy and management increases. If scant attention is paid to such data gathering and analysis, decision-making will become entirely *ad hoc*, and may simply degenerate into desperate steps by officials to hold on to power. Such an orientation does nothing to satisfy the developmental needs and demands of the millions of people who live in conditions of poverty and uncertainty in developing countries.

There is a final complication in dealing with the environment. The environment is not the same for everybody. Different people perceive it in different ways. They may 'enact' the environment creating the very information to which they then react (Weick, 1977). Thus, organizations or policy-makers respond to what they have con- structed – what is influenceable and what is appreciated. What they perceive and how they perceive it may vary. An organizational response may then be characterized as a 'strategic choice' which usually reflects the way in which the dominant coalition enacts the environment (Child, 1972). The environment is anything but a clear empirical reality. Information can be ignored or emphasized, institutions overlooked or awarded significance. It is a zone of contestation where political process and analysis are of great importance.

Elements of the environment

In this section we will describe some of the important elements of the environment which have been consistently appreciated, influenced and enacted by policy-makers and administrators in developing countries – and by academic analysts. Although we use convenient categories to package our environmental components remember that this is an analytical device and that life is not so easily compartmentalized in practice. There is a complex causal texture between parts of the environment and in their engagement with the organization. We should therefore beware of crude generalizations about cause and effect in explaining administrative and policy behaviour. With these considerations in mind we have modified Austin's (1990) model and divided the environment into economic, cultural, demographic and political components (see Box 2.1).

Economic factors

Making the economy grow and sharing out the results of such growth are fundamental concerns of governments and societies engaged in development. To pursue this strategy it is necessary to know what is happening in the domestic and international economy. Administrators and policy-makers need information about such items as growth rates of the gross national product, the availability of capital, changes in the structure of production and the labour market, and projections of international debt. They are simultaneously items which the government is trying to change and elements of the environment which affect those planned changes. They will offer opportunities or place constraints on policies in the economic and other sectors. Also, they are interrelated with the other variables in the environment and will both affect them and be affected by them.

BOX 2.1
Environmental factors for public sector managers

Economic	*Cultural*
Gross national product	Ethnicity
Structure of production	Family and kinship
Labour	Values and norms
Domestic capital	Gender
Foreign exchange	History
Foreign aid and debt	
Infrastructure	
Technology	
Poverty and inequality	
Informal sector	
Demographic	*Political*
Population growth	State–society relations
Age structure	Legitimacy
Urbanization and migration	Regime type
Health	Ideology
	Elites and classes
	International links
	Institutions

Source: Modified from Austin, J. E. (1990) *Managing in Developing Countries: Strategic Analysis and Operating Techniques* (New York: Free Press).

Gross national product

The most commonly cited statistics in the study of development are the closely related gross national product (GNP) per capita and gross domestic product (GDP) per capita. GNP per capita is calculated by 'estimating the money value of all goods and services produced in a country in a year, plus net factor income (from labour and capital) from abroad, and dividing by the estimated mid-year population' (Hulme and Turner, 1990, p. 18). GDP is GNP minus the net factor income from abroad. Both are measures of production and are utilized to compare levels of economic development between countries. The major division is between high income economies found in Western Europe, East Asia, North America and Australasia and the developing economies of Africa, Asia, Latin America and the Pacific.

The division is sometimes viewed as that separating rich and poor, North and South, wealthy OECD countries and the rest, or First and Third Worlds. However, these divisions are too crude, as within the developing world there is considerable differentiation. Since most of the nations of the world and the global population are classified as developing then such diversity should be no surprise.

The World Bank divides the developing world into three categories according to GNP per capita: low income (US$725 or less per capita in 1994), lower-middle income (US$726–2900 per capita in 1994) and upper-middle income economies (US$2901–8955 in 1994). It is questionable whether some upper-middle income economies such as Greece or Hungary would be recognized as 'developing'. Even excluding such cases the range is enormous – from Rwanda with US$80 per capita to Argentina with US$8710 per capita (see Table 2.1).

While the GNP measure does reveal a great deal about economic conditions there are limitations to its use. It says nothing about income distribution, it makes huge assumptions about informal and subsistence production which are ubiquitous in developing countries, and it is not an accurate guide to general levels of welfare. A human development index (HDI) constructed by the United Nations Development Programme (UNDP) is a far better guide to welfare as it incorporates indicators of life expectancy and educational attainment with national income to give a composite measure of human progress (see Table 2.1).

Structure of production
Other economic indicators help to elaborate the crude GNP per capita figure. Examination of the structure of production, for example, reveals that all developing countries have a greater reliance on natural resource exploitation including agriculture, mining, forestry and fisheries than the rich nations. For most rich countries agriculture provides under 5 per cent of GDP. The developing countries stand in marked contrast, particularly the low-income economies where an average of 28 per cent of GDP is derived from agriculture as compared to 10 per cent for all middle-income economies. But the range is considerable among the developing nations with middle-income economies often possessing substantial industrial sectors and sometimes revealing production structures nearer to the high-income than to the low-income economies.

TABLE 2.1

The economic environment

	GNP per capita 1994 $US	GNP Average annual growth rate (%) 1985–94	Agriculture as % of GDP 1994	Adult illiteracy (%) 1995	Total debt service as a % of exports 1994	Energy use per capita (kgs of oil equivalent) 1994	GNP rank minus HDI rank 1993
Low income							
India	320	2.9	30	48	26.9	243	7
Ghana	410	1.4	46	36	24.8	91	−4
Honduras	600	0.5	20	27	33.9	169	7
Lower middle income							
Philippines	950	1.7	22	5	21.9	364	8
Ecuador	1280	0.9	12	10	22.1	517	4
Tunisia	1790	2.1	15	33	18.8	590	−14
Upper middle income							
Brazil	2970	−0.4	3	7	35.8	691	0
Malaysia	3480	5.6	14	17	7.9	1711	−9
Gabon	3880	3.7	8	37	10.5	520	−46
High income							
Australia	18,000	1.2	3	<5		5173	11
UK	18,340	1.3	2	<5		3754	9
Japan	34,630	3.2	2	<5		3825	0

Source: World Bank (1996) *World Development Report 1996* (New York: Oxford University Press) and UNDP (1996) *Human Development Report 1996* (New York: Oxford University Press).

Labour

The human resources profile also provides contrasts both within the developing world and with the OECD nations. The latter invariably possess more educated populations and more highly skilled labour forces. Literacy rates within the developing nations vary widely and do not necessarily correlate with the GNP per capita figure. Some low-income economies such as Sri Lanka, Madagascar and China have superior adult literacy rates to middle-income economies such as Tunisia, El Salvador and Saudi Arabia. Skills are often in short supply. In some places, highly educated persons either do not have the particular skills needed by the economy or they migrate abroad for better opportunities. By 1987, for example, it was estimated that one-third of Africa's skilled people had moved to Europe. Even allowing for remittances this appears to represent a huge loss of investment in the type of skilled human resources required for national development.

Domestic capital

A further distinction between rich and poor countries is implicit in this very categorization. The latter generally demonstrate scarcity in both public and private domestic capital. The UNDP (1992, p. 63) has identified lack of finance as 'the most crippling constraint facing developing nations'. GDPs are low. Savings rates are also low with a few exceptions such as China and India. This is to be expected given the many persons who exist in poverty or near to it and who must attend to current consumption rather than to saving.

Other environmental features and problems relating to capital scarcity in developing countries include weak financial institutions which are unable to regulate the economy adequately and to mobilize savings. Inflation rates are frequently much higher in developing nations than in the OECD countries. In the 1980–93 period the annual inflation rates of all OECD countries averaged below 10 per cent, a figure attained by few developing countries. Over 30 developing countries averaged more than 20 per cent during this time, with some exceeding 50 per cent or even 100 per cent each year. Such inflationary environments make planning extremely difficult and demand management techniques in both public and private sectors which are unfamiliar to those used to operating in single digit inflation. Finally, capital flight, such as seen in Latin America in the early 1980s, may contribute to the shortage of domestic capital.

Foreign exchange

Foreign exchange is a form of capital which is frequently in short supply in developing countries and marks another distinctive environmental factor encountered by policy-makers and administrators in those countries. Foreign exchange is important because it determines the potential level of external purchasing power. Whether foreign exchange is used wisely for developmental purposes is another matter but it should be noted that even when countries enjoy the benefits of a commodity boom the foreign exchange bonanza can be frittered away in conspicuous consumption, prestige projects and inappropriate development programmes. However, foreign exchange scarcity is the common condition for developing countries with the poorer countries faring least well. Austin (1990, p. 50) cites a 1987 study which found that the average foreign exchange reserves were only US$17 per capita in low-income countries, US$128 for middle-income countries, but US$1148 for OECD countries.

Foreign aid and debt

Shortage of foreign exchange and scarcity of capital are reflected in the foreign aid relationship which binds the low and middle-income economies to the rich nations of the world in a dependent relationship. According to the influential neo-classical economist, Lord Bauer, developing countries can be defined as those which 'demand and receive aid from the West . . . The Third World is the creation of foreign aid: without foreign aid there is no Third World' (Bauer, 1981, p. 87). While this may have some empirical grounding as one possible classificatory device, Bauer's explanations of aid in terms of collective Western guilt certainly do not.

The flow of foreign aid from the governments of rich nations to those in poor nations has certainly been a leading feature of development in the post-war years, and the results of such flows have been disappointing and have contributed to another feature of the economic environment of developing nations – foreign debt. Two decades ago this was not a major element in the environment of administrators and policy-makers. Today in most developing countries it is a preoccupation, as the amount of debt in developing nations has grown rapidly to enormous and frightening levels: from US$100 billion in 1970 to US$650 billion in 1980 to around US$15 000 billion in 1992 (UNDP, 1994, p. 63).

OECD nations are by no means immune to debt but there are differences between them and the developing world. Most external debt in OECD countries is owed by private business while the level of production per capita is far greater than in developing countries. In developing countries it is governments which have the lion's share of debt. In the poorest countries there is little chance of repayment given the low levels of production while at the other extreme (for example, Brazil and Mexico) the amounts are so large that repayment problems are inevitable, permanent and affect the workings of the entire world economy. Furthermore, the level of debt for many countries has become so high that a large slice of government budget and an even larger portion of foreign exchange must go into servicing debts rather than into urgent economic initiatives and welfare projects (see Table 2.1). To exacerbate matters for poor nations, their real interest rates in the 1980s have been estimated as four times higher than those for rich nations (UNDP, 1992, p. 48).

Infrastructure
According to Austin (1990, p. 53) 'poor infrastructure may be the most visible distinguishing characteristic of developing countries'. This lack of capacity may be manifest in inadequate port facilities, roads in disrepair or unable to handle the increasing volumes of traffic, obsolescent railway rolling stock, an inability to maintain required electricity output and water supply systems which fail to satisfy personal and organizational demands. While large cities frequently outgrow and hence place insupportable demands on their infrastructure, rural areas are all too often characterized by their lack of infrastructural development. With good reason some authors have alleged a distinct and persistent urban bias in developing countries (Lipton, 1977).

Information is increasingly regarded as the most important commodity in advanced capitalist nations. Gathering, processing and disseminating information has become a leading activity in these countries. To service the insatiable demand for information, computers and telecommunications play a major role utilizing ever more sophisticated electronic machines with larger capacities and faster speeds. In the developing world one finds equivalent machines but in much smaller quantity, in many fewer places and processing information which is often less plentiful and less reliable. Only 20 per cent of the world's computers are to be found in developing nations. Thus, administrators and policy-makers must face an environment where information availability and accuracy may leave much to be desired and where the telecommunications infrastructure and computer availability may be poorly developed, fragmented or hardly present.

Technology

In large part, development is about technology. Whether one is promoting indigenous agricultural techniques, modifying machinery for small-scale production, building factories or re-equipping offices there are always questions about technology. As technology involves both hardware and techniques all technological activities have a human aspect. In OECD countries the speed of technological transformation during the past century has been unprecedented in human history. Some of what has been achieved is of dubious value for the present and future health of humanity. However, the industrial nations possess a massive store of technology and may be increasing their technological lead over the developing nations. This trend could accelerate as science and technology is increasingly privatized and made available only to those who can afford to pay.

By contrast, technology in developing countries is often less complex. It may also be inefficient and ineffective although one should exercise extreme caution before making value judgments about 'backward' technology in developing nations as compared to superior advanced technology in the OECD. 'Simple' can also be efficient, effective, well-tested and environmentally friendly. Technological innovation in developing nations is frequently concentrated in 'modern' activities such as large-scale manufacturing, the national airline, agribusiness plantations, and offices in the central business district of the capital city. This technology and much more is acquired overseas, in large part from the industrial nations. Third World research and development (R&D) capacity is highly restricted, constrained by capital shortages, foreign exchange shortfalls and other environmental factors. The UNDP (1992, p. 40) notes that despite having almost 80 per cent of the world's population, developing countries are responsible for only 4 per cent of global R&D expenditure.

Administrators and policy-makers face an environment where they must make continual technological choices. Many items on the shopping list derive from the industrial nations but what is appropriate in Australia or the UK might well be inappropriate in Nigeria or Pakistan.

Poverty and inequality

In 1990, the World Bank identified the reduction of poverty as the most pressing issue now facing the 'development community'. It still is and will remain that way for the foreseeable future. The poverty statistics make grim reading and are a shameful indictment of the world community. Over a billion people in developing countries were living in poverty in 1985, approximately one third of their total populations. Of these, 630 million were classified as extremely poor, their annual consumption being less than US$275 per person per year (World Bank, 1990, p. 28). Policy-makers and administrators in the OECD nations must also deal with poverty but its incidence is generally much less. Even among developing countries the amount of poverty can vary considerably while the degree of deprivation can be staggering when compared to what is defined as poverty in OECD countries. Furthermore, much poverty in rural areas goes unperceived as those officials concerned with bringing development perpetuate biases which overlook and misunderstand the nature and extent of poverty (Chambers, 1983).

In some developing nations there is also massive inequity in the distribution of resources and in incomes. For example, in Brazil the top 20 per cent of the population receives 26 times the income of the bottom 20 per cent. Many people in developing countries, especially in Asia and Latin America, have access to educational resources, health facilities, food, accommodation and consumer goods which are similar to people in Western countries. Some are fabulously wealthy but alongside them exist the millions in urban squatter settlements and those hidden in rural villages and remote locations who daily have to battle with poverty. They have few assets, live in larger households, have low incomes, have poor access to social services, and live shorter lives than the middle and upper classes. The details vary from country to country and region to region but the bottom line is always the same – an inability to attain an adequate standard of living.

But poverty should not be recorded simply as a matter of economic statistics. Vulnerability and powerlessness are two important characteristics which both define and perpetuate poverty. Chambers (1983) notes that the poor lack buffers against contingencies such as weddings, funerals, natural disasters, sickness and accidents. This makes them highly vulnerable. Attending to these contingencies frequently results in the sale or irreversible loss of their already meagre assets. The poor in rural areas have also witnessed the relative ease with which rural elites intercept benefits intended for the poor who lack the political resources to bargain. Such powerlessness, says Chambers, is especially common for women, and the physically weak, disabled and destitute.

Informal sector

A final and particularly distinctive economic feature of developing countries is the prevalence of the informal sector; that is, the multi-tude of unregistered micro-businesses that operate outside of state regulation. They typically include food preparation and sale, petty trade, transport hire, repair activities, scavenging and manufacture. It has been estimated that such unofficial economies employ between 35 and 65 per cent of the labour force of most developing countries and provide between 20 and 40 per cent of GDP (Chickering and Salahdine, 1991, p. 7). De Soto (1989) estimated that in Peru the informal sector accounted for 50 per cent of the full-time labour force, another 10 per cent part-time, 40 per cent of GDP, and 47 per cent of construction and 95 per cent of public transport in the capital city of Lima.

Such burgeoning informal sector activity provides an environmen-tal challenge to administrators and policy-makers. They cannot ignore the unofficial economy as it is ubiquitous, vast and frequently growing. But do they regulate it, do they encourage it or do they watch it erode the power and authority of the bureaucratic state?

Cultural factors

Policies and plans may be technically feasible but a group of cultural factors places limits on what policy-makers and administrators can actually achieve and indicates the acceptable directions for policy and management. Culture is manifested in beliefs, values, attitudes and norms of behaviour. It is the meanings we attach to behaviour. These meanings are the products of elements such as history, tradition and social structure. We have made a broad sweep of these elements in the group of cultural variables we discuss below. This complex cluster exercises a major influence on how actors will perceive the rest of the environment and how organizations and managers will operate.

Ethnicity

Ethnic identity may be perceived in various ways – according to race, culture, language, religion or place of origin. A unique combination of such attributes differentiates each ethnic community from others and provides the basis for self-consciousness particularly among members of ethnic minorities. According to both modernization and Marxist theories of development, ethnic identities would weaken as economic development proceeded. History has proved this assumption incorrect. In the late twentieth century this has been most graphically demonstrated in widespread inter-ethnic strife in the form of secessionist movements and civil wars. While ethnic differentiation and political action based on ethnic identity have occurred in the Western nations it is in the developing world that ethnic divisions abound. They are important environmental features for administrators and policy-makers which must be taken into account in framing policies, planning and implementation.

Ethnic configurations vary considerably within the developing world. In Latin America and the Caribbean the indigenous populations were decimated by the colonizers. Thus, ethnic diversity is not such a pronounced feature of these societies although relatively small indigenous ethnic communities survive in marginalized and disadvantaged conditions in some countries. In Africa and Asia there can be considerable ethnic diversity which can translate into sometimes violent competition over resources, the allocation of jobs, control of the state or can even challenge the existence of the state. For the administrator and policy-maker there is always the consideration that their actions can be interpreted by ethnic groups in a framework which focuses on inequity between ethnic groups and that such analysis can have severe repercussions. But rapid economic and social advancement is certainly possible in conditions of ethnic diversity as the example of Malaysia demonstrates.

Family and kinship
While family and kinship define important human relationships throughout the world, it is not an exaggeration to say that they have greater significance for determining behaviour in developing nations than in the Western world. There are a multitude of kinship systems in the developing world. Imagine Papua New Guinea where there are more than 800 language groups and so an equivalent number of kinship terminologies, each demonstrating some features which distinguish it from the next. Whatever the operating system, the affective relationships of kinship are important determinants of behaviour. In some societies where kinship links do not exist, fictive ones will be

sanctioned to cement significant personal relationships. In the Philippines, sponsors or godparents at a christening will be linked to the child, to its parents and perhaps to the wider family and even to the other godparents. One cannot generalize about the degree of intensity of particular kinship relations as differences between societies, individuals and contexts work against uniformity. The vital matter is that kinship forms an important frame of reference for individuals operating in society and the language of kinship has a wide currency in metaphors and analogies.

Values and norms

Among the most important components of culture are values and norms. They serve to both determine, explain and legitimate human actions, and they show extraordinary variance between societies and even within them. Their importance to the administrator and policy-maker is quite obviously profound although this has not always been appreciated. In the 1970s, Gert Hofstede (1980) asked the simple question 'do American theories apply abroad?' concerning motivation, leadership and organization. One hundred and sixteen thousand questionnaires later, Hofstede concluded that national cultures provided distinct patterns of mental programming which cast severe doubts on the appropriateness of certain American management practices in different national cultural contexts.

Administrators and policy-makers derive values from the wider society in which they live and from other collectivities to which they belong, such as ethnic groups, religions and classes. They import such values and norms into their work organizations, and perhaps add a few specific items of organizational culture from that particular office or department. The values and norms guide and give meaning to what they do and what is acceptable or feasible in their dealings with the wider society. The wider society also evaluates the actions of the policy-maker and administrator using values and norms as tools. There is no Third World value system, and even within a nation-state values can vary considerably between groups, or particular groups can operationalize the same values in different ways.

Gender

Women's issues have become major concerns for administrators and policy-makers only relatively recently. They were certainly part of the environment before the 1970s but their perception was generally undertaken using patriarchal instruments which both understated and misconceived the situation of women in development. The United Nations Decade for Women 1976–85 marked 'the acceptance of women's concerns as legitimate issues for national and international policy' (Tinker, 1990, p. 4). But this acceptance had been won through the political actions of women not as a result of some natural evolutionary process.

The overriding theme in the study of gender is inequity and its persistence in relations between men and women (see Table 2.2). The nature and degree of inequity varies between countries and social classes. The inequity between women in different social classes can in fact be greater than that between men and women. For example, the lives of middle class and elite women in Latin America are vastly different than those of poor rural and urban women in terms of status, power, life chances, education, work, health and conditions of existence. If we are to understand the status of women in development then it is important to see it in the context of an 'interweaving of class relations and gender relations' (Beneria and Sen, 1979, p. 288). Another element of our cultural environment – values – must also be taken into account as they furnish the ideological setting in which inequities are generated and maintained.

TABLE 2.2

Female–male gaps

	Females as a percentage of males			
	Life expectancy 1993	Literacy 1993	Tertiary enrolment 1990	Parliament: % of seats occupied by women, 1995
Mexico	109	95	76	14
Malaysia	106	86	89	11
Morocco	105	53	58	1
Nigeria	107	68	37	2
Mozambique	107	39	33	25

Note: All figures, except those in the 'parliament' column, are expressed in relation to the male average which is indexed to equal 100. The smaller the figure the bigger the gap, the closer the figure to 100 the smaller the gap, and a figure above 100 indicates that the female average is higher than the male average.
Source: UNDP (1996) *Human Development Report 1996* (New York: Oxford University Press).

But it is difficult to generalize about gender relations in the developing world as diversity is much in evidence. Programmes that work in one place might be failures in another. Leading issues in one situation can be of minor concern in another. Also, the historical experience of the West, including that of the women's movement, may be a poor guide for current developmental action.

While the administrators and policy-makers have often recognized the importance of women in development, whether because of perceived inequities or wasted human potential, the results of economic development for women are frequently disappointing. New technologies, greater opportunities for paid employment and the revitalization of religious values may even impose new burdens on women or may not seriously alter the overriding male-dominated power structures. For poor women, especially women-headed households, the global economic downturn has been particularly harsh leading to 'the feminization of poverty' (Tinker, 1990, p. 5).

History

Administrators and policy-makers seldom acknowledge history as a component of their organizational environments, yet it is one of the most significant. John Toye (1987) has argued persuasively that the Third World has acquired a common identity through anti-colonial and anti-imperialist struggles. While the details of individual cases may vary, all developing countries have engaged in these struggles. For most it has been the decolonization process. Even the relatively few developing nations which were not formal colonies of Western powers have been forced to fight against imperialism and to be vigilant in dealing with it. There is a collective psychology wrought in the process of anti-colonial struggles which leaves a deep and lasting imprint on nations. Whatever the specific experience the outcome is a sense of shared experience, a common history. And in the post-colonial era it can be expressed in the ideology and practice of development.

This notion should not be taken to extremes as historical diversity is also evident. The legacies of colonial rule are evident today. For example, national boundaries established by imperial powers often incorporated different ethnic groups. Such ethnic diversity may become a principal consideration in policy-making and even in the survival of the state. Economic structures established under colonialism which focus on export crop production may be difficult to dismantle in post-colonial times. Imported colonial values concerning gender relations may become deeply embedded and survive un-scathed long after the colonial power has departed. While at one level there may be a collective identity among developing nations forged out of broadly similar historical relations with the West, on another level one sees diversity between say the details of Hispanic colonialism in Latin America and British imperialism in South Asia. Both have left their mark and are addressed either explicitly or, more likely, implicitly by administrators and policy-makers engaged in the process of national development.

Demographic factors

The changing size, composition and location of populations is vital information for policy-makers and administrators. It enables them to know what services are needed, how fast they should grow, where they should be located and what to expect in the future. These population dynamics place societal demands on the state and must be monitored by government if informed decisions are to be made. Whether the needs and demands are fulfilled will depend on the interaction of these demographic factors with other clusters of environmental variables. Health is also included in this demographic grouping. Good health for the population is a major objective of development and it is vital to have knowledge of disease patterns and the availability of health services for the attainment of this objective. Furthermore, an unhealthy population produces at far below the optimum level and therefore acts as a constraint on development.

Population growth

Over three-quarters of the world's population live in developing countries and the proportion is increasing. This is because population growth rates in the developing world are significantly higher than in the rich nations. Growth rates in Europe and North America have never been more than 1.5 per cent; Japan's population grew at only 1.2 per cent per year between 1965 and 1990; while even a migrant society like Australia registered only 1.8 per cent population growth per year over the same period. By contrast the average annual growth rate of population for both low-income and middle-income countries between 1965–90 was 2.3 per cent. The growth rate has been much higher in many places, with African countries often exceeding 3 per cent. Many Asian countries have registered figures above 2.5 per

TABLE 2.3

Environmental features in population and health

	Population (millions) mid-1994	Average annual growth rate of pop. (%) 1980-93	Population 0–14 years as % of total pop. 1991	Life expectancy at birth (years) 1994	Population with access to safe water (% of total) 1991
Low income					
India	914	2.0	35.8	62	75
Ghana	17	3.3	46.8	58	56
Honduras	6	3.1	39.8	66	64
Lower-middle income					
Philippines	67	2.3	39.2	65	81
Ecuador	11	2.5	38.9	69	58
Tunisia	9	2.3	..	68	67
Upper-middle income					
Brazil	159	2.0	34.2	67	96
Malaysia	20	2.5	..	71	78
Gabon	1	1.7	39.7	54	72
High income					
Australia	17.6	1.5	22.1	78	100
UK	57.9	0.2	19.0	76	100
Japan	124.5	0.5	18.1	80	96

Source: World Bank (1995) *World Development Report 1995* (New York: Oxford University Press) and World Bank (1996) *World Development Report 1996* (New York: Oxford University Press).

cent. The explanation of this growth lies in health improvements which caused death rates to fall while birth rates remained high (see Table 2.3).

These percentages do not seem high but closer examination reveals another story – the effect of compounding. For example, a growth rate of 2 per cent entails a doubling of the population in 35 years. A rate of 2.77 per cent means doubling the population in 25 years, which is a single generation (Hull and Hull, 1992, p. 1). The challenge such growth rates pose for administrators and policy-makers are obvious. Each year they must provide more classrooms, more teachers, more health facilities and more services of all types to simply maintain current standards. Rapid population growth makes development more difficult especially in environments of resource scarcity.

Although population growth rates are slowing in the developing world, either through economic development, as in East and South-east Asia, or state policy, as in China, the growth in numbers of people will actually increase in the 1990s. This is because of the huge population base. Every day 250 000 people are added to the world's population, between 90 and 100 million people per year – the equivalent of another Nigeria or Bangladesh each year (*ibid.*).

Age structure
While the rich countries devise strategies to deal with ageing populations, the developing nations are characterized by young populations. In 1991, 35.4 per cent of the population of all low and middle-income countries were between 0–14 years of age as compared to 19.3 per cent for the OECD countries (see Table 2.3). For most low-income and over half of the lower-middle-income countries the figure was over 40 per cent. Such age structures have resulted from the rapid growth rates and the growth in absolute numbers which means that larger numbers of females are entering the reproductive stage each year. Thus, administrators and policy-makers must deal with a population whose age creates particular patterns of demand (for example, on education and health) and where family sizes and dependency ratios differ markedly from the rich nations. There is some divergence within the developing nations themselves, notably China where strict population policies have resulted in only 27 per cent of its population being in the 0–14 years category in 1991. But one should remember that even a 1 per cent growth rate for China means the addition of 11.5 million people to its population each year.

Urbanization and migration

While developing countries have larger rural populations than OECD countries one of the remarkable features of the past four decades has been the huge growth of urban population in the developing world. In 1970, only 18 per cent of the population in low-income countries and 46 per cent of the population in middle-income countries resided in urban areas. By 1994, the figure had risen to 28 per cent for low-income countries and 61 per cent for middle-income countries; and it should be remembered that this has taken place in the context of overall high population growth rates.

In all countries the urban population has been expanding at a more rapid rate than the rural population due to natural increase and migration from the countryside. Some believe that the most able and skilled rural inhabitants are those which comprise the bulk of the rural-urban flow. These are demographic patterns and processes which must be addressed by administrators and planners although all too often they appear to be overwhelmed by them. The poor who make up the vast majority of the developing world's urban population are all too evident in squatter settlements and slums throughout the world, living in cramped, insecure and often unhealthy conditions and displaying low levels of formal employment. The poor have in large part provided for themselves through the informal economy and have built their settlements despite the officeholders of the state rather than with their assistance.

The degree of urbanization varies considerably between developing countries. Some Latin American countries such as Argentina and Uruguay have over 75 per cent of their populations in urban settlements. By contrast some low-income countries such as Malawi and Bangladesh have under 20 per cent of their populations in urban areas. There has often been a tendency for the largest urban centres to grow most rapidly creating massive population centres, cities which carry populations far in excess of their infrastructural capacity and in which environmental problems such as air pollution have become acute. The world's largest cities are now in developing countries and this situation will become even more pronounced with continued urban growth. Mexico City leads the way with a staggering 20 million population.

In addition to the flow of rural populations to metropolitan centres there is a smaller but significant migration overseas. This flow is mostly comprised of skilled workers and has focused on OECD countries and oil-rich/labour-short Middle Eastern countries. Some of the migration is temporary, for example in the construction industry, while many may be making permanent moves in search of better opportunity. For administrators and policy-makers this 'brain drain' comprises a loss of highly trained human capital but it may be offset by remittances of foreign exchange and by an easing of pressure on domestic labour markets. In 1989, developing countries received about US$25 billion in official remittances from OECD and Gulf countries, and quite possibly another US$5 billion or more in unofficial remittances.

Health
One of the success stories of the development process has been improvement in health. However, there is still enormous scope for further improvement as the health status of populations in developing countries lags far behind that in the OECD countries. The life expectancy at birth for females and males in low income countries has increased from 50 years and 48 years in 1965 to 63 years and 61 years in 1993. Females in middle income countries now have life expectancies at birth of 71 years as against 60 years in 1965 while for men the 1993 figure is 65 years.

Despite these overall improvements some countries still have appalling health profiles while all have disease patterns and health problems which are both different and have a higher human toll than those in the OECD countries. A few examples will demonstrate this. In 1992, 1.2 billion people still remain without access to potable water (see Table 2.3), 1.7 billion people have no sanitary means of disposing of human waste, while water-borne diseases killed more than 3 million children in 1991 (*Source*, vol 4(2) December 1992). Ninety per cent of the world's blind people live in developing countries. Most of this blindness could have been prevented by the right diet, immunization against measles and other low cost preventative health measures. In Burkina Faso in 1990, there were 57 183 persons for every doctor, and infant mortality stood at 134 infant deaths per 1000 live births in 1990. By contrast, in Malaysia there were 1270 persons for every physician and an infant mortality rate of 16 per 1000.

Some diseases such as malaria are making a comeback. In the 1950s and 1960s, it was thought malaria had been brought under control by the lethal insecticide DDT and the drug chloroquine. Malaria has outsmarted this Western technology and is spreading. It is now present in over 100 countries infecting an estimated 267 million people and claiming 2 million lives each year (Dube, 1992).

Changed lifestyles can introduce new health problems. The spread of diabetes in certain South Pacific island nations following the Westernization of dietary habits is a case in point. New diseases, such as AIDS, can emerge with devastating effect. In India, by the year 2000 it is estimated that there will be 1 million AIDS cases and 5 million persons HIV-positive. The health situation is ever-changing and provides yet another series of considerations and contextual conditions within which and with which administrators and policy-makers must work.

Political factors

A message that we keep reiterating is that development administration is an intensely political affair. Thus, special importance attaches to the cluster of political factors that we discuss in this section. But, it is not an exhaustive list, and there will be considerably more reference to power and politics in the rest of the book. It is also important to note that all of the other factors discussed under different headings have political aspects to them. Political scientists used to search for explanatory models which could encompass the entire developing world. Their demise was an acknowledgment of diversity and 'that peculiar open-endedness of history that is the despair of the paradigm-obsessed social scientist' (Hirschman, 1971, p. 356). There was no ideal-type Third World state and no ubiquitous Third World political processes. But equally we should not advocate anarchic exceptionalism where dissimilarity makes conceptualization and the comparative method redundant. It is still possible to identify regularity in diversity. For example, states in sub-Saharan Africa may share some (never all) experiences and features. The histories of East Asian states may also reveal commonalities. Even then, certain historical patterns such as the nature of leadership or the origins of institutions can transcend such classifications. The items discussed in this section reveal these paradoxical themes of similarity and diversity.

Social class

One of the most fundamental divisions in society is that of social class. Although there are competing definitions, classes are 'large-scale groups of people who share common economic resources which strongly influence the types of life-style they are able to lead' (Giddens, 1989, p. 209). While there has generally been a weaker development of classes in the Third World as compared to the industrial nations, the class structures of developing nations display far greater diversity and complexity than found in the First World.

Developing countries have large rural populations and a variety of class arrangements which not only distinguish Third World from First World but also differ between countries of the Third World and even within countries. The 'peasant' is ubiquitous in the literature and is found in different relationships with landlords, other peasants and landless labourers. There are often upper, middle and lower peasantries in addition to the landless who have only their labour to sell. Some peasants own their land, others enter a variety of rental agreements with landlords – a direct payment, a share of the crop, a set proportion of the production expenditures. In Latin America there are large landowners known as *latifundistas* who control vast armies of landless labourers either on 'traditional' farms or modern agribusiness estates. Especially in middle-income economies, rural class structures are often more complex as rural inhabitants may have access to urban employment and to rural non-farm employment in marketing, transport, repair and other services.

The level of development may also affect the size and nature of the middle class. In the rapidly expanding Asian economies there has been substantial growth and rising affluence among the middle class. In many of the poor countries it is the meagre development of anything resembling a middle class which is most noticeable. At the upper ends of the class system other complexities may arise as different fractions of a dominant class compete for policy supremacy: landed interests, industrial exporters, manufacturers for the domestic market and technocrats of the state machinery.

The critical political issue relating to social class is whether people belonging to social classes or fractions of them move beyond a simple awareness of their similar class position to taking action based on their class interests. This class consciousness is expressed in class conflict where particular classes or class fractions pursue political strategies to promote their own interests. Revolution is the most extreme expression of class action, and while it was regularly pursued by armed insurgency in earlier decades, its appeal has waned considerably. Institutions are sometimes interpreted as being established to articulate class interests in the political arena – labour unions for the urban working class and peasant farmers, business organizations for the bourgeoisie and consumer groups for the middle class. Political parties may have a class character and adopt policies which benefit their membership and class supporters. Leaders can mobilize support from particular classes and use it in opposition to other groups, institutions or classes. Finally, classes may engage in strategic alliances with other classes in the furtherance of mutual interests.

Legitimacy

Concern over regime legitimacy is something which affects developing countries far more than OECD nations. Military juntas, democratically elected parties and self-appointed presidents-for-life all share an interest in attempting 'to justify their holding of power in terms other than those of the mere fact of power-holding' (Lewis, 1982, p. 125). Policy is one mechanism by which claims to power can be legitimated.

In sub-Saharan Africa, for example, 'regime uncertainty has been the norm', making the search for 'workable political arrangements' a leading issue (Chazan, 1989, p. 325). Multi-party democracies had short lifespans and were replaced by one-party states, tyrants, military rulers and other authoritarian variants. But they too were often overthrown as their legitimacy was tenuous. In the late 1980s, in line with international trends, many African countries, such as Zambia and Nigeria, began to plan the reintroduction of democratic rule. Regime type was a leading issue and the arrangements for a transition were central policy concerns.

President Marcos of the Philippines demonstrates how, even under authoritarian rule, there can be close attention bordering on preoccupation with claiming legitimacy for a particular type of regime and its incumbents (Turner, 1990a). He employed a variety of techniques: establishing the legality and constitutionality of martial law, using performance in socioeconomic development, manipulating history and culture, and securing international support. And all this was done to establish the obedience-worthiness of the institutional order which he had imposed.

Policy concerns and capacity

The history of the modern Western state has been one of bureaucratization and of the encroachment of the state via the policy process into almost all aspects of everyday life. Rules, regulations, policies and officials determine much of what is done and the manner in which it is done. Even given the recent market orientations of some

Western governments the policy coverage of the state is enormous as are the resources gathered by the state for this purpose. Quite obviously the Third World state cannot hope to have the same scale of policy coverage especially in the area of social welfare. It simply does not have the same resources at its disposal. This is immediately apparent from our discussion of socioeconomic and demographic indicators in this chapter. One should take care, however, to avoid simply reading off policy coverage from indicators such as GNP per capita. Other contingencies such as regime type, political ideology and budgetary tradition can profoundly influence which policies are given priority. For example, low-income Sri Lanka has operated a form of welfare state for more than 40 years.

Nevertheless, it is evident that developing countries have less reliable knowledge and technical analytical capacity than are available in OECD countries. In the latter, the state institutions collect and analyse enormous quantities of information on the grounds that policy decisions can only be made with expert knowledge and specialized information. Even the realization that political processes rather than rationality determine decisions has not diminished the passion for data gathering and processing. While greater knowledge and analytical capacity do not guarantee more successful policy decisions and outcomes they have the potential to be of considerable assistance.

Developing country policy-makers and implementors are frequently hamstrung by a lack of knowledge. Their actions are more likely to be guided by guesswork rather than systematic analysis. Their environments are necessarily and undeniably 'enacted'. The cost of generating information is high, the logistical difficulties are numerous while the immediate political returns are minimal. Furthermore, governments and bureaucrats have frequently had a Western or technocratic orientation and have ignored the contributions that indigenous knowledge can make to the policy process. What farmers know, for instance, has often been treated as inferior knowledge when in reality it can be of great use and can be gathered by cheap innovative methods (Chambers, 1993).

A further difference both between the OECD and Third World and within the Third World is not in the scale but in the nature of policy coverage. There are issues, areas and activities which are of concern to the state in developing countries but which are of little concern in the West. Horowitz (1989) identifies matters of morality and religious freedom which can be 'zones of immunity' into which

Western policy-makers rarely wander but which may be of great importance to their developing country counterparts. Many contrasting policy concerns are simply a product of environmental differences. For example, land reform can be an area of vigorous policy conflict in developing countries but not on the agenda in the West. Reducing population growth is often of major importance especially in large-population countries such as China and Indonesia while in the West it is the ageing of populations which is the major issue.

Generic labels such as economic policy or agricultural policy apply to all types of country but conceal major differences and orientations. While the European Union policy personnel may focus on the level of agricultural price subsidy and wonder what to do about butter mountains and milk lakes, in the Third World the policy personnel are analysing how to increase food production and how to reach the poor tenant farmer with low-cost technologies.

The weak state
This is the most critical item for understanding the policy process in much of the developing world, and not surprisingly the topic which has generated the most debate.

In the early days of development planning it was often assumed that states had a far greater degree of control over the environments which they wished to change than was actually the case. The falseness of this assumption was soon realized and academics began exploring the ways in which state–society relations in the developing world were different from the West. Myrdal (1968, p. 66) identified 'soft states' where 'policies decided on are often not enforced, if they are enacted at all'. Huntington (1968, p. 1) argued that 'the most important political distinction among countries concerns not their form of government but their degree of government' The developing countries, said Huntington, often have a shortage of political community and of effective, authoritative, legitimate government – 'in many cases, governments simply do not govern' (*ibid.*, p. 2). More recently Migdal (1988) has written of 'weak states and strong societies' where there is an ongoing struggle between the state and societal actors over who has the right and ability to make the rules that guide people's social behaviour; and just because state legislation exists it does not necessarily mean that it is enforced. Migdal points to the power of 'traditional' institutions and practices and to various forms of 'strongmen' organizations which both thwart and penetrate the state.

Expressions of the weak state are many and widespread. They can be seen in the inability of the state to collect taxes and in the ability of the society to avoid them. The administration of official statutes can be altered by corruption, by the force of custom or by the demonstrated capacity for violence of local strongmen. Land reform legislation may be passed but minimally implemented. Tenancy arrangements may lay down a particular division of the crop between landlord and tenant but local practice may enforce another arrangement. The state may establish upper limits for interest rates but usurious rates may prevail. Representatives of the state may recast their official roles in rural locations to better fit with the expectations and practices of the local populations. Official mechanisms of accountability may be weak so that the occupants of state office can simply use those offices for personal gain or for the benefit of groups based on kinship and ethnicity.

At the extreme, the weak state can simply disintegrate as in the Lebanon or Somalia. Its only claim to existence may be international recognition of something which is not actually there. In Africa, Richard Sandbrook (1985) has identified many such states classifying them as 'fictitious'. O'Brien (1991) refers to the 'state of nothingness' but nevertheless demonstrates how, in Francophone Africa, rulers have been adept in the 'show' or 'display' of state to satisfy international actors – despite the 'nothingness'. For example, in Togo, General Eyadema built a regime on entertainment and fear relying especially on a cult focused on himself – yet 'the structures of the Togolese state appear to be virtually non-existent' (*ibid.*, p. 161). Toulabor (1986, p. 313) sees this as proof that the Western graft of state has now been 'adapted, tropicalized and steeped in the ethos and the rationality of social actors who have reshaped it to their own purposes'.

But the weak state is not ubiquitous. China, Malaysia, Indonesia and many other developing countries are inadequately described or totally misrepresented by the uncritical application of the weak state model. Back in 1953, Maurice Zinkin wrote that 'There is in Asia less mental resistance to State intervention than in the West, for Asia has a long history of effective and helpful State action' (p. 214). Recent experience confirms this. The enormous economic success of the East Asian NICs is not simply the triumph of the market but also has much to do with strong state institutions. For example, South Korea's economy grew at an average rate of 8.3 per cent between 1962 and 1985, in large part *because* of government intervention:

Presidential political leadership and a significant proportion of the bureaucratic elites have given their top priority to economic development . . . there has been a host of price controls, distribution controls, and other government interventions through direct and indirect taxes, tariffs, quotas, export subsidies and the protection of import-substituting industries . . . Through government intervention the Korean economy was directed more to export promotion than to a neoclassically efficient allocation mechanism.   (Kim, 1991, p. 136)

Care should be taken not to assume that authoritarian regimes and strong states go hand in hand. Authoritarian rule has undoubtedly been associated with economic success stories but it has also been party to economic and social disasters. Military juntas frequently return to barracks because they fail to live up to their claims for legitimacy based on performance (for example, more jobs, less corruption, better social services). Dictators are often primarily concerned with staying in power. Policy can then all too easily focus on survival rather than on the broader needs of the nation, as with President Mobutu in Zaire. In some cases this can mean that there is minimal state penetration of the routines of everyday life apart from the threat of state violence to maintain consent (but not necessarily legitimacy). In short, authoritarian regimes are often associated with weak states.

But we should not force an all or nothing categorization of weak or strong on Third World states. As Clapham (1985, p. 39) observed, its distinguishing feature is 'the combination of power and fragility'. We should be aware that elements of the weak and the strong can be simultaneously present.

Neo-patrimonialism

According to Weber's ideal type, the modern state is based on principles of rational-legal authority. This involves legally defined structures of authority and power oriented towards the achievement of widely accepted goals. The public officials follow rules, regulations and laws in an impersonal manner and maintain strict distinction between their public and private lives. While this theory may live on in ideological form as a legitimating device we know that the ideal type does not exist anywhere in its pure form.

Greater insight into the nature of the state is provided by invoking the notion of neo-patrimonialism. According to Weber, and historical experience, the traditional ruler frequently lacked the coercive capacity to impose his rule. His power depended on his ability 'to win and retain the loyalty of key sections of the political elite' (Crouch, 1979, p. 572). Assuming that the masses could be kept in a state of apathy and acquiescence then the successful patrimonial ruler could focus on keeping his potentially troublesome élite loyal through awarding them fiefs and benefices. The contemporary environments enacted by developing country rulers differ from those of their traditional patrimonial forebears. Most importantly, the trappings of the rational-legal authority are very apparent in such institutions as formal constitutions, legislative bodies and huge state bureaucracies. However, patrimonialism seems not only to have survived in the Third World but has prospered in the context of development. The impersonal universalistic systems and rules of the rational-legal have been employed for private, particularistic purposes (Findlay, 1991, p. 18). The modern ruler fulfils the patrimonial role by rewarding followers and kinsmen by giving them jobs, contracts or licences which should go to those satisfying the rational-legal requirements.

The neo-patrimonial ruler depends on the state being pervasive in the formal economy. Thus, the ruler can protect followers from competition by enacting tariffs and quotas, and by access to subsidized credit, grants and foreign loans. The rent-seeking state is the home of the neo-patrimonial ruler. This is where one finds the dual political systems – of the verandah and of the air-conditioner (Terray, 1986). The latter can be viewed in the form of 'State . . . President, Ministers, Parliament, Administration, Party, Constitution, Laws, Rules and airport with VIP lounge, company of paratroopers . . . motorcycle outriders with siren' (*ibid.*, as quoted in O'Brien, 1991, p. 151). Bureaucracies headed by highly trained technocrats should be added. These are the symbols of the rational-legal which give legitimacy or the appearance of substance to the regime and state, especially for outsiders bearing gifts in the form of loans and grants.

Meanwhile on the verandah the real business of government is conducted according to the informal practices of patron–client ties. It is here that significant decisions are made and loyalties secured. If the patrimonial ruler cannot maintain control over scarce resources then loyalties falter and replacement becomes possible. Political arts are employed to avoid the admonitions of the World Bank and IMF to 'get the prices right'. The patrimonial ruler's success in many instances reflects the ability to communicate the image of the air-conditioner while practising the politics of the verandah. Survival also depends on maintaining mass acquiescence. Signs of disquiet among the masses are frequently met with repression especially if economic development is not happening.

This approach goes a long way to identify apparent irrationality in policy-making. We can understand why certain policy choices are made and why seemingly inefficient government expenditures are sanctioned. It certainly assists in explaining policy failure or the maintenance of the status quo but it often overlooks the question of how change occurs. How do you explain successes in patrimonial contexts? How can reformist policies be introduced? If politics is always seen as negative and élites are always exclusively self-interested then the answers to such questions are difficult. Policy simply cannot be explained in exclusively neo-patrimonial terms. Grindle (1991) suggests an alternative political economy model in which we should not examine the pursuit of self-interest as if it existed in a void but look at the bargains, pacts and compromises of politics in terms of 'problem-solving through negotiation and the use of political resources in the context of great uncertainty' (*ibid.*, p. 66). She acknowledges that the results of these processes can be good, bad or indifferent for the economy, society or for sectors of the society. However, that such a range of possibilities exists means that there is 'space' in which policy élites can manoeuvre to achieve policy choices that are both economically and politically wise.

The public sector and its environment

Having placed various environmental components under the microscope and examined them in isolation it is time to put them together in order to make some general observations about public organizations and their environments.

Distinctiveness

We have presented enough evidence to demonstrate that the environments encountered by administrators and policy-makers in the developing world can be distinguished from those facing their OECD counterparts. While there may not be one typical developing country environment there are clusters of interrelated environmental factors and forces which give some distinctiveness to development administration. It is this contextual distinctiveness of administration and policy which is one of the most important defining features of development administration, what makes it a specific field of enquiry and practice.

Frequently, the differences are a matter of degree. For example, poverty affects OECD nations as well as the developing world although the criteria for distinguishing the poor and the incidence of poverty vary. Particular values found in developing nations may also be present to a greater or lesser extent in rich countries. Rich countries have often some colonial history. But the causal texture, that interrelationship between the environmental parts and between them and the public organizations, invariably gives distinctiveness to the developing world.

Diversity

It seems somewhat paradoxical that having made the case for distinctiveness we now argue for diversity in developing country environments. However, within the group of countries collectively identified as the South, the developing world or the Third World there is considerable differentiation which perhaps questions the appropriateness of such labels. What constitutes the environment for public administrators and policy-makers in Bangladesh varies considerably from that facing similar persons in Botswana, Barbados and Brazil. Whether one uses GNP per capita, female participation in education, level of foreign debt, or any other indicator of develop-ment the findings are always the same: there is considerable variation between developing countries. There are groups of nations which are quite alike. For example, many small states face similar adminis-trative problems which may be amenable to similar, but never identical, solutions. Many Latin American countries have similar profiles. Common problems are found among many sub-Saharan African nations. However, there are also contrasting historical ex-periences and developmental trajectories and these have become more marked over time and have created increasing differentiation between developing countries.

Turbulence

Focus on the statistics of development can easily lead to static images of the environment. Nothing would be further from the truth. The environments of policy-makers and administrators in developing countries are characteristically uncertain and have become increasingly turbulent. For example, there may be new technology, the ascendancy of a political party, rapid population growth, the rise of pressure groups and externally determined resource constraints. There may even be war. The environments have moved towards a situation 'in which the very ground on which the actors stand is shifting' (Sagasti, 1988, p. 436). In a study of organizational environments in Africa, Munene (1991, p. 455) found that 'extreme environmental uncertainty is a defining characteristic and . . . predictability is almost nil'. Uncertainty does not make success unattainable. It means that administrators and policy-makers need certain techniques, organizational structures, implementation capacities and moral commitment which can be used to deal with such flux if developmental interventions are to be successful.

Opportunities and constraints

A basic aim of development administration is to change the environment. Practitioners are trying to bring about improvements in people's lives and as such are attempting to alter environmental conditions; for example, make water more available, increase rural income-earning possibilities, provide more educational opportunities. But, the environment can be seen as presenting both opportunities and constraints in the pursuit of such goals. Certain conditions, such as resource scarcity, limit policy options while others, such as labour surplus, suggest avenues of action which could utilize such surplus. Some environments are more restrictive than others and much literature seems to dwell on these constraints rather than on the opportunities. Encouraging creativity which would both identify and make use of the latter while not losing sight of the constraints would seem to be a leading requirement of development administration in the late 1990s.

Competing perceptions

We have already noted the diversity and interrelatedness of components in developing country environments. Now we can add a further complexity: different people perceive the environment in different ways. Peasant farmers, top bureaucrats, rural teachers, NGO workers and politicians will have different ideas on what is important in the environment, what happens in the environment and what actions should be taken to alter the environment. Within the public sector there may be considerable divergence in environmental interpretation, in forecasting what will happen if certain actions are taken and on what are the existing conditions. Environmental perception is not some universal science with a single inviolate set of rules and tools – despite the apparent finality of World Bank statistics. We bring values and interests into our understanding of the environment. We look at the environment and make judgments. We may express different rationalities. But what this means is that interpreting the environment and taking actions to improve it (the tasks of the policy-maker and administrator) has a strong political component.

Cause and effect

Public organizations are affected by their environments. Much literature in organization theory has been devoted either to the ways in which organizational structure and behaviour is determined by the environment or to how organizations must adapt such features to achieve 'fit' with their environments. Making such conscious adaptations will allegedly make organizations more efficient and effective (Emery and Trist, 1965; Lawrence and Lorsch, 1967). But we should be equally aware that public organizations exist interdependently with their environments and that these organizations adopt various strategies to alter their environments (Pfeffer and Salancik, 1978). More recently there has been focus on the complexity of environments and the interrelationship between environments and public organizations, where 'connectedness in action' should be the object of study, where boundaries between organisations and environments are at best vague and where organising rather than organizations should be our principal concern (Cooper and Fox, 1990). The recent establishment of 'growth triangles' in East and Southeast Asia is an example of such flexible organizing (Turner, 1995).

Foreign models and Third World realities

Following from all these general points about the environment is the observation that we should be extremely cautious in applying models of management structure and action imported from the West. One review of the literature on administrative theory and practice in developing countries summed up the situation as follows:

. . . whenever the organization can function as a closed system then what we know about organizations from North America seems to work fairly well. Whenever the organization interacts with its environment, however, the resulting behaviour cannot be understood without significant adjustments to the theories developed in industrialized nations.   (Kiggundu *et al.*, 1983)

We should not automatically reject Western ideas as inappropriate. There may be lessons to be learned and advantages to be gained. But we must also accept that many ideas from OECD managerial experience may be unworkable and undesirable in developing country contexts. The institutional, demographic, economic or social environments are different and often require alternative responses. Political behaviour and structures are also different despite superficial similarities.

3

The Policy Process:
Politics and Technics

Both the public and development professionals identify the formulation, and to various degrees the implementation, of policy as the prime task of government. It is believed that governments should be generating economic growth, providing education, guaranteeing personal safety, expanding job opportunities, and taking many other initiatives which should lead to development. They should be pursuing these objectives through public action, cooperating with NGOs, the private sector and other institutions in civil society. The official goals and activities of Third World governments (or any modern government for that matter) focus on the policy process even if at the operating level some incumbents of political office are more absorbed in strategies to retain power and to secure material gain for themselves and their followers.

Policy is vitally important whether one is concerned with its quality, quantity, direction or symbolic value. Governments often use their own versions of policy outcomes and initiatives to legitimate their hold on power while opposing forces denigrate these same policies in order to justify their claim for office. But the outcomes of policy initiatives are more than just influences on who occupies the offices of state. On the performance of policy also hangs the future of the billions of people who inhabit the developing nations.

In this chapter we will examine the nature and context of public policy in developing nations. As the policy process is an intensely political matter great attention is paid to the nature of politics and of the state in the Third World. This is the political environment of policy and administration as discussed in Chapter 2. In addition, we will investigate the question of who makes policy and why. Finally, we will move from the policy-making phase to policy implementation and examine the fierce political battles which can be fought at this stage in the process. But first we will look at a few conceptual issues to furnish a strong foundation for the ensuing discussion.

What is policy?

A recurrent problem in the social sciences is that many terms, such as 'development' and 'policy', have multiple meanings, and it depends on who is using the term and in what context as to its meaning. The crucial issue is not which one is right but that students develop an awareness of multiple meanings and identify the versions which have greatest analytical insight. Hogwood and Gunn (1984) have provided a useful classification of the meanings of policy for those trying to intervene in the 'real world'. We have recast their various meanings in a developmental context in Box 3.1.

We regard policy as process. This gives policy a historical dimension and alerts us to different foci (for example, policy-making and policy implementation) during that process. Policy is also about decisions – series of decisions in fact – and decisions are about power. Sometimes such expressions of power may be revealed in the capacity not to act, the 'non-decision'. Policy is also purposive behaviour although officially stated goals may mask other intents, and rationalizations about policy initiatives and outcomes may come after decisions have been made and actions taken. Finally, policy is constructed by human agents and we need to understand their behaviour. For this we need to appreciate that these agents have multiple, often conflicting and sometimes changing political goals and that they may enter and exit the policy process at different stages. What must be banished is any lingering idea that policy is some highly rational process in which expert technicians are firmly in control using highly tuned instruments to achieve easily predicted outcomes. Such an image is inappropriate for the OECD countries let alone the developing world where environments are more unpredictable and turbulent. Dror's (1986, p. 98) notion of policy-making as 'fuzzy betting attempting to influence the probability of future situations' is particularly appropriate for the developing world.

BOX 3.1
How do people use the term 'policy'?

● *As a label for a field of activity*
For example, broad statements about a government's economic policy, industrial policy, or law and order policy

● *As an expression of general purpose or desired state of affairs*
For example, to generate as many jobs as possible, to promote democratization through decentralization, to attack the roots of poverty

● *As specific proposals*
For example, to limit agricultural landholdings to 10 hectares, to devalue the currency by 10 per cent, to provide free primary education

● *As decisions of government*
For example, policy decisions as announced in the national assembly or by a president

● *As formal authorization*
For example, acts of parliament or other statutory instruments

● *As a programme*
For example, as a defined and relatively specific sphere of government activity such as a land reform programme or a women's health programme

● *As output*
For example, what is actually delivered such as the amount of land redistributed in a reform programme and the number of tenants affected

● *As outcome*
For example, what is actually achieved such as the effect on farmer income and living standards, and of agricultural output of a land reform programme

● *As a theory or model*
For example, if you do x then y will happen; if we increase incentives to manufacturers then industrial output will grow; if more opportunities are provided in rural areas then migration to cities will slow down

● *As process*
As a long-term matter starting with the issues and moving through objective-setting, decision-making to implementation and evaluation

---

The contribution of policy

While many factors influence the developmental record of countries, it is certainly the case that good policy choices and their effective implementation are major explanatory variables. Examination of the success of the eight East and Southeast Asian countries (Japan, Hong Kong, the Republic of Korea, Singapore, Taiwan, Indonesia, Malaysia and Thailand) in the period 1965–90 is the clearest manifestation of this proposition.

These high-performing Asian economies (HPAEs) enjoyed rapid and sustained economic growth rates and were 'unusually successful' in sharing the fruits of this growth among the population (World Bank, 1993). The HPAEs were the only group of economies with high economic growth and declining inequality. Shared growth has meant improved human welfare; for example, life expectancy in the developing HPAEs increased from 56 years in 1960 to 71 years in 1990, while the proportion of people living in absolute poverty decreased from 58 per cent to 17 per cent over the same period.

Although the World Bank have dubbed this experience, 'the East Asian Miracle', officials actually admit that there was little that was actually 'miraculous' (see Box 3.2 for a critique of the miracle). Instead, they point to 'fundamentally sound development policy'. Effective macroeconomic management (for example, low inflation, competitive exchange rates) provided the strong and stable framework for private sector development. Banking policies improved the integrity of the banking system, encouraged non-traditional savers to utilize it and so raised the level of financial saving. An emphasis on developing human capital was evident in policies that focused on primary and secondary education. Agricultural policies stressed productivity and were not biased against the rural population. Policies to limit price distortions resulted in flexible markets for capital and labour while there was a high degree of openness to foreign ideas and technology.

The World Bank classifies this policy approach as the 'market-friendly' strategy which it advocated in its *World Development Report 1991*. Rapid growth is achieved by governments doing less where markets work but doing more in areas where markets cannot be relied upon for the desired outcomes. The Bank does acknowledge that market failure can be an 'important impediment' to rapid growth but argues that government failure can have very high costs as well. Government responsibilities are to 'ensure adequate investment in people, provide a competitive climate for private enterprises, keep the economy open to international trade, and maintain a stable macro-economy' (World Bank, 1993, p. 10). If the government tries to do more, says the Bank, then it may do more harm than good – unless its interventions are market-friendly. The northeastern HPAEs have intervened extensively in their economies while the Southeast Asian countries have been far less interventionist. Box 3.3 presents a framework which links rapid economic growth to three functions (accumulation, efficient allocation and technological catch-up) and to varying combinations of policies ranging from the market-oriented to the state-led.

BOX 3.2
How much does a miracle cost?

Various East and Southeast Asian countries have experienced a development phenomenon often referred to as the 'Asian Miracle' and characterized by rapid and sustained economic growth and considerable improvement in socioeconomic indicators such as income, housing, health, life expectancy and poverty. There is considerable evidence to support this. However, there is an additional perspective that these gains have come at a high cost.

(a) *Loss of identity*
    In Singapore it is alleged that 'Many Malays feel sadly out of place in the anonymous concrete corridors of the housing estates' and that 'two decades of public housing have done nothing to replace the lost solidarity of the kampong'.

(b) *Exploitation of labour*
    In Taiwan 'Whole factories are now said to be run on foreign labour . . . Their average wage rates were reported at . . . less than half the average monthly earning of workers . . . By employing workers outside the jurisdiction of the Labor Standards Law, firms are under no obligation to provide them any benefits such as health insurance, vacation time, severance pay or pension.'

(c) *Lack of participation in decision-making*
    In Korea, 'Park Chung-Hee promoted high-speed industrialization in order to gain legitimacy, working on the theory that if you deliver growth and higher living standards, people will willingly forego democratic choice'.

(d) *Urban environmental degradation*
    In Korea, 'So polluted is Seoul's air, that according to a Seoul National University study, 67 per cent of the rain falling on that city contains enough acid to pose a health hazard to human beings. . . None of Korea's coal-burning power plants contain pollution treatment facilities for noxious gases.'

(e) *Rural environmental degradation*
    In Taiwan, 'Twenty percent of farm land, the government admits, is now polluted by industrial waste water . . . 30 per cent of rice grown in Taiwan is contaminated with heavy metals . . . many of the island's rivers are little more than flowing cesspools, devoid of fish, almost completely dead.'

Source: All of the above quotes are taken from Walden Bello and Stephanie Rosenfeld (1992) *Dragons in Distress: Asia's Miracle Economies in Crisis* (London: Penguin).

62

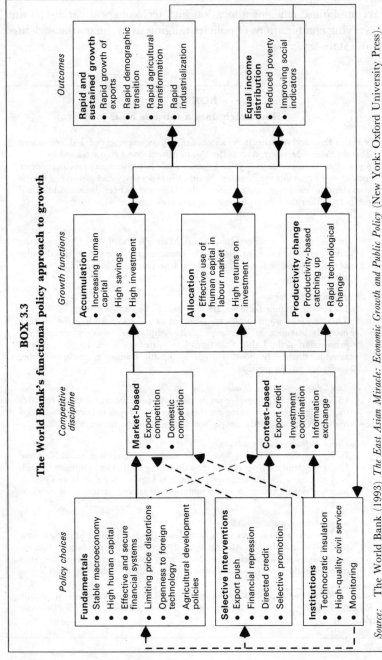

BOX 3.3

The World Bank's functional policy approach to growth

Policy choices

Fundamentals
• Stable macroeconomy
• High human capital
• Effective and secure financial systems
• Limiting price distortions
• Openness to foreign technology
• Agricultural development policies

Selective Interventions
• Export push
• Financial repression
• Directed credit
• Selective promotion

Institutions
• Technocratic insulation
• High-quality civil service
• Monitoring

Competitive discipline

Market-based
• Export competition
• Domestic competition

Contest-based
• Export credit
• Investment coordination
• Information exchange

Growth functions

Accumulation
• Increasing human capital
• High savings
• High investment

Allocation
• Effective use of human capital in labour market
• High returns on investment

Productivity change
• Productivity-based catching up
• Rapid technological change

Outcomes

Rapid and sustained growth
• Rapid growth of exports
• Rapid demographic transition
• Rapid agricultural transformation
• Rapid industrialization

Equal income distribution
• Reduced poverty
• Improving social indicators

Source: The World Bank (1993) *The East Asian Miracle: Economic Growth and Public Policy* (New York: Oxford University Press).

This would seem to indicate that there are multiple paths to growth as 'it is not easy to identify a single recipe followed across the region' (*ibid.*, p. 86). But being market-friendly is obviously viewed as a necessary path. 'Pragmatic flexibility' is also seen as an important characteristic of economic policy-making with governments ready to abandon policy instruments which seem to be performing poorly. However, this does not really answer the burning question of whether the 'Asian Miracle' is replicable. This is an issue on which the Bank is somewhat evasive. Different environmental conditions may well mean that replication is not possible. Where weak states and quite different cultures prevail, the Asian Miracle model may well be inappropriate.

What policy-makers and administrators need to define, and business managers need is to understand, is what a country's national strategy actually is. Lindenberg and Ramírez (1989) offer a useful classificatory device for this purpose. They acknowledge national differences and warn that 'no recipes for development can be passed blindly from one to another' (*ibid.*, p. 5) but identify some common questions for leaders ask in order to make national strategies (that is, objectives and policies) realistic:

1. *Reconstructing the past and understanding the present.* What economic strategy has the country pursued in recent years and how successful was it? What current problems exist?
2. *Shaping the future: short- and medium-term options.* What short- and medium-term economic options might be viable for the country? What policies might be required? Which options might be the most attractive and why?
3. *Managing winners and losers.* Which groups might perceive themselves to be winners and losers in the scenarios developed? What tactics might be used to maintain support for new economic strategies?
4. *Adjusting the organization to change.* What organizational adjustments must be made should any of these scenarios become a reality? (*ibid.*, p. 5)

Such an approach – a policy-oriented form of environmental scanning – is broader than the economistic methodology adopted by the World Bank in *The East Asian Miracle* and gives due importance to political factors (Killick, 1994). It specifically identifies political management as an integral component of policy and points to the importance of organizational reform.

Explanations of the Third World policy process

National experiences with development have varied considerably. Some policies have been effective in one place and not in others. There are countries where policy success in one sector contrasts with failure elsewhere. In other countries, policy choices and outcomes have consistently disappointed. Alarmingly, the lessons from past policy have often not been learned. To understand this situation we must enter the realm of politics and power and examine some of the leading models which attempt to explain policy behaviour in the developing world, especially the apparent paradoxes in that behaviour.

To accomplish this we have adopted (and slightly modified) a useful typology of policy models constructed by Grindle and Thomas (1989). They draw a distinction between society-centred and state-centred models of policy change. In society-centred models, explanations of the policy process are based in terms of the power relations between social groups such as classes and interest groups. The mechanics of decision-making take a minor role. By contrast, in the state-centred models analysis focuses on 'decision-making within the organizational context of the state' (*ibid.*, p. 219). The decision-maker is awarded 'considerably more capacity for choice' while societal constraints are less emphasised as investigators debate complex actor motivation and delve into the organizational politics of the state.

Society-centred models

Social class analysis
This mode of analysis is characteristic of Marxist and dependency approaches. Policy is the outcome of the conflicts between social classes. These struggles have their origin in the economic relationships between classes which, at least in dependency theory, transcend national boundaries to incorporate a dominant metropolitan bourgeoisie. A major concern is to delineate dominant and subordinate classes. Policy is seen as the prerogative of the former and is one method of securing the reproduction of the existing inequitable societal relations of the capitalist mode of production or even 'articulated' modes of production. The crude instrumentalist view of the state as simply being the executive committee of the bourgeoisie

is now rare. But the state has often been portrayed as functioning to provide 'the legal, institutional and ideological hegemony of the dominant class or class alliance over subordinate classes' (*ibid.*, p. 217). In this formulation the state is an instrument of domination used by the ruling classes and policy is a reflection of dominant class interests. These may incorporate concessions, incentives or palliatives to the subordinate classes – especially if the latter seem to be finding some political muscle.

Diversity and sophistication have been introduced to the class model. Some authors have examined the struggles and alliances between more than one dominant class (for example, feudal-style landowners and industrial capitalists) or between fractions of the bourgeoisie (for example, export-oriented capitalists and import-substituting capitalists) for control of the state. Others have awarded the state a certain degree of autonomy in promoting capitalist development and bourgeois interests. A class of the 'bureaucratic' or 'state' bourgeoisie which derives its privileges from control of the state has sometimes been recognized in this formulation (Shivji, 1976). Many have considered such a classification as too narrow, and have argued that in transitional societies diverse elements (for example, top bureaucrats, leading entrepreneurs, and politicians) combine to form a 'managerial bourgeoisie' (Sklar, 1979) or 'organizational bourgeoisie' (Markowitz, 1977). The dominant components in such coalitions are likely to change over time but they may retain a policy orientation towards the management of wealth rather than to its creation. With the impressive records of economic growth in many Asian countries there has been a renewal of interest in the identification and influence of the middle class on policy (Johnson, 1985; *The Pacific Review*, 1992).

Pluralism
In this approach 'public policy results from the conflict, bargaining and coalition formation among a potentially large number of societal groups, organized to protect or advance particular interests common to their members' (Grindle and Thomas, 1989, p. 218). It is an idealized model of Western democracy, especially the US version, in which assumptions are made about power being widely distributed among a variety of groups, and that channels for the expression of grievances are numerous and open. The state acts largely as an arbiter in this democratic competition and responds to pressures coming from society.

This model is simply inappropriate for many developing countries. Where were the plurality of interests in Paraguay under Stroessner, Malawi under Banda or contemporary Myanmar? Such authoritarian regimes do not encourage or allow the formation of diverse and active interest groups as routinely found in Western democracies. Even in robust Third World democracies, such as Sri Lanka, interest groups which actually influence policy-making may be few in number (Hulme and Sanderatne, 1995). However, interest groups do exist and in some Third World countries are increasing in the wake of economic and political liberalization. Business groups, professional associations, labour unions, consumer groups, squatter associations, religious institutions, women's groups and NGOs are evident in many developing countries. They all try to influence the policy process with varying degrees of success, and because formal channels are often poorly developed they utilize personal ties and other strategies to secure a voice in the policy process. Even in authoritarian regimes or partial democracies they may exert influence. But in no case does practical experience conform to the plurality of participatory opportunities offered in Western models of pluralism.

Public choice
The public choice perspective has a kinship with the pluralist approach in its basic assumption about political society being composed of organized interests. These interests are concerned with obtaining access to public resources. The benefits are frequently referred to as 'rents' where a particular group or individual obtains some form of preferment from the state; for example, an import licence, a logging concession, exclusive rights in a particular industry. Both elected and non-elected officials facilitate favoured access to public goods, services and regulations. Such rent-seeking behaviour is common in Third World states and goes a long way to explain why policy often appears irrational; for example, why agriculture has been overtaxed in predominantly agrarian societies; why import substitution protection is maintained yet consumers pay high prices for inferior products.

The paradox of such apparent irrationality is that public choice theory is based on the view that 'people are rational, self-interested, opportunistic, maximisers' (Larmour, 1990, p. 64). It is the furtherance of narrow interests and not the public interest which dominates. The weak and poor are losers unless they can organize and articulate their interests. Often they appear unable to accomplish this especially as obstacles, such as other interests, prevent it.

The difference between pluralist and public choice approaches is in the perception of politics. The former sees wise policy resulting from competing interest groups while the latter has no illusions about politics, characterizing it negatively as an often cynical and always self-interested struggle for resources.

But public choice may not focus exclusively on venal rent-seekers. It is frequently associated with economic ideas of efficiency and can support policy recommendations which come from consumer preferences and which take advantage of market opportunities. Public choice can thus be used as a method of criticizing the public providers of services and of looking to consumers to find what is wanted and how it can be supplied most efficiently. This is why public choice has often been associated with New Right formulations in the West and with the neo-classical economic leanings of the New Political Economy in the developing world (Meier, 1991).

State-centred models

Rational actor

As its name suggests, the rational actor model shares with public choice the belief that actors (whether persons, governments or other agencies) behave as rational choosers between alternative courses of action. But the rational actor model does not assume the actors' preoccupation with self-interest which takes such a central role in public choice. Also, the focus of both analysis and action in rational actor models is on the decision-makers and the decision-process and not on the societal players. They take supporting roles in this approach.

In its pure form the rational actor model involves a sequence in which goals are identified, translated into objectives and prioritized. Alternative course of action for achieving the objectives are evaluated, chosen and implemented. It is the stuff of a perfect world in which there are no constraints in time, resources, and knowledge. It is an ideal-type model which is never achieved although we have regularly encountered planners who aspire to reach some approximation of this scientific approach in their own work.

What has been proposed in the place of the rational ideal-type is a series of softer rationalities in which the effect of constraints and the sub-optimal conditions of the real world are incorporated. Thus, decision-makers may opt for 'satisficing' behaviour in which they do not search for the best possible use of resources but seek outcomes that are satisfactory and sufficient (Simon, 1957). They operate in conditions of 'bounded rationality' where time and resources are acknowledged constraints. Decisions are thus made by rule of thumb with limited search and information, especially as many policy problems are recurrent. Lindblom both described and prescribed such decision-making as incrementalist (Lindblom, 1959 and 1979). Policy-making is seen as 'muddling through' rather than a search for the best policy possible. How else could it be, argues Lindblom, in a complex and changing world where human intelligence and decision-making capacity are limited. This is why he prescribes 'successive limited comparisons' as the wise policy process because it eschews large leaps into the unknown, avoids expensive errors, makes decision-making easier and allows decisions to be reversed.

Although this incrementalist model can be used to describe some policy-making activities in developing countries it is inappropriate in many circumstances. On prescriptive grounds incremental solutions are not the requirement for severe problems of development which require urgent and major attention. On descriptive grounds incrementalism does not incorporate enough of the extra-rational considerations which are evident in the politics of developing countries and which impinge so much on the policy process.

Saasa notes that public policy-making in the Third World cannot be fully covered by the rational actor model or even incrementalism as they do not do full justice to the complexity and turbulence of the environments in which the decision-makers operate:

> It is, thus, prudent that when attempts are made to apply the contemporary, largely Euro-centric, policy-making models to developing countries with relatively unstable regimes, minimum inputs from the environment, resource scarcities, and rapid societal change, one needs to be aware of these societies' unique circumstances. (Saasa, 1985, p. 320)

Taking the critique of rational and incremental models to its limits, some authors have described such choice theories as 'improbably precise guesses about the future' (March, 1984) and have argued that much decision-making actually results from problems, solutions and participants happening to come together at a specific time (Cohen *et al.*, 1972).

Bureaucratic politics

This decision-making model views the structure of the state as an arena in which public officials engage in political manoeuvres to secure desired policy outcomes. They build coalitions, bargain, compromise, co-opt, guard information and devise strategies in order to further their personal or organizational objectives (Clay and Schaffer, 1984). The objective is control over the policy process in areas which are of particular concern to the actors involved. As Allison (1971, p. 176) succinctly observes 'where you stand depends on where you sit'. For example, the determination of health policy would involve the interaction of persons in the health department. Hospital staff and administrators would usually try to prevent reduction in spending on hospital facilities. Other departmental players might favour the extension of low cost primary health care in rural areas. Specialist units, such as malaria eradication, would also be lobbying to maintain or increase their budgets. The department of finance might be attempting to reduce health spending as part of a structural adjustment package while other departments could well support such initiatives to save their own funding.

It is a useful perspective which dispels the lingering myth of politicians deciding policy according to some objective criteria for neutral administrators to implement. The bureaucratic politics model identifies the organizations of the state as being embroiled in constant political conflict to determine which policy options are selected and how they are to be implemented. Where it may be criticized is that it awards great autonomy to officials in the determination of policy. Where are the social classes and interest groups? Also the bureaucratic approach credits officials with clear policy preferences which may simply not be there. We rediscover our rational actor in a new context. But what of the force of normal bureaucratic routines, inertia, incorrect reasoning and the state-society relationship? The narrow focus of bureaucratic politics thus omits or undervalues some considerations which could have a profound impact on the policy process.

State interests

The state interests approach moves away from the micro-political processes occurring between public officials and adopts a broader perspective in which 'the state appears to have some autonomy in defining the nature of public problems and developing solutions to them' (Grindle and Thomas, 1989, p. 220). It has even been evident in some neo-Marxist literature where the state demonstrates relative autonomy in making decisions against the expressed interests of the dominant classes.

The state is seen to have interests – or to avoid reification, officials of the state identify and pursue collective interests because of their shared location in the state. These state interests can refer to any aspect of human activity ranging from defence of the state to attempts to change public morals. Different states can be seen as having different degrees of autonomy and perhaps different interests *vis-à-vis* those of societal actors.

The great strength of this approach is that although its analytical focus is the state, the nature of state-society relations is also of concern as this will determine the degree of autonomy of policy élites in the state. As Nordlinger (1987, p. 386) notes, 'Taking the state seriously involves bringing statist and societal accounts of state autonomy together in empirically meaningful, mutually illuminating, and analytically integrated ways'. We will pursue one of these ways in the next section where we make deeper investigations of who actually participates in policy-making and who does not.

Participation in the policy-making process

While the majority of Third World leaders invoke the name of the people and democracy the level of popular participation in policy-making has been generally much less than in the OECD nations. There are fewer participants in the policy-making process and the official channels for participation are more restricted. Such restriction can lead to the use of non-democratic forms of mobilizing power including violent challenges to the government.

In sub-Saharan Africa the typical contemporary regime has revolved round the person of the ruler (Gulhati, 1990). A varying combination of patronage and coercion secures compliance while factional struggles and regime uncertainty are endemic. Policy circles are narrow. In Zambia, for example, there is a history of parliamentary debate and some airing of critical commentary in the press. In cabinet and the bureaucracy there were conflicts over policy but President Kaunda acted as the princely arbiter of disputes, sometimes overruling cabinet or simply ignoring it. In Malawi, President Banda demonstrated little tolerance of dissent over his policies. In some instances, such as Idi Amin in Uganda, it is not even possible to talk of a policy circle as the extreme unpredictability of life and arbitrariness of decision-making render the notion of policy obsolete.

As in much of the developing world the regimes of sub-Saharan Africa have frequently been authoritarian in character. Such regimes by definition restrict decision-making to relatively few individuals and groups. Democratic forms such as parliaments and congresses are typically closed or shorn of power, regime opponents may be imprisoned, the media are tightly controlled and mobilization of the population is at the behest of the state. While personal rulers such as Banda, Marcos and Somoza feature prominently in authoritarian regimes there are in fact other significant actors in the policy circle.

The most obvious of these actors is the military. In Latin America, for example, military intervention in politics and prolonged military rule have been common. Contemporary Latin American armies are professionalized, self-conscious and hierarchically organized forces which began to intervene in politics in response to economic collapse and perceived civilian incompetence in the 1920s and 1930s (Cammack *et al.*, 1988). They have ruled for considerable periods, especially in the more developed countries on the continent, and even when not in office have exerted considerable influence on policymaking. In the Middle East, the military has played a 'decisive role'. Since, 1958, the monarchies of Iraq, Egypt and Libya have fallen to officer-led initiatives while contemporary Syrian politics focuses on factional shifts within the military. Middle Eastern military regimes have sometimes been radical pursuing policies of land reform and nationalization. They have sometimes returned to the barracks but like all militaries which have led or participated in government they are reluctant to leave national affairs to civilians and remain 'a force behind the scenes, and at minimum a powerful pressure group whose interests and views must be taken into account' (*ibid.*, p. 146).

Less obvious but perhaps more pervasive in Third World policymaking circles are the leading public servants and their vast bureaucracies. We will make more detailed examination of these bureaucracies in the next chapter but we will make a few comments on their policy role now. In many instances, public servants do not simply wait to be issued implementation orders, they are actively involved in various ways and to varying degrees in the business of policy-making. In Bangladesh, for example it has been reported that:

Due to the absence of an effective extrabureaucratic power structure, bureaucratic domination has become so extensive that it pervades the entire social fabric. Bureaucrats have taken upon themselves the responsibility of public decision making, and there is no efficacious means of holding them accountable for their actions (Khan and Zafrullah, 1991).

Also active in the authoritarian, and indeed democratic, policy-making circle is the bourgeoisie, the owners of big businesses. In Latin America businesses have organizations that represent their commercial, financial and industrial interests. These organizations do not work through political parties but lobby legislative bodies and get members onto government commissions and boards. Members of the bourgeoisie deal directly with public officials using personal ties and perhaps bribery to pursue their policy options. There is not a consistent set of bourgeois policies. These are determined by historically specific factors and the bourgeoisie are always only one of the players vying for policy control (Wynia, 1990).

For example, while the transitions to 'uncertain democracies' in Ecuador and Bolivia in the 1980s were greatly influenced by business organizations, the latter were unable to guide the transitions completely to their liking. They were always constrained by other players in civil society and the state – trade unions, popular organizations, the military and political parties (Conaghan, 1990). Such experiences lead to the general point that capitalism in Third World countries does not automatically entail unfettered business élites exerting a free hand in policy-making. They are always constrained by other actors from neo-patrimonial rulers to elected legislatures.

The bourgeoisie may also be fragmented into competing interests and engage in internal squabbles about the direction of economic policy. In some instances the national bourgeoisie may be weak allowing public officials to extend the economic interests of the state, thus promoting the ascendancy of a bureaucratic bourgeoisie whose class position and privilege is directly dependent upon the state. A weak national bourgeoisie may also allow foreign capital to exert dominance in the local economy and permit transnational corporations to become major actors in the domestic policy circle.

There are other actors in the policy circle but they may be nation or issue-specific, and their relative strength can vary over time. The Roman Catholic Church exerts influence in Latin America; in some countries trade unions wield power; and where higher levels of economic growth have been recorded the emergent middle classes may start to participate in defining policy issues. But there are many whose participation is weak, sporadic or non-existent. Policy is determined by élites. Some members of these élites may claim to represent the interests of the less-powerful masses but it is evident that the majority of the populations in developing countries have not enjoyed access to, or influence over, policy circles.

Authoritarian regimes by definition have narrow policy circles. Democratically elected assemblies may have restricted powers or consist of members of privileged classes. Mass organizations have often been discouraged or made illegal. Coercion by state agencies or private forces has been common. The result is exclusion from the policy process of the bulk of the population in the developing world. Perceived apathy of these populations may result from the rigours of attending to daily subsistence needs, the demands of patron–client networks, the difficulty of organization in hostile political environments and the systematic closure of policy circles by élites. A couple of examples of who does not make policy will help to clarify these general points.

Sub-Saharan African societies are predominantly agrarian. Therefore, one might suppose that the peasant farming families who make up the majority of the population have exerted some influence on policy-making or have been represented by particular élites. But, we find a history of neglect and exploitation. Policies have been characterized as follows:

(i) maintaining unduly low producer prices; (ii) extracting public revenue through taxes on export crops or surpluses of agricultural marketing parastatals; (iii) overvalued currencies; (iv) maintaining low-cost food for urban dwellers; (v) raising prices of locally manufactured items above international prices via tariffs and import restrictions; and (vi) a marked urban bias in the pattern of public expenditure. (Gulhati, 1990, pp. 1152–3)

Such policies have been constructed by a coalition of rulers, bureaucrats, urban workers, local industrialists and occasionally multi-national corporations. The poor African farming family is notably absent from the circle. Each of the participants in the circle benefits in some way from the policies; for example, cheap food for urban workers, protection for urban manufacturers, subsidized imports for commercial farmers, rents for the bureaucrats and rulers. By keeping the coalition happy and the smallholder denied, the ruler will survive. But what has been the smallholder's response? According to Bates (1981), smallholders search for crops with better prices and will move into informal or black markets. They may see better opportunities in the towns and migrate to the urban areas. Thus, they may avoid or attempt to make the best of the discriminatory policies but they are not admitted to the policy circle.

Smallholders find it difficult to organize interest groups because they are numerically large, diverse and scattered. Costs of lobbying are high and there is the incentive to free ride. Commercial farmers do not provide leadership because they are seduced by input subsidies. Parties or factions that try to mobilize peasants into interest groups are repressed by the government.

A second group which has limited access to the policy circle and hence to decision-making which directly affects their lives is women. Gender is one of the social bases of inequality but cross-cuts others such as class and ethnicity. Thus, women may have common interests as women but sometimes may perceive themselves to have conflicting interests as women of particular ethnic groups or classes. As we saw in the previous chapter women appear to have fared less well in the development process than men. This can be conceptualized in terms of the relative powerlessness of women.

One way in which this can be seen is in the heavy male domination of parliaments, congresses and other assemblies at all levels of the state. While the overall figure for developing countries (14 per cent of male parliamentarian figure) is marginally above that for the OECD countries (13 per cent), both figures are low and hide considerable discrepancies. Fifty-five developing countries are below 10 per cent while only 30 are above. Also, there are no data for 42 countries, among which are nations such as Saudi Arabia and other Middle Eastern states which have few or no female representatives in the formal political institutions of state.

But some countries which have been associated with patriarchy have produced politically prominent females – Benazir Bhutto in Pakistan, Corazon Aquino in the Philippines, Aung San Suu Kyi in Burma, Begum Khalida Zia and Sheikh Hasina in Bangladesh, Indira Gandhi in India and Chandrika Kumaratunga in Sri Lanka. In these countries, and many others, politics has been presumed to be the natural sphere of men while women's natural sphere has been determined as the private and domestic (Richter, 1990). Allocation to this sphere has worked to exclude women from political competition and office because experience in this sphere is said to limit their horizons and loyalties. Conversely, masculine characteristics are cited as the requirements for politics. Thus, women are made ineligible for political roles.

So how have a significant number of women in South and South-east Asia achieved such political prominence? Richter (*ibid.*, p. 526) argues that 'women are accepted as behaving appropriately in politics when they are perceived as filling a political void created by the death or imprisonment of a male family member.' All of the above examples corroborate this. One can further generalize that female politicians come from privileged social classes where domestic work is performed by servants. What this adds up to is that women politicians tend to be in office for reasons other than being women and that their primary loyalty may be to class or family interests. As one female lobbyist in the Philippines observed to us in early 1993, up to that time any progressive legislation for females had been tabled by males in the Philippine Congress.

Rising levels of education and greater participation in the labour market are no guarantees of more women in elective politics. Japan, South Korea, Argentina and Chile are a few examples of that. In each case, women parliamentarians make up less than 6 per cent of their male counterparts. Perhaps, women have made their greatest gains outside of the formal electoral structures in non-governmental organizations, which can be linked nationally and internationally in networks and which can apply pressure on the formal system of policy-making and implementation. Such organizations may yet provide the foundations for greater female representation in politics and greater attention to gender issues in policy.

Policy, politics and implementation

There is a persistent myth or perhaps naive assumption that politicians make policy and public servants implement it rationally 'as if implementation was something utterly simple and automatic' (Lane, 1993, p. 93). While both politicians and bureaucrats are frequently active in promulgating and maintaining this myth, the reality is somewhat different. Implementation is not easy and straightforward and cannot be simply classified as a technical exercise involving calculated choices of appropriate techniques (see Box 3.4 for common implementation problems). Implementation is frequently a highly

BOX 3.4
The notorious nine implementation problems

These implementation problems of projects of the US Agency for International Development (USAID) were found to occur frequently enough to impede the progress of implementation. In the original article, the authors suggested 'solutions' to these problems. What solutions can you suggest?

1. *Political, economic and environmental constraints*
   There are four sets of constraints which project designers and implementors ignore at their peril: donor foreign policy, national politics, macroeconomic policy, and physical and sociocultural factors in the local environment.

2. *Institutional realities*
   The institutional context in which development activities take place is a major determinant of project success. Important institutional factors include administrative capacity, selection of project agencies for implementation, access to resources by development agencies and structures that support effective information flow.

3. *Host country personnel limitations*
   Many developing countries have only a small cadre of personnel with appropriate technical and administrative skills. These people are often overextended.

4. *Technical assistance shortcomings*
   There can be criticism of the quality of technical assistance (TA) personnel, confusion about the appropriate function of TA, and disagreement over the roles that such personnel should play. The ability to motivate and teach is often perceived to be vitally important by recipients as this promotes sustainable development.

5. *Decentralization and participation*
   Decentralization and participation are commonly believed to increase the likelihood of project success but lack of political commitment, bureaucratic resistance and inadequate resources have contributed to often disappointing results

6. *Timing*
   Three types of timing problem interfere with effective project implementation: delays between project identification and start-up; delays during project implementation; and inappropriate time-phasing of project activities.

7. *Information systems*
   Information generated by development projects is often used ineffectively or not used at all: information systems are designed but never implemented; data are collected but never processed; or the results are made available but are only used by researchers.

8. *Differing agendas*
   The principal actors in development projects try to achieve different and sometimes contradictory ends. When these agendas differ, project success and benefit sustainability will rarely achieve priority attention.

9. *The bottom line: sustaining project benefits*

Although development projects are intended to foster a process of self-sustaining development, they have often provided little more than a temporary infusion of assets, personnel and services. Sustainability has been adversely affected by factors of a political, economic, institutional and financial nature. Financial factors include the use of excessively costly technologies and service delivery systems in a setting where revenues are insufficient to cover future financial needs.

Source: Gow, D. D. and Morss, E. R. (1988) 'The Notorious Nine: Critical Problems in Project Implementation', *World Development*, vol. 16(12), pp. 1399–418.

political process. It is an arena where those with interests in a policy engage in negotiation over the goals of the policy and conflict over the allocation of resources.

This 'politics of implementation' has been a special interest of Merilee Grindle over many years, and it is to her work we will now turn. She notes that in the United States and Western Europe policy activity is focused on the input (policy-making) stage but that in the Third World, where interest aggregating structures are often weak, 'a large portion of individual and collective demand making, the representation of interests, and the emergence and resolution of conflict occur at the output stage' (implementation) (Grindle, 1980, p. 15). This is the stage where those interested in particular policies are best able to participate. Also, politics based on factions, patron–client ties, and other affective forms is highly suited to 'individualized demand on the bureaucratic apparatus for the allocation of goods and services' (*ibid.*, p. 18).

The implementation phase may thus be seen as an arena in which those responsible for allocating resources are engaged in political relationships among themselves and with other actors intent on influencing that allocation. The cast would typically include national level planners; national, regional and local politicians; economic élite groups; institutions such as the church and military; recipient groups; groups seeing themselves as suffering adverse consequences from the policy; multilateral agencies such as the World Bank; and bureaucratic implementors. The intensity of participation by an actor will depend on a range of factors including the strength of interest in the policy and the organizational capacity.

The prevalence of politics in implementation has led Grindle to a rejection of the popular linear model of implementation (see Box 3.5).

78

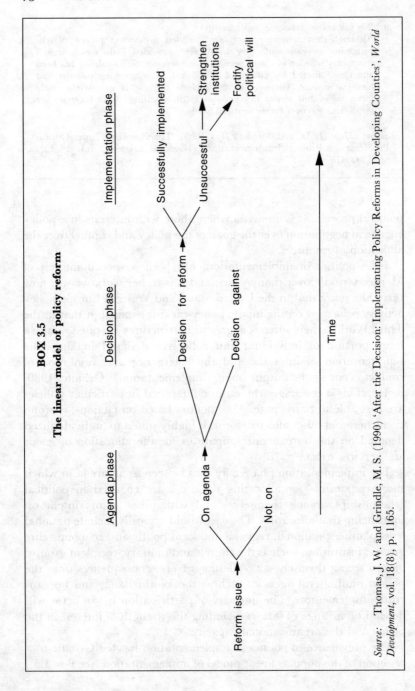

BOX 3.5
The linear model of policy reform

| Agenda phase | Decision phase | Implementation phase |

Reform issue → On agenda / Not on

On agenda → Decision for reform / Decision against

Decision for reform → Successfully implemented / Unsuccessful

Successfully implemented → Strengthen institutions

Unsuccessful → Fortify political will

Time →

Source: Thomas, J. W. and Grindle, M. S. (1990) 'After the Decision: Implementing Policy Reforms in Developing Counties', *World Development*, vol. 18(8), p. 1165.

This scheme is related to the Whitehall myth mentioned earlier as it anticipates implementation is simply about doing what has already been decided. Failure to implement is interpreted either as 'a lack of political will', surely the woolliest phrase in the developmental lexicon, or as weak institutional capacity. Much effort has gone into resolving the latter in programmes designed to strengthen institutions and to improve policy analysis. We agree with Grindle and Thomas (1990) that such initiatives are necessary and often valuable but that they represent only a partial solution to the search for successful policy implementation.

Grindle and Thomas identify key decision-makers and implementors in the policy process and suggest that:

> [They] face opposition in attempting to pursue reformist initiatives; in consequence, they need to consider feasibility in terms of support and opposition to change, what stakes they and the government they serve have in the pursuit of reform, and the political and bureaucratic resources needed to sustain such initiatives. (*ibid.*, pp. 1165–6)

Analysis of implementation feasibility should thus become an essential part of policy analysis. The linear model treats this as a technical matter or even omits such considerations. But the case studies of Grindle and Thomas lead to an interactive model in which policy is viewed as a process not as a series of discrete stages (see Box 3.6). Analysis commences with looking at the characteristics of any public policy in terms of the reaction it will generate. Then governments must assess what their resources are and how they can be mobilized to promote successful implementation. Decision-makers must evaluate political resources while public managers attend to bureaucratic resources. Such analysis can lead to a more realistic approach to policy where the question of implementation feasibility assumes major importance. Failure can be better anticipated, modifications can be better judged and resources can be more efficiently and effectively allocated.

Conclusion

In this chapter we have examined public policy and its political context. People everywhere expect governments to make and implement policy, and there are increasing pressures for this to be done

BOX 3.6
The interactive model of policy implementation

Issues

↓ ↓ ↓

Policy agenda

Decision
stages

Policy characteristics

Arena

Bureaucratic — — — — Public

Reject / implement   Implement / reject

Resource requirements:
Political
Financial
Managerial
Technical

Multiple potential outcomes

Source: Thomas, J. W. and Grindle, M. S. (1990) 'After the Decision: Implementing Policy Reforms in Developing Countries', *World Development*, vol. 18(8), p. 1167.

with consultation and assistance from non-state actors. There are multiple meanings to the word policy. None is wrong but we should be aware of these alternate usages and for analytic purposes adopt a meaning in which process is emphasized. In a few Asian countries there has been great success with policy which has made a major contribution to rapid economic and social gains. Whether this 'Asian Miracle' model is replicable remains open to doubt as environmental conditions vary so much between developing countries.

This diversity may partially explain why various models have been applied to Third World policy processes. Some are society-centred and focus on the interplay between societal actors such as classes or interest groups. Others are state-centred and emphasize the interactions of those involved in the decision-making of the policy process. We believe that both perspectives have explanatory validity and that elements of both need to be combined to illuminate the nature of the policy process in any specific developing country. Looking at who actually makes or influences policy decisions is useful data for the policy models. There is also the question of implementation. At this stage in the policy process many political battles are fought over the allocation of scarce resources and any policy model must incorporate this reality. Indeed, politics and power permeate the entire policy process rather than rational and technical matters. To understand the policy process in the developing world we must first understand the political context, and to secure improvement in policy-making and policy outcomes it is not enough to simply increase the capacities of state bureaucracies.

There must also be action on the political front. We should move beyond the shrugging of shoulders accompanied by references to lack of political will and attempt to construct a politics of policy improvement as Grindle and Thomas (1990) have done, or actively encourage wider participation like the advocates of public action. As we have seen, there are structural constraints to effective policy-making and implementation but even under typically adverse conditions in the developing world there is room for manoeuvre. Both public and private actors do have some autonomy in decision-making which means that getting more policies right is possible. The politics is not going to be removed from the policy process but it can be made to produce policies and outcomes which are more equitable and effective and which make more efficient use of scarce resources.

4

Bureaucracy: Obstructing or Facilitating Development?

The growth of bureaucracy has been a leading feature of twentieth century development. Whether one looks at OECD countries, former and present communist countries or the nations of the Third World bureaucratization is ubiquitous. In developing countries the organizations of the state have high visibility and assume great importance but interpretations of what they do and how they do it vary considerably. In many cases the public service is blamed for poor developmental performance. Bureaucracy is, nevertheless, an essential and vitally important instrument of development. Even the most ardent proponents of the virtues of the market now admit this. In some instances bureaucracies have made a considerable contribution to development. Such desirable outcomes are possible and with appropriate action can become more frequent.

In this chapter we will briefly examine some of the voluminous literature on bureaucracy in the developing world, investigate the leading issues and controversies, and even expose a few myths. We commence with a conceptual warning about the multiple meanings attaching to the term 'bureaucracy' and then describe the origins of these vast state organizations. In the main section of the chapter we will look at major issues relating to bureaucracy and development.

What is bureaucracy?

There are many answers to this question. Jan-Erik Lane (1987), for example, identifies ten different usages of the term! We will, however, confine ourselves to four leading meanings of bureaucracy which are found in popular sentiments and academic literature on bureaucracy in the developing world.

Rule by the bureau
This was the original nineteenth century use of the term to indicate 'a system in which ministerial positions were occupied by career officials, usually answerable to a hereditary monarchy' (Beetham, 1987, p. 3). It should be contrasted with representative forms of government. In the contemporary Third World, it can be employed to describe military dictatorship, one-party authoritarian states and neo-patrimonialism.

Professional administration
This is a sociological approach which looks at bureaucracy as a particular type of organization. Its principal reference point is the ideal-type bureaucracy constructed by Max Weber (Gerth and Mills, 1948). This is characterized by a clearly defined division of labour, an impersonal authority structure, a hierarchy of offices, dependence on formal rules, employment based on merit, the availability of a career and the distinct separation of members' organizational and personal lives. Such a form of organization represented, said Weber, the 'rationalization of collective activities' and was 'capable of attaining the highest degree of efficiency'. It was increasingly found in the professionalization of administration in the modernizing societies of the late, 19th century both in the public and private sectors, but Weber's model is still widely employed today as a comparative tool by which we can assess the degree and form of bureaucratization in a society or organization.

Public administration
In this usage bureaucracy is another way of saying public administration. Private organizations are excluded on the grounds that there are distinct aspects to public administration because of its location in the state. Beetham (1987, p. 3) identifies some of the characteristics as

'its compulsory character, its particular relation to the law [and] the public accountability of its operations'. While managerialism in many countries has led to attempts to incorporate private sector management techniques into the public sector, the public administration view of bureaucracy is still strong both in the popular imagination and within the organizations of the state. When people say 'the bureaucracy', more often than not they mean the public sector.

Negative characteristics

This meaning focuses on popular perceptions of the workings of bureaucracy, and is most often associated with the organizations of the state rather than the private sector. It encompasses a range of negative assessments of all that is wrong with these organizations. Crozier provided a concise summary in 1964, and his observations are still valid today:

> [Bureaucracy] evokes the slowness, the ponderousness, the routine, the complication of procedures, and the maladapted responses of 'bureaucratic' organizations to the needs which they should satisfy, and the frustrations which their members, clients, or subjects consequently endure.   (Crozier, 1964, p. 3).

We will review many of these charges later in the chapter when we deal with the problems of bureaucracy.

Bureaucracy thus means different things to different people and sometimes different things to the same people depending on their situation. The above meanings are not mutually exclusive but can be used together in analysis provided the reader is made aware of which meaning is being employed. For simplicity's sake and to eliminate Western cultural bias embodied in Weberian notions of rationality one could opt for a minimalist definition as advocated by Brown (1989). Such a definition makes few assumption about how bureaucracies should work but looks at how they actually work. Brown cites Jacques's (1976) definition of bureaucracy as a leading example of the minimalist genre: 'a hierarchically stratified managerial employment system in which people are employed to work for a wage or salary'.

In this chapter we will be focusing on the bureaucracies of the state and while trying to elucidate their organizational features we will attempt to avoid the cultural biases implicit in much Western managerial literature.

The origin of Third World bureaucracies

There are numerous books, movies, television series and other forms of remembrance devoted to European explorers, conquistadors and pioneers who discovered and exploited the colonial possessions which now form the Third World. However, one major legacy of European colonialism in the Third World which is of greater significance but seldom if ever celebrated is bureaucracy. The African example is instructive:

> Colonial states all created an administrative hierarchy through the concentration of political and administrative functions in the hands of the colonial civil service. [The colonizers] went about the task of governance by establishing a bureaucratic network staffed by officers who had charge of specific duties (such as revenue collection, public order, medicine, education, infrastructural organization, adjudication, social services, and even in the later colonial period, development projects). (Chazan *et al.*, 1988, p. 40)

Public administration undertaken by organizations with bureaucratic features was, however, in evidence in some ancient civilizations of what is now the Third World centuries before Max Weber observed their emergence in Europe. Heady (1984, pp. 150–1) comments on the 'impressive' bureaucracy of Old Kingdom Egypt where before 2180BC complex patterns of delegation, specialization and institutional longevity were evident. By the time of Confucius's death in 478BC, the Chinese army 'already had the character of a disciplined bureaucracy' while state officials were developing a penchant for 'bureaucratic meddling in everything' (Weber, 1948, p. 421). Other ancient civilizations such as the Incas and Aztecs in the Americas also developed complex and effective systems of public administration which carved out and maintained vast empires.

The ancient bureaucracies were frequently patrimonial displaying only some of the ideal Weberian characteristics. If one takes the long view of history, then such characteristics may have survived European colonialism and be in evidence today albeit in modified form. Many colonial rulers followed ancient practice in relying on traditional institutions as 'carriers of order'. Offices were awarded on the basis of some combination of merit and personal ties. The idea of state officials as an élite caste was universal while centralization was a common theme in administrative structures.

The colonial state is best characterized as an administrative unit, a bureaucratic state. Politicians were largely absent or severely restricted in their powers. The roles of administrator and politician were usually amalgamated. The precise arrangements of the bureaucracies varied between colonial powers but they were all designed to regulate (laws and rules) and extract (taxes and raw materials) and were backed by strong coercive force. Control was the theme of colonial bureaucracy but this did not necessarily entail penetration of all or even many of the routines of everyday life. Much could be left to 'traditional' institutions. Nevertheless, bureaucratic control is an issue which has been prominent in post-colonial states especially in the context of weak political institutions. Bureaucracy has often been the strongest institutional inheritance of the post-colonial state.

Bureaucracy even conquered without colonialism. Strong external impulses for defence of the state or to modernize could induce rulers to introduce elements of modern bureaucracy. For example, British and French threats in the nineteenth century helped precipitate modernizing reforms in Thailand which included the adoption of Western administrative methods, while the overthrow of absolute monarchy in 1932 facilitated the consolidation of military-bureaucratic rule. This alliance has only recently been challenged seriously following the Bangkok uprising of 1992 and subsequent democratization measures.

Bureaucracy and development

As we have already learned, bureaucracy is ubiquitous in the developing world. It is also the subject of considerable debate and criticism. In this section we will review some of these leading issues relating to bureaucracy and development.

Size

A widespread criticism of bureaucracy is that it is too big, a lumbering juggernaut which absorbs enormous resources but actually produces very little. The World Bank, for example, makes reduction in the size of the public service a condition of most structural adjustment loans. Sometimes the reason is that there are simply too many personnel. Alternatively, and in line with neoclassical thinking, it is argued that some functions should be opened to the market and that government should concentrate on core regulatory functions.

The post-independence period has normally seen the expansion of state bureaucracies as new governments moved beyond the restricted regulatory focus of colonial administration and took on new responsibilities (for example, foreign affairs) and embarked on ambitious schemes of planned development. This necessitated the creation of new institutions and the expansion of existing ones. For example, within a decade of India's independence the government had created the Central Secretariat Service, the Central Health .Service, the Central Legal Service and the Central Information Service. Then came the Indian Economic Service and the Indian Statistical Service (Maheshwari, 1990). In 1951, there were 1.529 million central government employees. By 1960, there were 2.025 million and in 1980 there were 3.678 million. The story at state level is similar with figures revealing the numbers of state functionaries growing from 1.202 million in 1958 to 4.414 million in the 1980s (*ibid.*).

But do such figures represent the bloated bureaucracies of popular imagination? Donald Rowat (1990) has provided some interesting insights on this question in his comparative statistical analysis of developed and developing-country bureaucracies. From his sample, Rowat found that the number of public employees in proportion to population is much greater in the developed countries – 6.4 employees per 100 population in the developed countries compared to 2.6 in developing countries but with wide variations in each category. The large number of workers in local government in the developed countries accounts for this difference. They are in areas of 'personal services' such as education, health and social welfare which are frequently poorly provided for at the local level in developing countries. But workers in public enterprises make up a greater percentage of public sector employment in the developing countries while public sector employment as a percentage of total non-agricultural employment is far higher in the developing countries. Rowat cites a 1983 IMF study which gives a range of 10 per cent (Japan) to 36 per cent (New Zealand) for public sector employment as a proportion of total non-agricultural employment in developed countries as compared to a range of 17 per cent (Guatemala) to 85 per cent (Benin) in developing countries.

There is no simple formula to determine how big a public service should be (see Box 4.1). In very poor countries public bureaucracies may be the only way to provide certain services, particularly primary

---

BOX 4.1
The challenge of big beaucracy

China's bloated bureaucracy – stuffed with 500 000 idlers according to official figures – is to be streamlined. Premier Li Peng is heading a top-level Communist Party committee charged with trimming the fat of a civil service that is draining state coffers and meddling in business, the official media reported yesterday.

China has 33 million bureaucrats at all levels the *China Daily* said yesterday. About 500 000 were 'paid but doing little'. Each year, one million university graduates and demobilized troops joined the ranks of the civil service, the newspaper said. Only 400 000 retired. Zhang Zhijian, Vice Minister of Personnel, was quoted as saying it would be difficult enough to stop the growth let alone cut overall numbers. Without drastic measures, he predicted a civil service of 40 million people by the year 2000.

Smashing the 'iron ricebowl' – a cradle-to-grave system of employment and social security – is a politically explosive issue for China's hardline leaders. But propping up state industry and subsidising inefficiency at all levels is breaking budget targets and threatens another round of raging inflation. Reducing the size of the bureaucracy has become the most hotly debated issue in government and is shaping up as the new battleground between orthodox Marxists and economic reformers.

Source: *The Canberra Times*, 13 October 1991.

---

education and primary health care. One must also take into account what the public expects from the state, and what are the state's development plans. Concern with size may be misplaced and our attention should be fixed more on promoting efficiency and effectiveness in what exists rather than with 'downsizing'. But bureaucratic growth may reflect government's unwillingness to trust other partners in development and the bureaucrats' self-interest. In such cases there may be good arguments for decentralizing functions to NGOs and private businesses as a way to overcome poor bureaucratic performance thus forcing the public sector to compete and to fulfil participatory goals of development.

Capacity

In the ideal Weberian model, bureaucracy is an efficient instrument of policy implementation. But in many developing countries the practice of implementation has been disappointing (see Box 4.2). The leading explanation for this state of affairs has been poor administrative capacity.

BOX 4.2
Project implementation and capacity

• The efficiency and effectiveness of government administrative and legal procedures directly influenced the implementation of the institutional strengthening components of many UNDP-funded urban development projects. A project executed through the United Nations Capital Development Fund (UNCDF) to provide low-cost housing in Conakry, Guinea, could not be implemented as originally planned because of inefficient or ineffective government procedures. Many of the other UNCDF-assisted projects were delayed by the long and complex processes of obtaining supplies.

• The slowness with which government agencies cleared operational plans in Nigeria delayed implementation of the waste disposal and drainage project in Ibadan, as did the lack of an effective organizational arrangement for carrying out the health education component of the project. Progress on the regional cities development project in Thailand was also slowed significantly by time-consuming committee and sub-committee procedures. The financial planning component of the Eastern Seaboard development programme in Thailand was affected by the delays in completing funding negotiations, signing of contracts and implementation.

• In Liberia, legal procedures for acquiring land seriously delayed implementation of the low-cost housing construction components of the UNDP-UNCHS assistance to the National Housing Authority. Complicated processes of land acquisition resulted in a delay of nearly two years in the housing program in Monrovia and in a decision not to acquire land in Matadi for housing.

• The impact of many UNDP urban developments was weakened by the lack of qualified counterpart staff in project organizations. The project in Liberia to upgrade the capability of the National Housing Authority was also undermined by a shortage of trained and motivated technicians and by a lack of candidates to participate in project-supported fellowships. Changes in counterpart personnel, and government limitations on recruitment of staff, impeded the ability of the technical expert to train and develop the capabilities of Thai personnel in the financial-planning aspect of the Eastern Seaboard development programme. Evaluations of the project also point out that on-the-job training was drastically limited both by the failure to design the projects to build institutional capacity, and by the failure of the government to provide sufficient counterpart staff to learn from the international experts provided by UNDP.

Source: Rondinelli, D. A. (1992) 'UNDP Assistance for Urban Development: An Assessment of Institution-building Efforts in Developing Countries', *International Review of Administrative Sciences*, vol. 58(4), pp. 519–37.

Administrative capacity is a broad concept which refers to the managerial abilities of organizations – whether they are equipped to do what they are supposed to do:

> Capacity in government is the process of identifying and developing the management skills necessary to address policy problems; attracting, absorbing and managing financial, human and information resources; and operating programs effectively, including evaluating program outcomes to guide future activities. (Umeh, 1992, p. 58)

There are frequent reports of inadequate management skills and qualifications. A 1984 survey in Papua New Guinea estimated that 40 per cent of public servants lacked the appropriate qualifications for their positions (Turner, 1991). Regular suspensions of provincial governments for financial irregularities in the same country may be less to do with corruption than with a shortage of the whole range of accounting and financial management skills. In assessing pro-grammes for providing services to the urban poor, Cheema (1986, p. 12) has noted that in some Third World cities the availability of professionals for such public service work has not kept pace with demand. In rapidly expanding economies such as Thailand there may be acute shortages in some professional areas of the public service (for example, engineering, computer systems management) as the private sector provides superior terms and conditions of employment to the holders of such skills.

But skill shortage may not simply be a matter of supply failing to keep pace with demand. In Latin America, attempts to introduce merit reforms into the personnel practices of public services over three decades have met with considerable difficulties (Ruffing-Hilliard, 1991). Political responsiveness has often been maintained against professional competence and a spoils system has frequently been able to hold out against a merit system despite administrative reforms. Qualified personnel may exist but this does not necessarily mean that they will be the ones employed.

The human resource profile is only one aspect of capacity. The nature of administrative structures and procedures provides another focus. The concern has often been with the dysfunctions of develop-ment bureaucracies. Criticism has targeted red-tape, poor commu-nication, centralization of decision-making, delays in operation, and distance of public servants from their clients. It is argued that the bureaucratic structures generate dysfunctions which adversely affect efficiency and effectiveness. Far from being responsive organizations which react flexibly to the turbulent environments in which they are set, bureaucracies, in this conceptualization, are seen to be rigid and suffering from a bad case of goal displacement. The operating goals of these organizations are about system maintenance not developmental outcomes. Thus, Umeh (1992) found that in Southern Africa the least reported management skills were 'adaptation' and 'community relations'. Such shortcomings mean that bureaucracies are not well equipped to implement change. In fact, they display a close affinity to the regulatory orientation of their colonial forebears – and they may not even be efficient at that.

So far we have looked at administrative capacity from an intra-organizational perspective. But inter-organizational links are also important:

> A local project staff is related to regional coordinating bodies, a national planning bureau to international donor agencies, a private voluntary agency in a donor country to its funding ministry and its counterpart organizations in the Third World.
>
> (Van Ufford, 1988, p. 13)

A vital management skill for development concerns shaping the relationships between organizations. Any bureaucracy's environment is increasingly populated with other organizations. Agreements need to be forged with such organizations, coordination arranged, resources distributed, action jointly planned and, more recently, performance jointly assessed. Such activities have frequently been neglected by bureaucracies which are intent on maintaining their traditional areas of functional responsibility rather than sharing an orientation to outcomes and efficient patterns of resource utilization. The neglect can lead to the obvious gap which so often emerges between policy intention and implementation outcome.

Culture

The administrative capacity frame tends to portray development bureaucracies in terms of 'instrumental rationality'. They are tools which can be designed to perform particular tasks but which currently have some components missing. In some hands a rather narrow view is taken in which the effects of the environment on the organization is underestimated or ignored. But for those writers who focus on culture the reverse is true. They look at the way in which a nation's culture (that is, non-bureaucratic elements from the environment) penetrates the 'rational instrumentalities' to create deviant bureaucratic patterns.

Explanations of bureaucratic behaviour in terms of culture date back to the seminal work of Fred Riggs (for example, 1964 and 1966) while Hyden (1983), writing on Africa, has been a particularly influential recent exponent. He has identified an 'economy of affection' penetrating state organizations. He is referring to such particularistic relations as kinship, tribe, ethnicity and religion. Officials' commitment to these non-bureaucratic ties can override the 'rational' features of the imported bureaucratic structure. The economy of affection finds expression in favouritism, the importance of personal ties of patronage within bureaucracy, promotion based on who you are and not qualifications or experience, resource allocation to one's own group or region, and the appropriation of public resources for private purposes. Such behaviour takes place in the context of the soft state (Myrdal, 1968) or the weak state (Migdal, 1988) where state and society are engaged in conflict over who will make and impose the rules which actually govern the routines of everyday life – and strong societies often win over weak states.

Culture is generally portrayed as a problem of management although such an approach has been strongly criticized as a 'form of ethnic stereotyping that moves blame for failure off the shoulders of donors and reformers and onto the backs of Third World people' (Honadle and Rosengard, 1983, p. 5). The 'culture as problem' view sometimes carries an echo from scientific management with the implicit assumption of a universal technical rationality which characterizes the efficient and effective organization. In practice there may be multiple rationalities which differ between nations. For example, Bjur and Zomorrodian (1986) advocate a 'context-based' approach to administration in which cultural values influence the success or failure of administrative techniques. An example of the ways in which cultural values can affect administrative practice is given in Box 4.3. There can be no doubt that the bureaucracies of East Asia, particularly Japan, are heavily influenced by endogenous cultural factors. In terms of development performance, such factors must be interpreted as strengths rather than as problems.

BOX 4.3
Cultural values and administration

An exemplar religious–institutional cultural value set

1. No dichotomization of church and state. Church and state are one.
2. Market is one social enclave among others; mosque dominates political and social value arenas.
3. Family-clan the dominant organizational model.
4. Goals–means compatibility; how one pursues goals as important as the goals themselves. No deviation permitted.
5. Total subordination of instrumental values to religious values. Direct implications for meanings of concepts like efficiency, effectiveness, rate of return, etc.
6. Emphasis on personal fulfilment in a spiritual or otherworldly sense as the main goal rather than material achievement.
7. Any comparative individual superiority admitted only in terms of the religious piety or virtue possessed.

An exemplar secular–instrumental cultural value set

1. Church and state constitutionally separated.
2. Market values and institutions dominate most political and organizational value arenas.
3. Commercial firm the dominant organizational model.
4. Pragmatism; results-oriented; means utilized much less important than achieving ends. Means-rewarded if economic benefit accrues.
5. Values of efficiency, effectiveness, equality of opportunity utilized in evaluation of nearly all institutions, public and private.
6. Material goals dominate the individual's search for meaningful achievement.
7. Individual achievements measured in wealth, education, material accomplishments – almost never in personal piety.

Source: Bjur, W. E. and Zomorrodian, A. (1986) 'Towards Indigenous Theories of Administration: An International Perspective', *International Review of Administrative Sciences*, vol. 52(4), p. 406.

Power, politics and authority

There has been a tendency to view bureaucracies as technical instruments of administration. In such a model, inefficiency and ineffectiveness are recognized but are ascribed to rational capacity problems such as lack of skilled human resources or to the existence of irrational elements grouped under the residual category of culture. But such a picture is incomplete. We believe that a useful addition is to perceive bureaucracies in a political context – as political systems in which coalitions form to pursue particular policy options and where there are relations to wider political structures within society.

Anybody who works in a bureaucracy must be acutely aware that personnel in their organization are engaged in multiple political interactions. Some are highly visible such as lobbying by one division for a particular approach on a policy issue or for a larger share of budget. There may be differences of opinion within a ministry and major stakeholders will seek to form a dominant coalition to determine what the official ministry line might be. Some expressions of power are less visible. For example, experts within a ministry may recommend particular policy options and exclude others, thus determining what is considered by politicians and what is not. This manipulation of what actually comes onto the decision-making agenda has been described as non-decision-making, an apparent non-action which in fact may be just as effective as overt bargaining.

But the critical political concern is the interaction of political leadership and the public service. This is of great importance in developing countries where regimes and governments often change more rapidly than in OECD countries and are always more concerned with demonstrating legitimacy or simply maintaining a hold on office. Ledivina Cariño (1991a and 1992) has facilitated our understanding of this matter by constructing a matrix of possible regime–bureaucracy interactions (see Box 4.4).

In cell 1 we have 'the legally expected interaction of a political leadership and bureaucracy in a democracy', whereby the political regime maintains control over what a bureaucracy does. But such dominance is not specific to democratic regimes. In the Philippines, bureaucratic subordination has been maintained through all post-independence regimes whatever the degree of democracy or authoritarianism of the regime.

Cell 2 delineates a 'bureaucracy-dominated democracy' where the bureaucracy is ideally participatory and non-hierarchical, dealing directly with public interest groups representing racial, gender and class minorities. But, in practice, such coprimacy may be used by bureaucracies to further their own interests. Cariño cites examples from Latin America and South Asia to demonstrate how bureaucracies only permit reforms or implement them when the reforms are seen to be in the interests of the bureaucrats.

Cell 3 depicts bureaucratic subordination under an authoritarian leadership. Such concentration of power may be evident in some of

---

BOX 4.4
Regime–bureaucracy interactions

Power Distribution in Society	*Power Distribution in Government*	
	Executive ascendant	*Executive sublated*
	1	**2**
Democracy	Democratic political regime controls bureaucracy	Bureaucracy dominates democratic political regime
	3	**4**
Authoritarianism	Bureaucratic subordination to authoritarian political regime	Authoritarian political regime shares power with bureaucracy

Source: Modified from Cariño, L. V. (1992) *Bureaucracy for Democracy* (Quezon City: University of the Philippines Press).

---

the highly personalized regimes in Africa. The 'prophetic' Julius Nyerere in Tanzania, the 'princely' Kenneth Kaunda in Zambia, and the 'autocratic' Hastings Banda in Malawi are contrasting examples (Jackson and Rosberg, 1986; Gulhati, 1990) Other cases for Cell 3 occur where strongmen such as Park Chung Hee in South Korea or Ferdinand Marcos with his martial law in the Philippines succeed in subordinating the public service on the grounds of its inefficiency and corruption to the instructions of the political leader.

The final cell 4 is especially common in military regimes which secure the willing participation of the bureaucracy in government. The technocrats approve of such arrangements as they allow them to get on with development (usually top-down) without the encumbrance of interfering politicians and other democratic forces. For example, the 1932 coup in Thailand against the absolute monarchy was executed in a context of mass civil service lay-offs and has led Wongtrangan (1988, pp. 49–50) to describe it as 'a revolution of the bureaucrats, by the bureaucrats, and for the bureaucrats'. Thus, Fred Riggs was able to characterize Thailand as a 'bureaucratic polity', a classification which still has currency despite the 1992 uprising. Pakistan provides another post-war example of bureaucratic coprimacy. Military regimes have relied heavily on bureaucratic cooperation to rule and have rarely invoked policies with which bureaucrats disagree or which go against bureaucratic interests.

Cariño stresses that there are tensions and struggles in the regime-bureaucracy nexus. Regimes try to dominate bureaucracies. Bureaucracies fight back. Sometimes bureaucracies persist largely unchanged through differing political regimes while in other cases new political leadership may obtain bureaucratic commitment to change especially if other civil institutions and social forces are involved in such a movement. This is the arena of 'public action'.

Bureaucratic bias

Development bureaucracies are biased against the rural poor argues Robert Chambers (1983). This huge group which are most in need of development receive the attention of 'rural development tourists' from government ministries, aid agencies, academic researchers, civic delegations and other urban-based groups with an interest or stake in rural development. Chambers has identified six manifestations of bias against the rural poor by the 'rural development tourists' (see Box 4.5).

Chambers (1992) has continued his bureaucratic critique in the notion of 'the self-deceiving state'. He uses India to illustrate his thesis and, while giving the bureaucracy some credit for developmental initiatives, still maintains that developmental progress for the poor is held back by a combination of culture, conservatism and corruption in bureaucracy. He claims that the state misrepresents the reality of what is actually happening in rural areas and because of such self-deception continues to apply inappropriate models of rural development. The 'false positive feedback' which fuels the self-deception occurs through misreporting especially in the exaggeration of government performance; selected perception using unrepresentative sources of information; methods such as the questionnaire survey which mislead; diplomatic prudence by the researchers, monitors and evaluators; and evidence is simply ignored.

The important constructive task, says Chambers, is to get the development professionals and administrators in closer touch with reality. We will explore this matter further in Chapters 5 and 6.

BOX 4.5

Rural poverty unobserved: the six biases

- *Spatial biases*
  A preference for tarmac roads and travel close to urban centres where the more favoured rural population live. Even in villages the poorer people may be hidden from the main streets.

- *Project bias*
  Visitors are directed to see projects which are 'atypical islands of activity'.

- *Person biases*
  These are the persons with whom the officials, visitors and researchers have most contact and by doing so acquire impressions and information which is biased against the poor. They include local élites rather than representatives from the poorer social classes; men rather than women; the users of services and the adopters of innovations rather than non-users and non-adopters; and those who are active such as fit and happy children rather than the sick or inactive.

- *Dry season bias*
  Many of the world's rural poor live in climatic regimes marked by distinct wet and dry seasons. Rural visits by the urban-based are concentrated in the dry season when socioeconomic conditions are relatively good rather than in the wet season when roads are difficult to negotiate and rural welfare is at its worst.

- *Diplomatic biases*
  Urban visitors are often deterred by combinations of politeness and timidity from approaching, meeting and listening to and learning from the poorer people.

- *Professional biases*
  Professional specializations make it hard for visitors and practitioners to understand the web of deprivation linkages which cause and constitute rural poverty

Source: Adapted from Robert Chambers (1983) *Rural Development: Putting the Last First* (Longman: Burnt Mill).

Gender and bureaucracy

In 1981, the UN Assistant Secretary General stated that women would not make a full contribution to development 'until there were more women involved in the planning process, in the administration at all levels, and in all sectors' (Col, 1991, p. 711). This would increase women's participation in decision-making in public bureaucracies leading to 'increase in overall productivity, to increase public sector responsiveness to women's needs, and to provide opportunities for women's advancement' (*ibid.*).

Women often make up a significant and increasing proportion of the staff of public sector bureaucracies. However, there are still major impediments to women's advancement in many public services. They are frequently concentrated in the lower bureaucratic ranks. For example, in Indonesia women constitute only 0.1 per cent of the top 'echelon' of the public service, while according to the official Islamic authorities in Iran 'a woman's participation in social activities does not necessitate her continuous and physical daily presence at the office' (BRIVAS, 1992, p. 73). It was in 1988 that Kenya appointed its first woman permanent secretary, whilst in China, despite growing female participation at high levels, there were still only 6 per cent of cadres at the ministerial and director levels in 1990 who were women (Peiqing, 1992).

The obstacles, and also opportunities, women face in advancing themselves in public administration can be seen in Box 4.6. The diagram should be perceived as 'a potentially restrictive pipeline'. In order to enter and then progress through the pipeline women must negotiate the restrictions whose dimensions will vary quite widely between countries. For example, in the Philippines women have made remarkable advances in public bureaucracies (Domingo-Tapales, 1992). Women dominate the 'professional/technical level' (59 per cent) although the incorporation of the female-dominated teaching profession into this category should be acknowledged. However, women also constitute 29 per cent of top-level posts, a figure which exceeds most OECD countries. But women from 'élite' families are over-represented in this group thus suggesting that there are still restrictions in the pipeline for women from other social classes.

But even if women do gain increasing representation in public bureaucracies does this necessarily mean that women's issues and perspectives are awarded greater prominence? Even in the Philippines, Domingo-Tapales (1992, p. 5) notes that the female bureaucrats do not have feminist orientations and 'do not look at public policy in terms of both class and gender'. This gives some support to Goetz's argument that:

> public administration is in itself a gendered and gendering process, such that the outcomes, internal organization and culture reflect and promote the interests of men. (Goetz, 1992, p. 6)

In this conceptualization, bureaucracy is not the Weberian domain of rational value-free activity. Men have shaped bureaucracies – their

BOX 4.6

**Barriers and opportunities for women's advancement
in the public service**

PROMOTION

Objective Evaluation   Effective Performance   Visibility in Workplace/Profession   Opportunities for Training

STRUCTURAL   **BEHAVIOURAL**

STRUCTURAL	SUPPORT	BEHAVIOURAL
Vertical Job Segregation	House Care	Role Modeling Networking
Horizontal Job Segregation	Child Care	Contacts
Salary Differentials	Orientation	Training
Careers: Ladders/Bridges	Mentors/Sponsors	Success Seeking
Promotional Rules	Collegial Peers	Risk Taking
Distribution of Positions	Solidarity Among Women	Flexibility
Career Planning	Women's Organizations	Positive Attitude Toward Power
Evaluation Systems	Professional Associations	Supervisory Skills
Management By Objectives	FACTORS IN WORKLIFE	Team-Building Skills
Rotational Assignments		Absence of Stereotyping
Non-Discrimination Laws		

Women Clustered In Lower Ranks

ENTRY POSITIONS

Employers Believe   Employers Provide   Employers Believe
Women Can Get Along   Maternity Leave   Women Can Do
With Men   the Job

Creates Labor Pool of Qualified Women

EDUCATION AND TRAINING

Parental Decision   Availability to   Girls Decision to
to Send Girls   Girls of Full Range   Develop Ambition and
to School   of Subjects   Pursue Goals

BASIC SOCIALIZATION TO ATTITUDES AND VALUE

Media   Family   Religion   Community   Culture

Source: Col, J.-M. (1991) 'Women in Bureaucracies: Equity, Advancement and Public Policy Strategies', in A. Farazmand (ed.), *Handbook of Comparative and Development Public Administration* (New York: Marcel Dekker) p. 713.

structures, cultures, authority relations, management styles and divisions of labour – so that they represent the interests of men.

For example, Goetz's (1992) study of state bureaucracies and NGOs engaged in development administration in Bangladesh found organizational structures which restricted women staff to women's programmes, thus ghettoizing the latter. Opportunities for management roles were limited by 'gender-typed' training. Such institutional patterns found legitimation in Bangladesh's 'purdah culture' which prescribes rural development as a man's job. It requires mobility, close involvement with strangers, and commitments beyond office hours, all of which are features of 'male prerogative' and 'female forfeiture'.

Such an analysis points to political action as the way to promote more equitable gender relations. Women's empowerment is necessary. But the nature of such empowerment is not a matter for external agents to decide. Western experience may inform in many instances but the environments, priorities and local rationalities of developing countries mean that the programmes of women will vary according to such contingencies.

Corruption

Corruption is found in all countries of the world from Australia to Zambia. It is not a peculiar property of the Third World but it has been a persistent feature of the political and administrative landscape of developing countries for many years. Myrdal (1968) noted that it was 'rampant' among lower level officials in colonial India. Harrison (1981) has written of Nigeria that 'corruption riddles every part of the public edifice like a bad infestation of woodworm'. In 1981, the head of the Indonesian Financial Audit Board stated publicly that no department was clear of corruption while the country's vice-president spoke of corruption reaching 'epidemic proportions' (Robison, 1986, p. 393). And corruption can be a leading issue with the public. For example, in the 1992 presidential elections in the Philippines, Miriam Santiago almost won on a one-issue platform of anti-corruption despite having far less resources for her campaign than her rivals.

But what is administrative corruption? Gould (1991, p. 467) has defined it succinctly as 'the institutionalized personal abuse of public resources by civil servants'. Typical examples would include 'kickbacks' on construction contracts; bribery to secure a favourable decision on the granting of an import licence; 'tips' after a decision has been made on the allocation of land; the use of public resources such as labour, vehicles, travel and accommodation for personal consumption; providing unqualified family, friends and co-ethnics with public sector jobs; selling state property such as construction materials or weapons and pocketing the income; payment of salaries of 'ghost' staff into one's own bank account; or hiring a middleman to 'grease' appropriate personnel to speed up the issuance of a passport (see Box 4.7). The details of what constitutes corruption vary between regions and countries. What is seen as polite and culturally necessary gift-giving in one place may be deemed as unfair attempts to win favour in another. But culture itself can be manipulated and mobilized by the corrupt to legitimate their corrupt practices; for example, by labelling them as 'traditional'.

Corruption has a number of effects. First, political legitimacy and stability may be threatened. People may become morally outraged or alienated by corrupt behaviour. Alternatively, there may be resentment by those excluded from receiving the benefits of corruption. In

---

BOX 4.7

Evading the rules in Pakistan

There is an argument that corruption is efficient: that it is simply the market asserting itself in the face of government inefficiency. But a lot of corruption is extremely inefficient – it prevents governments from collecting taxes, allows people not to pay for utilities, enables people to buy jobs and to pocket government spending.

I went to see a businessman friend in his office to ask him what sort of payoffs he made. There was excise duty, he said, levied according to what and how much he produced. He made a deal with the excise boys to declare half his production, and gave them a third of the value of the tax he would have paid on the rest. Then there was the old age benefit tax, which depended on the number of employees in an industrial establishment of over ten people. Again, he would agree with the taxman to understate the number of employees. There was a similar deal with social security tax. His cousin, he said, spent at least 20 000 rupees a month in international telephone charges. By paying the telephone men 1000 rupees, he reduced his bill to 2000. For electricity, there were three levels of charges – residential, commercial and industrial. Residential was the cheapest, so people paid the electricity man to register their business consumption as residential.

Source: Duncan, E. (1989) *Breaking the Curfew: A Political Journey through Pakistan* (London: Arrow) pp. 41–2.

both cases political opposition may be mobilized to destabilize or overthrow the regime. Secondly, there is a negative effect on productivity as the public interest is subsumed by the individual bureaucrat's pursuit of private gain. Action is delayed until corruption greases the administrative machinery. Thirdly, inequity is likely to increase as those who can afford corruption secure the desired outcomes while the poor lose out. Fourthly, there is an opposing view which believes that 'if the prevailing system is bad, then corruption may be good'. It cuts red tape, makes decision-making predictable, substitutes for social welfare, gives motivation to underpaid workers and enables out groups to buy into political power thus avoiding violence. But such a view overlooks the millions of dollars diverted from productive investment to Swiss banks and conspicuous consumption.

The idea that corruption may be a rational substitute for the market is also dubious as it fails to recognize that competition is reduced to a 'money talks bottom line' (Gould, 1991, p. 471) which facilitates unqualified job-seekers, wasteful projects and policies which may be against the public interest. Often, the corrupt are monopoly suppliers and thus do not compete. Such resource utilization does little to contribute to economic production or social welfare.

If the majority of analysts and the public believe that corruption produces predominantly negative effects, then reforms to combat corruption must incorporate a clear understanding of its causes. These can be broadly classified as follows (Gould, 1991):

- *The nature of the state* The soft or weak states which we encountered in the previous chapter are fertile grounds for corruption as there is little accountability for official action. Colonial traditions of non-participation by large sections of the community may be maintained by postcolonial regimes. Such conditions facilitate the appropriation of public office for personal gain. Patrimonial and authoritarian regimes rely on patron–client ties for survival. Rewards are passed down through these ties in exchange for loyalty and subservience rather than for upholding the public interest. Finally, the frequent expansion of the state, especially if it is weak, into new areas of socioeconomic activity through public enterprises provides a corresponding expansion of opportunities for corruption.

- *Low pay* In many countries, especially in Africa, public service wages and salaries have remained low for many years while inflation has often been high and currency devaluations regular. Public officials thus use their positions for private gain for 'sheer survival' or simply because everybody else does it (Ouma, 1991).
- *Cultural factors* In the context of weak states where primary loyalties lie with social institutions such as kinship and ethnicity, there may be pressure on officials to look after their own group's well-being above all else. Also, practices from traditional society such as gift-giving may be carried through to the contemporary context even though official norms stress impersonal values and behaviours in line with the Weberian ideal-type bureaucracy.
- *Organizational factors* Certain organizational features can provide favourable conditions for corruption. For example, highly centralized structures may remove decision-makers from the public gaze thus ensuring little interference should they choose to pursue private ends. Centralization can result in cumbersome processes which are speeded up by clients' payments. Corruption becomes institutionalized with public officials resisting attempts to decentralize and reform bureaucratic structures. The inaccessibility of decision-makers and the lack of public understanding of complex bureaucratic procedures also leads to the emergence of middlemen. They derive income from facilitating transactions between members of the public and bureaucrats and so form a 'group with an unambiguous interest in spreading the belief that corruption is pervasive' (Oldenburg, 1987, p. 533).
- *External influences* One way of looking at corruption is to argue that corrupt officials exist because there are those who corrupt them, and among the latter are foreign actors. Multinational corporations have frequently been accused of bribery in order to secure favourable decisions in host countries. Foreign governments may be accessories to corruption by supporting regimes despite rampant corruption. There is evidence in Sri Lanka that the 'aid avalanche' created by donors in the late, 1970s fuelled corruption in the public service and contributed to its entrenchment (Hulme and Sanderatne, 1994). Foreign support may be maintained to safeguard foreign economic interests, to ensure that foreign military bases remain or to secure desired votes in the UN. Measures for combating corruption will be discussed in the next chapter.

Conclusion

Bureaucracy is ubiquitous in developing countries. It is important and will remain so. We commenced our excursion into Third World bureaucracy by examining the concept of bureaucracy and discovering that there are several meanings for the term. We have mainly employed the idea of bureaucracy as the public service, the most common identification in developing countries. However, this has not prevented us – nor should it stop you – from using other definitions such as particular organizational features to assist in analysis. We have also traced the evolution of developing country bureaucracies and emphasized their important colonial heritage and variations which exist between countries and regions. Contemporary bureaucratic structure and practice cannot be understood without knowledge of history. This observation is also important for our discussion of leading issues in development bureaucracies.

Our list of issues is far from exhaustive but the items discussed appear to be those which assume importance in developing country discourses and in the thinking of international agencies concerned with the development process. In presenting these issues we have indicated that all is not well with the bureaucracies in developing countries. They should be providing better performance for their clients, especially the poor and powerless. Remedial actions are required. These are the subject of the next chapter.

5

Administrative Reform: The Continuing Search for Performance Improvement

Just as bureaucracies are ubiquitous in developing countries, so are efforts to reform them. The reform agenda has varied through the development decades but it has always been there. It used to be that consultants and multilateral organizations nodded approval for the creation of new agencies and the expansion of existing ones. They talked of modernizing bureaucracies, recommended the construction of training institutions and designed schemes for rapid localization. In more recent times the leading themes have included privatizing state institutions, reducing the size of bureaucracies, building management capacity and promoting greater accountability. All are undertaken in the name of performance improvement in the public sector.

Despite the longevity of administrative reform, its importance for development was not fully acknowledged until the 1983 World Bank *World Development Report* which focused on the management of development. This official confirmation of the importance of management in the public sector occurred at a time when the dominant economic paradigm was stressing efficiency and the efficacy of the market. Development failures and disappointments were now seen not simply as the result of inappropriate policy choices but also because state institutions were performing poorly. The public organizations that had been encouraged to expand and multiply in earlier years were now perceived as obstacles to development – and expensive ones at that. Public sector management required reinvigoration and redesign as a vital component of strategies to 'redimension the state'. Organizations needed to be efficient, effective and to provide value for money. Administrative reform was therefore universally sanctioned as the means to bring about the desired changes to the public sector. A state was no longer credible (and might even be without credit!) unless it had an ongoing programme of administrative reform.

In this chapter we will briefly examine the meaning of 'administrative reform'. Then we will deal with the actual strategies which have been employed in reform programmes. Because so many actions are classified as administrative reform we cannot hope to cover all of them in this short space. Also, the major reform issues of decentralization, privatization, planning systems and government–NGO relations are dealt with in other chapters. Here we will concentrate on the reform of bureaucracy paying special attention to restructuring, human resource development, participation and accountability.

Defining administrative reform

There are a range of definitions for administrative reform – not surprising since so many diverse activities have been progressively incorporated under this label. Some definitions emphasize the outcomes of administrative reform by identifying it as the means 'to make the administrative system a more effective instrument for social change, a better instrument to bring about political equality, social justice and economic growth' (Samonte, 1970, p. 288) Other writers focus on process. Khan (1981), for example, sees reform in terms of changing established bureaucratic practices, behaviours and structures. Authors such as Quah (1976) and Jreisat (1988) incorporate both views by linking the processual changes to the production of a more effective and efficient bureaucracy.

Despite the differences there are some common elements in the various definitions. First, administrative reform is about deliberate planned change to public bureaucracies. Second, it is synonymous with innovation. Third, improvements in public service efficiency and effectiveness are the intended outcomes of the reform process. Fourth, the urgency of reform is justified by the need to cope with the uncertainties and rapid changes taking place in the organizational environment (de Guzman and Reforma, 1992).

On some issues there is disagreement or ambivalence. Administrative reform may sometimes be targeted at particular institutions but equally it may be dealing in system-wide innovations. It also overlaps with concepts such as 'administrative evolution' and 'administrative change' and may even be inseparable from them. Many writers currently favour the term 'public sector reform' as it appears to be more encompassing and is less associated with earlier administrative reform failures. But the content of public sector reform definitions and practice reveal little or no difference from those delineating administrative reform.

Many definitions lack an appreciation of the politics of reform thus making it difficult to comprehend why reform programmes are introduced, what measures they incorporate and why they may succeed or fail. Too many operational definitions contain an excess of instrumental rationality. This presumes that the reformers have accurate knowledge of cause and effect and can calculate precisely the results of the actions that they take. It reduces administrative reform to a technical problem, like fixing a machine, and omits the political interactions of stakeholders which actually determine the course of events. Caiden (1969, p. 8) is the most quoted of those who move beyond the technical emphasis of the above definitions by stressing the important political aspects of administrative reform. He characterizes it as 'an artificial inducement of administrative transformation against resistance'.

Administrative reform strategies

Restructuring

Many of the strategies and techniques that comprise administrative reform can be classified as restructuring. Eliminating red tape, downsizing, decentralizing authority and improving organizational responsiveness to clients are a few of these restructuring devices. Drawing from organization theory, the rationale of restructuring is that the structure of organizations can be designed to improve organizational effectiveness and efficiency.

Structure is not simply boxes and lines arranged in a hierarchy on an official organization chart. It is 'the sum total of the ways in which the organisation divides its labour into distinct tasks and then achieves coordination among them' (Mintzberg, 1979, p. 2). The components of structure are complexity, formalization, and centrali-zation. Complexity refers to the degree of differentiation in an organization. This is expressed in specialization in the division of labour; the grouping of activities into departments, divisions and sections; the number of levels in the organization; the number of positions controlled by a supervisor; and the geographical dispersion of work activities.

Formalization is 'the degree to which jobs in the organization are standardized' (Robbins and Barnwell, 1994, p. 57). For example, a highly formalized clerical job would have specific rules and proce-dures which would determine precisely what to do, how to do it and when to do it. A job low in formalization, such as for some university lecturers, would give the incumbent considerable discretion in the performance of work.

Centralization concerns the degree to which decision-making is concentrated. High centralization would entail top management making all the decisions. When decision-making is dispersed through the organization, decentralization has occurred.

There are an infinite number of ways in which these structural dimensions can be put together in organizations. But while all public bureaucracies are different, there are also similarities. This leads to the observation that there are in fact only a few basic types of structural configuration but that each has considerable potential for variation in detail. For example, Hage and Finsterbusch (1987) identify four basic organizational models (and later add two more) in their work on improving bureaucratic performance in developing countries (see Table 5.1). They adopt a contingency perspective which argues that different organizational structures are required for different organizational contexts. For example, if a large volume of a standardized product or service is required then the high formalization and centralization of the mechanical bureaucratic model is the most efficient and effective organizational form. If, however, there is a need for flexibility, innovation and responsiveness, then the organic professional model will be appropriate. In many cases, a hybrid using structural elements from different models will be necessary to cope with multiple tasks and variations in relations with the environment, and the inherent uncertainty of that environment.

A few examples will assist in understanding these structural principles in practice. Agricultural extension aims to provide assis-tance to large numbers of small farmers so that they can modify their agricultural practices to achieve higher outputs and higher incomes.

TABLE 5.1

Four basic organization structures

Structure	Appropriateness
Mechanical–bureaucratic	
Small variety of specialists	Large demand for services
Generalists as administrators	Standardized services
Highly centralized	Economies of scale
Authority based on position	Simple technologies
Fixed leader	
Highly stratified	
Clear roles and responsibilities	
High formalization	
Organic–professional	
Large variety of specialists	Small demand
Professionals as administrators	Non standardized services
Highly decentralized	No economies of scale
Authority often based on skill	Complex technologies
Shifting leadership	High quality
Highly egalitarian	Adaptable to changing conditions
Low formalization	
Nondefined roles and responsibilities	
Traditional–craft	
Craft and semiprofessional skills	Moderate local demand
Centralized but job autonomy	Partially standardized services
Often dominated by founder	No economies of scale
Small administrative component	Simple technologies
Low formalization	Easy to start up
Small size	Adapted to local needs
Mixed Mechanical–organic	
Engineers and specialists	Moderate to large demand
Professional field agents	Multiple products from same technology
Centralized and decentralized	Economies of scale
Large size	Complex technologies
Some components mechanically structured and some organically structured	Diversification as strategy
Sophisticated technology	Productive and adaptable
Capital intensive	High start-up costs
Domination by committees	Possible value conflicts

Source: Adapted from Hage, J. and Finsterbusch, K. (1987) *Organizational Change as a Development Strategy: Models and Tactics for Improving Third World Organizations* (Boulder: Lynne Rienner).

The problem for developing countries has been how to organize such extension activities to achieve the desired objectives. In India during the 1970s, the government adopted the 'training and visit' system (T&V) in an effort to increase food production. This model demonstrates mechanical bureaucratic features with simple routinized technology for delivering information to farmers using a rigid schedule of activities (see Table 5.1).

The T&V system was regarded as a successful example of organizational restructuring (Hage and Finsterbusch, 1987; Israel, 1987) and was exported under the auspices of the World Bank to other countries. But there have been subsequent critiques which question whether such a mechanical model is appropriate for many agricultural systems in developing countries. The T&V approach has certainly not worked everywhere and may have produced far less spectacular results than its adherents have claimed (Hulme, 1992).

BOX 5.1

The training and visit system

1. *A single line of command* – all village extension workers (EWs) are brought under a unified extension service within a structure that permits supervision at all levels but ensures that each 'span of control' is manageable.
2. *Precise task definition* – the EWs' time should be devoted purely to agricultural extension. They should not be involved in other agricultural functions (e.g. credit, inputs, marketing, regulation) nor in activities for other sectors (e.g. electoral duties, censuses).
3. *Systematic EW training and farmer visits* – EWs must follow a fixed programme of field visits which is overseen by supervisors who have an equally rigid schedule. Frequent one-day training sessions ensure that EWs know the three or four most important agricultural recommendations for the next one or two weeks.
4. *Concentration of efforts* – EWs concentrate on only one or two of their region's most important crops, and for these only on a small number of high-return practices. To bolster morale and EW status, an initial 'immediate success' is pursued by the extension organisation.
5. *Manageable workloads* – as EW areas include large numbers of farmers, they must focus their efforts on a limited number of selected contact farmers, each of whom passes recommendations on to approximately ten follower farmers.
6. *Improved extension-research linkages* – the extension service must forge close links with research organisations which can generate future recommendations and receive 'feedback' from EWs about 'the real problems farmers face'. Subject matter specialists (SMSs) within the extension service and joint 'research and extension committees' can assist with these linkages.

Source: Abstracted from Benor, D. and Harrison, J. Q. (1977) *Agricultural Extension: The Training and Visit System* (Washington D.C.: World Bank).

For example, greater flexibility is essential to cope with different environments. T&V needed to pay more attention to inter-organizational linkages. The machine bureaucracy tends to deliver and not listen and learn, while the costs of T&V interventions may be unsustainable for many countries.

In many instances the reform agenda has attempted to address the rigidities and dysfunctions associated with mechanical structures. These actions are sometimes classified as debureaucratization. In the 1980s, the Indonesian reputation for red tape, slowness in decision-making and corruption was perceived to be discouraging investment and economic growth. For example, a person wanting to establish a fabric factory would start seeking permissions and permits at the sub-district level where the factory was to be located. The entrepreneur would then go to the district office, to the municipality or county office, to the office of the governor, and finally to the Department of Industry at the central government level (Pamudji, 1992). In each office the application would need to be seen by at least five desks before the required recommendation was given. This tortuous procedure was streamlined so that applications could be sent directly to the office of the governor which provides the lower-level offices with copies. While this has reduced local government income, it has speeded up the application and approval procedure, reduced chances for corruption, and encouraged business activities.

Task forces are a favoured organic structural device for promoting reform. They tend to be loosely structured organizational devices with low formalization and high communication between the specialized members. This gives them the structural flexibility for rapid and appropriate response taking maximum advantage from the mix of professional skills. Despite their own 'adhocratic' form, task forces may not recommend such adhocratic structures for the better future performance of the organizations being reformed. In Guyana, starting in 1979, management improvement teams (MITs) were created and trained for work in the Ministry of Agriculture and the electrical utility (Hage and Finsterbusch, 1987). These teams focused on problem-solving and were temporary features of the structure. The MIT in the electrical utility was successful. Recommendations and new practices in the structure of this organization often had a mechanical bureaucratic nature which were relevant to the organizations role and internal configuration.

In Papua New Guinea until the 1980s, restructuring could be more correctly described as reshuffling. Sections of departments were amputated and attached to other departments while top bureaucrats were regularly shifted, sacked and reassigned. Following a World Bank report on the nation's public sector management in 1983, the Project Management Unit (PMU) was established (Turner, 1991). This small group of highly qualified Papua New Guineans and expatriates commenced detailed diagnostic reviews of organizational structures and other management issues. The initial work focused on individual departments which were given advice on how to improve management – but no quick-fix remedies were advocated. The PMU also engaged in system-wide reforms by assisting in the formulation of the *Public Service (Management) Act 1984* which relegated the Public Services Commission from a position of centralized power to a role as peripheral advisory body.

The new Act continued the theme of decentralizing personnel functions by allocating many day-to-day personnel functions to departmental heads. However, the new 'streamlined' Department of Personnel Management (DPM) was in practice a renamed and slightly reorganized Department of the PSC with the same staff, the same equipment, the same premises, and the same culture of hierarchy and formalization. Given this, it is doubtful whether these interventions have improved organizational performance. The persistent weakness of monitoring and evaluation processes means that information on performance is frequently lacking in Papua New Guinea, and even where hard data have been available certain stakeholders have chosen not to learn from these lessons (Hulme, 1989).

The popular practice of restructuring embodies a pronounced faith in instrumental rationality; that is, that the most efficient and effective reform measures will be taken and that the outcomes are calculable in advance. Experience reveals that a softer rationality is more appropriate. Environmental changes or initial misinterpretation of the context in which reform must take place are frequent occurrences and suggest that revision of plans should be a normal part of the reform process. The plans which guide administrative reform should not be immutable blueprints but should accommodate a learning process in which errors are admitted and modifications become a normal part of organizational life. This, in itself, is a characteristic of the organic mode of organizing.

The most frequent environmental misinterpretation is to underestimate or ignore the resistance to administrative restructuring. Such political considerations are all too easily overlooked by analysis and planning which emphasize technical feasibility and formal structures. Informal structures are important determinants of behaviour and performance. Civil servants may feel no urge to introduce a new administrative system which is more efficient and effective. These values may not be the top priorities of many public servants. A system which focused on such values might even be viewed with suspicion. It could be perceived as a threat to employment.

Patronage may result in ministries being staffed with people who are ill-equipped for their work. Their positions and the patron's power could be threatened by reforms. Expatriate experts who are recruited to work on organizational reform projects may lack sensitivity to counterparts and generate resentment leading to project failure. Organizations may have cultures which fit uneasily with reforms. Resistance may simply be a lack of interest by bureaucratic and political leaders whose activities focus on short-term crisis management and high visibility projects which shore up legitimacy. Administrative restructuring is long-term, unexciting and does not win votes or political popularity polls.

Participation

A pervasive feature of public administration in the Third World is its emphasis on management of the public. The public have little influence over that management. Bureaucratic cultures and structures emphasize centralized top-down decision making, a relative autonomy in determining who gets what services and an assumption of technological superiority. Individuals, groups and organizations in society have often had little or no input into deciding what services they receive and little influence over their quality. Parallelling this long-diagnosed problem have been continuous calls for participation by the public in shaping the activities of public bureaucracies so that they provide services that are both required and desired.

Experiments in participation have been around for a long time. In the 1950s and 1960s there were great hopes that government-led cooperatives and community development would restructure social and economic interactions to raise the living standards of the poor especially in rural areas. Both movements incorporated democratic ideals and stressed the notion of participation by beneficiaries. But the state organizations and officials responsible for these initiatives most often regarded group formation as a standardized bureaucratic product. They lacked commitment to such participatory measures as bottom-up planning or designing programmes to meet felt needs. Flexibility was generally absent. Many of the intended beneficiaries believed that large ministries were imposing a bureaucratic version of development on an unwilling but less powerful clientele. Thus, many cooperatives and community development programmes failed to meet the early developmental expectations of both government and participants. This experience demonstrated that conventional bureaucratic methods of group formation and mobilization were inappropriate among poor disadvantaged groups (Hulme and Turner, 1990).

But could large bureaucracies be reformed to include beneficiaries in decision-making and the management of significant activities? A 'learning process approach' proposed by David Korten suggested that it might be possible (Korten, 1980). This approach advocates villagers and officials sharing knowledge and resources in designing programmes which achieve a fit between the needs and capacities of the beneficiaries and the officials. It is a contingency approach which demands organizational flexibility in order to respond to the environment and an ability to learn from action. Participation is stressed and redesign is a normal and expected activity.

Although Korten's initial formulations provided little advice for would-be implementors, other authors stepped in with practical suggestions. Johnston and Clark (1982, p. 171), for example, provided a strong warning to those who regarded participation as 'a free good, desirable in unlimited quantities'. Participation has a large cost for the poor and they will 'invest their participation when they believe it will secure them valuable benefits not otherwise available at comparable, cost, time and risk' (*ibid.*, p. 172). This and other lessons were learned by the reformers of the National Irrigation Administration (NIA) in the Philippines. This large government organization saw itself as a constructor of physical facilities when, in 1974, it was ordered to provide support for communal irrigation systems. In order to implement this presidential directive, staff at the NIA gradually developed a participatory approach to the management of communal irrigation systems. This required a change in organizational culture with NIA staff adopting a more interactive style in their relations with farmers. Evaluation shifted to indicators which reflected farmer needs and actions. Also, partial funding of provincial NIA offices by farmers' equity and amortization payments meant that budget level became dependent on client satisfaction.

This financial incentive provides additional encouragement for consultation with farmers (Korten and Siy, 1988).

The NIA example shows that large government organizations can be redesigned to be less top-down and bureaucratic, and that they can successfully embrace participatory modes. However, in the majority of instances this does not happen. Chambers (1983 and 1993, p. 3) blames this on 'normal professionalism' which refers to 'the thinking, values, methods and behaviour found in a profession or discipline.' It represents the knowledge, attitudes and interests of those who are not poor and disadvantaged. According to Chambers, it is urban, industrial, high technology, male, oriented to quantification and of primary benefit to the rich. It is prevalent among those who determine the course of development: professionals in multilateral development agencies, consultants, government officials and academics. It is quite obviously anti-participatory as it relegates all characteristics, values and practices of the rural poor to an inferior status.

Chambers maintains that such biases can and should be overcome by adopting the new professionalism which reverses power relations by putting the last (the rural poor) first. Poor people define development and classify their own needs and wants. Research priorities are identified by the poor who join with the professionals in experiments and knowledge-building in field conditions. Evaluation is by the clients, not the peers. In this process, the professionals cease being experts and become learners. This is somewhat idealized and it is the remotest of possibilities that all development bureaucracies will adopt the new professionalism. However, if we treat Chambers' new professionalism as an ideal type then state organizations can be encouraged or cajoled into moving towards such new behaviours.

There are, however, dangers for the new professionalism. In Papua New Guinea, the adoption of a bottom-up planning process, the Resource Management System, resulted in the generation of a multitude of expressed needs, wants and demands for projects. The state does not have the capacity to respond to such demands, and so risks alienation and anger among the rural population.

So far, we have looked at participation in terms of the relationship between bureaucracies and their clientele. But, greater participation could also be a reform strategy inside government organizations. The problem is that it runs against the grain of the strict hierarchical principles of mechanistic organizations and against directive leadership styles. The advantage of incorporating the organization's members into decision-making about reform is that individuals are less likely to oppose a plan in which they have participated. Even if they do not engage in such participation but are kept informed, they may be more amenable to reform and less likely to offer resistance. In Jamaica, ignorance of a major administrative reform programme was widespread below senior management (Kitchen, 1989). Reform was thus viewed with suspicion, and associated with job loss in some minds. There was a regular information bulletin but it was obviously an ineffective communication tool and more creative solutions to winning popular support were necessary.

Administrative reforms may aim to provide greater scope for continuing participation in significant decision-making by organizational members. This can also be described under the heading of decentralization which we encountered in the section on restructuring. The claimed advantages of such participation include a lesser need for coordination and control, a more effective utilization of human resources and a greater commitment to organizational objectives.

Human resource issues

An organization's most valuable resources are its staff. They perform the tasks, coordinate them, organize the inputs and produce the outputs. Without them there would be no organization. It is not surprising, therefore, that attention to matters of human resource development (HRD) and human resource management (HRM) are of great concern to reformers aiming for greater efficiency and effectiveness in state bureaucracies.

The term HRD is open to different definitions. In the broad sense it applies to investments and outcomes in education, health and population across entire societies. In the narrower sense that we will employ it, HRD refers to the organizational activities directed to improving the skills and capacities of its workforce. Human resource management (HRM) focuses on selection, recruitment, appraisal, reward and career development within an organization. HRD and HRM are the principal means used to promote increases and improvements in organizational capacity – a highly favoured and oft-repeated objective of administrative reform. Improving human resources is practised in a variety of ways. For example, a conference of heads of the public service in the South Pacific in 1992 identified the following HR initiatives in their countries:

- Increasing emphasis on training and the development of interpersonal skills;
- Providing career advice and mentoring;
- Encouragement of mobility and broadening experience;
- Introducing participative management styles;
- Providing performance feedback;
- Introducing human resource planning systems;
- Human resource development planning;
- Devolution of personnel management functions and powers (EDI and ISAS, 1992)

We cannot hope to cover all human resource issues here. Therefore, we will concentrate on two particularly important areas of intervention – management training (usually central to HRD) and remuneration (central to HRM).

Since the dawn of administrative reform, training has been the major HRD strategy. It has come in many shapes and forms – long courses, short courses, specialized courses, one-day workshops, overseas training, bachelor degrees, masters degrees, in universities, in public sector training institutes, overseas, on-the job, and in the field. It can range from teaching keyboarding skills and how to process simple forms to management skills for senior executives. Hundreds of millions of dollars have been poured into such training and the flow continues unabated especially as it is a favoured activity of multilateral and bilateral donors. It has even been suggested that a widely spread ideology – 'trainingism' – sustains the belief in training as the way to remedy inadequate organizational capacity (Schaffer, 1974; Turner, 1989).

Paradoxically there has been considerable criticism of the training that has taken place. Many have asked why public sector management has improved so little in many countries despite the management training of the past few decades (for example Reilly, 1987; Kubr and Wallace, 1983). A possible political reason is that training is a safe response to big problems as varied as poor bureaucratic performance and the political legitimacy of the incumbent regime. Training is a technical, non-threatening and widely popular answer to these political problems. All stakeholders will embrace training and extol its virtues whereas many may offer resistance to restructuring or more participatory modes of management. Training may fulfil latent functions such as forestalling other changes to the public service, providing career opportunities in training, permitting overseas visits and meeting the disbursement targets of aid agencies. In such a context there may be little attention paid to the outcomes of training. Evaluation may be overlooked or found impossible to undertake because of non-evaluable goals which studiously avoid specific targets. Staff development and training sections of government organizations are frequently weak politically, understaffed, and perceived to be at the margins of the organization. They may therefore lack the clout to promote stricter evaluation regimes, the motivation to do so and the expertise to carry out such activities. Evaluation of training is, however, a vital activity and, in the future, one which should be awarded more importance and into which more critical and creative energies should be directed (Action Aid, 1990).

There is an increasing recognition that other aspects of training require attention. Woodrow Wilson once declared that public administration was a foreign science and that it needed Americanizing to make it of benefit to Americans. The irony of this statement is that there has been an alleged 'over-Americanization' of public administration education in Asia and that this has not been of benefit to the region's inhabitants (Cariño, 1991b). The content and assumptions of the alien import often fail to fit with the realities and needs of Asian environments. Cariño does not argue that there should be a complete break with the past. Rather, she advocates retaining what is useful from this heritage while pursuing greater indigenization of the field. Middle-range theory arising from the specifics of each nation's experience is vital both domestically and for wider regional utilization and refinement.

While training has disappointed, there is not a feasible alternative to it. The future tasks would seem to be more attention to diagnosing what training is required, orienting training to client service, continuing experimentation with training delivery systems, a move away from over-academic and Western-derived syllabuses, a greater concern with outcomes (not outputs), and a recognition that training is not a discrete activity but is one of several interrelated components for organizational change and administrative reform. There will always be the difficulty of relating the results of training to management improvement. There are too many variables for neat correlations which perhaps means that training will continue to be a popular reform strategy. The recommendations by Merrick Jones (Box 5.2) for the future education and training of Malawian managers would seem to have application far wider than that country.

BOX 5.2
Suggestions for desirable training outcomes

You should reflect on the practical training strategies and techniques that might be used to produce the following outcomes:

1. In an environment of turbulent change, learning should become a conscious and continual process for managers.
2. Managers should develop a profound awareness of, and sensitivity to, the sociocultural context in which they operate.
3. Managers should have a clear understanding of the implicit demands of Western management ideas and practices, and of the facets of their own societies that might be congruent and incongruent with such demands (e.g. deference and dependent relationships).
4. Managers should develop a skeptical, critical approach concerning the possible adoption of Western (or other alien) organizational and management theories.
5. Managers and educators should acknowledge, analyze and reflect on the experiences of organisations in their own countries and from them work on the development of indigenous explanatory concepts.
6. Managers should develop more confidence in the validity of their own experiences and their views on management (rather than deferring to outsiders)

Source: Modified from Jones, M. (1992) 'Management Development: An African Perspective', in M. Jones and P. Mann (eds), *HRD: International Perspectives on Development and Learning* (West Hartford: Kumarian), p. 117.

The HRM issue of greatest concern to most public servants and their cash-short governments is remuneration or who gets paid what. Israel (1987) has identified distortions in salaries and wages as being among the most costly obstacles to improvement in public sector performance. Governments find that excessive wage bills crowd out non-personnel recurrent expenditures. This leads to teachers without books, doctors without medicines and postal workers without stamps. There are frequent allegations that surplus numbers of public servants populate state bureaucracies. For example, in 1990 the Management Service Division (MSD) in Pakistan undertook a 'scientific analysis' of workloads in 33 of the 43 divisions of the federal government. Out of a total of 14 400 posts at the Secretariat level, 1294 (9 per cent) were found to be surplus (Choudhry, 1991).

Meanwhile, international agencies urge governments to get value for money from their public services. Many public servants have experienced reductions in real pay, sometimes by large amounts. For example, in Tanzania and Sierra Leone between 1975–85 real salaries of public servants declined by about four-fifths (Robinson, 1990). In El Salvador, real salaries of public servants declined by between 48 to 89 per cent during the 1980s (World Bank, 1995). Thus, the benefits of civil service employment expected at the time of recruitment may not be met. Efficiency and effectiveness suffer as a result. Workers lose motivation, leadership qualities remain undeveloped and there is a drain of skilled personnel. Public servants take up other jobs, often during office hours, or engage in corruption to supplement their low official salaries.

The elimination of non-existent public servants – 'ghosts' – is a popular measure as it is the least politically sensitive method of employment reform. Ghana claims to have eliminated 11 000 ghosts through head-count and public service census exercises in the late 1980s, while in Cameroun 5000 fictitious names were removed from the public payroll (Nunberg and Ellis, 1990). Freezing or restricting civil service recruitment is another favoured technique for reducing government employment. Complications can arise if jobs in the bureaucracy are normally guaranteed to graduates of government training institutions. Also, freezes can prevent government agencies from achieving the desired skill-mix while natural attrition may be more effective in some instances than freeze-and-hire cycles.

The cost savings on ghost-busting and freezes may be wiped out by increments and other automatic salary increases. Various countries, such as Dominica and Mauritania, have used the suspension of automatic pay increases while others, such as Burkina Faso and Côte d'Ivoire, have made promotion more selective (*ibid.*). Enforcement of retirement for over-age public servants has been used successfully in some countries but the cost saving may be minimal if the target group is small. Early retirement packages have been proposed but the need to make lump-sum payments can negate salary savings unless aid donors provide grants for 'golden handshakes' (as in Uganda). Also, the loss of experienced officers would possibly have an adverse effect on performance. The same observation applies to voluntary redundancy schemes even though the absence of coercion makes them more politically acceptable.

By contrast, political difficulties accompany retrenchment schemes. Governments have tried to avoid such compulsory dismissals as they undermine the patronage and social welfare functions of public bureaucracies. Also, retrenchment can contribute to political instability and strengthen opposition to the government. Despite these risks, some governments have implemented retrenchment measures. In the late 1980s, 27 791 public servants were retrenched in Ghana, 4245 in Guinea and 3350 in the Gambia. In many cases of retrenchment there may be external pressure on governments from multilateral agencies.

Various additional measures have been utilized to cut aggregate costs of public services. In Guinea, competency exams were held to determine which personnel would be retained and which would be given severance packages. Some who passed the exams were not guaranteed public sector employment but were placed in a personnel bank. If they could not find jobs within six months they would be dismissed. In 1990, 14 487 public servants and public enterprise employees were in the personnel bank. It has, however, proved complicated to administer while the presence of an 'officially idle class' of employees may be damaging to wider public service morale (Nunberg and Ellis, 1990). Also, it is not clear whether the government would risk sacking so many personnel over a very short time.

Opportunities for retraining or for transitional employment have been made available for former public employees. Demand has usually been low and the activities have posed administrative difficulties. The targets of such programmes often use alternate strategies to find work or to enter into informal sector business activities. The need for further government-sponsored training does not appear to be strongly felt.

Reforming wage structures has been a common strategy in many countries. Wage freezes have been a major component of the strategy and have sometimes been imposed in loan agreements with multilateral agencies such as the IMF. Rationalization of the remuneration structure has also been popular. This has focused on reducing the proportion of non-wage benefits in remuneration, for example housing, vehicles, food rations and telephones. The World Bank reports little progress in this area of reform. This is perhaps a reflection of the underlying salary distortions which led to the introduction of non-wage items in the first place.

Inequities in pay and other benefits between different parts of government have been rationalization targets. If such inequities prevail, the best managers and technical personnel will gravitate towards the better paying organizations leaving lesser-qualified staff to occupy equivalent positions in the lower paid agencies. Simplifying salary structures is another reform technique. In Dominica, over 100 pay scales for middle and lower management were converted to 14.

In many developing countries there has been a narrowing of the range of public service salaries by giving relatively large increases in pay to the lower grades. However, if differentials are too compressed there may be a loss of motivation among upper level officials and even an exodus from the public service. For example, in Zambia in 1971, an assistant director was paid 17 times more than the lowest-paid worker, but by 1986 only 3.7 times as much (World Bank, 1995). In some countries there has been decompression to counteract this trend, that is increasing the ratio of top workers' pay to that of the lowest workers. Also, salary supplements have been utilized to compensate for low pay received by upper-level public servants. In Mozambique and Bolivia some officers obtained supplements which exceeded basic pay by up to 400 per cent (Nunberg and Ellis, 1990). While such topping up helps to retain the brightest and best it may simultaneously demotivate and disillusion those who do not receive such benefits.

The results of World Bank programmes to contain the cost and size of public services and to correct pay structure distortions have been disappointing. The programmes have often been short-term solutions rather than taking the long view. Also, the World Bank has perceived them largely in technical terms thus leading to an underestimation of the highly political nature of these issues. By contrast, governments have been acutely aware of the risks of radical reform in public service size and pay structures, and hold off such reforms despite the World Bank's admonition to be bolder. But as the majority of developing countries have strictly limited resources to fund public services and public employment, they will need to strike a compromise between the level of civil service employment and the level of civil service pay (Robinson, 1990). This means satisficing compromises between the various stakeholders rather than the ideal-type programme of rationalist reform favoured by World Bank technocrats (see Box 5.3).

Accountability

Accountability is a complex concept. Its attainment is a leading objective of most public sector reforms and involves much more than simply tackling corruption. It is 'the driving force that generates the pressure for key actors involved to be responsible for and to ensure good public service performance' (Paul, 1991, p. 5). It may focus on 'regularity' where public servants are expected to follow the formal rules and regulations of a bureaucratic type of organization. They

---

BOX 5.3
The World Bank's 'rationalist' reform progamme

- Installing in civil services personnel information and management systems, more tightly linked to payrolls, and including clear and appropriate career development schemes;
- Staff audits to determine what personnel is on hand;
- Improved training systems;
- Revision, usually meaning simplification, of the legal framework governing the civil service; and
- Getting the right people into the administration, partly by stronger incentives to attract and retain them, partly by changing objectives and procedures in an effort to make the work situation more challenging and rewarding.

Source: Nunberg, B. and Ellis, J. (1990) 'Civil Service Reform and the World Bank', *Policy Research and External Affairs Working Papers*, No. 422, World Bank.

---

should turn up on time, do their work in specified ways, and observe the formally prescribed authority pattern. More recently, the notion of 'performance accountability' has embraced effectiveness and the achievement of goals. Financial accountability, for example, is no longer simply a matter of probity but also encompasses evaluation of whether project goals were achieved or a particular amount and quality of a service was delivered.

Another important question is, to whom is the public servant accountable? In traditional bureaucratic forms of organization, accountability is through a hierarchy of supervisors until the organization's chief executive is reached. There may, however, be informal structures of patronage superimposed on the formal structures of organizations. If such conditions prevail then an informal system of 'accountability' will focus on the patron and have little or no concern for responsibility towards the public. In all political regimes, public servants are expected to be accountable to the country's leaders. The level of this accountability will vary in practice according to the nature of the relationship between political authorities and public servants. Democratization potentially opens up accountability as it creates a variety of avenues through which public service performance can be monitored and political pressure can be applied. Even in authoritarian regimes, certain representative organizations (for example consumer groups, chambers of commerce, religious authorities) may be permitted or encouraged to assist in making government organizations more accountable.

A variety of tools are available to make public servants accountable. As Table 5.2 demonstrates, particular tools are designed to suit particular purposes. It is likely and desirable that countries will simultaneously employ several tools in their pursuit of accountability, which, as we have seen, is a multi-dimensional concept. There will be a range of institutions such as national assemblies, public accounts committees, Ombudsmen, Auditors General and the media to be the tools or to employ them. However, the existence of a particular tool does not necessarily mean that it is effectively used.

In Guyana, the Office of the Auditor General (OAG) had been established at independence in 1957 but entered the 1990s with an unenviable reputation for inefficiency and ineffectiveness. The OAG had failed to present a report on the country's public accounts for a

TABLE 5.2

Choosing the tools for accountability

Ends *To facilitate/enhance*	Means *Tools*
Legitimacy of decision-makers	Constitutions; electoral systems for governments and decision-making bodies; bureaucratic systems of representation; Royal Prerogative; legislation; letters of appointment; formal delegation of authority; standing orders
Moral conduct	Societal values; concepts of social justice and public interest; professional values; training/induction programs
Responsiveness	Public participation and consultation; debates; advisory bodies; public meetings; freedom of speech
Openness	Parliamentary question times; public information services; freedom of information laws; public hearings; green and white papers; annual reports
Optimal resource utilization	Budgets; financial procedures; rules of virement; parliamentary public accounts committees; auditing; public enquiries and participation; formal planning systems
Improving efficiency and effectiveness	Information systems; value for money audits; setting objectives and standards; program guidelines; appraisal; feedback from public

Source: Modified from Hayllar, M. R. (1991) 'Accountability: Ends, Means and Resources', *Asian Review of Public Administration*, vol. 3 (2), pp. 10–22.

decade up to 1992 (Goolsarran, 1994). The 1992 report was also the only one to have been completed within the statutory deadline since 1957. A new Auditor General was appointed in 1990 and reported problems including 'a culture of a lack of accountability', shortages of skilled personnel, and cumbersome accounting and information systems. He instituted a range of reforms which have resulted in marked performance improvement. The OAG informed both the Ministry of Finance and the National Assembly of leading problems and made specific recommendations for action. The OAG was also instrumental in the reactivation of the Public Accounts Committee, that important institution in parliamentary systems where ministers and public servants are grilled on their expenditures. Accounting officers in government agencies were informed of their statutory obligations, given detailed reports on deficiencies in their organizations and offered assistance by the OAG. To demonstrate the importance of these matters, direct supporting action was provided by the President while the media were used to publicize them.

Within the OAG, a 3-year training programme for entrants was introduced while staff were encouraged to engage in training provided by international agencies and auditing institutions in other countries. Job descriptions and salary scales were revised to give due recognition to performance and higher levels of training. International standards of auditing were formally adopted, planning and review functions were strengthened and the auditing of 20 public corporations was contracted out. UNDP funding was obtained to pay for a programme to improve efficiency.

Recent innovative schemes in the Philippines and Malaysia indicate a trend towards the closer linkage between performance improvement and accountability. They also show greater concern with accountability to the public rather than simply to political and bureaucratic superiors as has been the case in the past. In 1994, the Philippines Civil Service Commission (CSC) launched a citizen satisfaction campaign called Citizen Now, Not Later (Sto Tomas, 1995). It was seen as a reform mechanism to improve employee performance by using external pressures to reinforce internal systems. The campaign involves the adoption of standard norms of conduct and courtesy to clients. There are specified modes of greeting clients which incorporate the values of assistance and service. Employees are personally identified either by easily read IDs or by stating their names on the phone. Employees are expected to explain procedures clearly to clients. The campaign is being publicized by the media which are making a telephone complaint system well-known. Action on complaints is taken far more rapidly than in the past and the emphasis is on deterrence rather than punishment.

Included in the Malaysian Civil Service's pursuit of institutionalizing a culture of excellence has been a focus on meeting the expectations of customers in the provision of quality services (Rahman, 1995). The Malaysian Administrative Modernization and Management Planning Unit (MAMPU) has designed and supervised an initiative called the Client's Charter in which each government agency should produce a charter. This is a written commitment relating to the delivery of outputs or services to the agency's clients. It is an assurance that an agency's services will comply with declared quality standards that are in conformity with the expectations and requirements of the customers. Should an agency fail to comply with the stated quality standards in its charter, the public can use this as a basis for complaints against non-compliance. Information or complaints received from the public should enable the management of an agency to improve their services if necessary.

Accountability is prominent in contemporary public sector reform. The driving force in all cases is to improve public sector performance. However, there is often a range of contrasting accompanying goals which differentiate the various national drives for accountability. In Iran, a strong spiritual and moral element has been evident in the effort to create an Islamic approach to public sector accountability. In Indonesia, the Fifth Five-Year National Development Plan identified control with accountability and emphasized the importance of improved control (functional, legislative, social and managerial) for sustained economic and social development. In many cases, making the existing institutions for accountability more efficient and effective would represent a considerable advance. But such a solution is not simply a technical matter. It is an exercise in power and politics.

Public–private mixes

As we will see later, the international financial agencies have developed a passion for privatizing public enterprises. But they have also been encouraging cooperation of public and private organizations in the field of social welfare as another technique of administrative reform. Governments in developing countries have become major providers of health and education services. The 'public goods' argument which considers education and health as basic human rights has been the justification for massive public sector involvement in these activities. Progress has been 'substantial but uneven' (van der Gaag, 1995, p. 4) and large disadvantaged populations still have inadequate access to education and health services. Furthermore, 'in almost all countries where social services are provided publicly on a large scale, the burden on public resources is crippling and the quality of services has suffered' (*ibid.*, p. 7). These changed circumstances have prompted a search for alternative approaches, one of which is for government to invite the private sector to collaborate in attempting to reduce the 'social deficit' in education and health. It is argued that equity, quality and efficiency are not the exclusive properties of either public or private sectors. Such objectives are better served by examining the specifics of each situation and designing a response which takes account of the advantages offered by each sector and both in combination.

A few examples from the education sector illustrate some of the possible public–private combinations (see also Box 5.4 on Latin America's innovative Social Funds). One option is to provide public funding for private schools. For example, when Chile began its educational reforms in 1980, the government introduced per student payments to both public and private schools. Payment was based on the costs in public schools which were higher than in the private sector. Thus, private sector schools competed strongly for students and by 1986, enrolments in private sector primary schools had more than doubled while enrolments in secondary schools had almost quadrupled.

A second option is to place public schools under private management. In Bolivia, the government contracted the church-based Fey y Alegria to manage some public schools. Fey y Alegria appoint teacher graduates from the same pool as public schools and receive the same level of income as public schools. But the Fey y Alegria schools are highly popular. They have generated an exceptional *esprit de corps* among students, parents and staff, and families are willing to pay extra school fees for their children to attend. A third option is to provide choice to parents or students. In Kenya, the government established the Micro and Small Enterprise Training Fund which enables informal-sector workers to purchase the training they want. Vouchers to the value of US$150 (for management training) and US$200 (for technical skills upgrading) can be used at either public or private institutions. The system gives clients the purchasing power to select the trainer and the training they want and helps to prevent

---

BOX 5.4
Latin America's social funds:
innovative public–private cooperation

In 1985, Bolivia, one of Latin America's poorest countries, turned its economy round with new fiscal and economic policies. At the same time, it established the Emergency Social Fund (ESF) to help displaced workers. The fund supported public works that generated new (if temporary) employment and at the same time improved services in education, nutrition and health. Most of the projects were carried out by NGOs, community groups and private entrepreneurs. Supported until the project's end by US$190.8 million from many donors, the results directly benefited 1.7 million people.

Because of the efficiency of the ESF in channelling resources to poor people it was decided to establish a similar fund to support the activities of private agencies and coordinate them with those of line ministries in the areas of health, water supply, sanitation and education. Since 1990, Bolivia's Social Investment Fund (SIF) has targeted Bolivia's neediest communities, complementing rather than replacing public social services. Like the ESF, the new SIF is a convenient mechanism to mobilize external assistance.

To keep it flexible and responsive to local concerns, the SIF primarily sponsors proposals identified and prepared by local communities. A third of the organizations asking for SIF financing are privately run, and small or medium-sized local contractors have been involved in all of the 1473 subprojects approved as of December 1994. In addition, the SIF trains public and private institutions and local engineering and social service consultants to prepare and supervise projects.

The SIF has performed multiple functions: helping to develop Bolivia's private sector, giving assistance to poor people, especially those in remote areas, and creating numerous temporary jobs.

Other Latin American countries have adopted the SIF model with considerable success. SIFs have become effective financial mediators – linking government and donors with the poor they wished to serve – largely because they have been allowed to operate with a high degree of autonomy. SIF managers and staff have been drawn from the private sector and paid at private sector rates. Their support has not been linked to the annual national budget cycle, and they have been exempted from cumbersome procurement and disbursement procedures. Frequent audits have ensured that SIF dealings remain above board and financially sound, and computerized information systems have further contributed to their efficacy.

Source: van der Gaag, J. (1995) *Private and Public Initiatives: Working Together for Health and Education* (Washington DC: World Bank), pp. 35–7.

an oversupply of a particular type of training. To ensure that the recipients value the services available under the voucher system they are required to pay a small part of training fees.

The World Bank argues that governments should focus on what they do best which is providing public goods and services and a regulatory framework that ensures minimum standards of quality and prevents fraud. Governments should also focus on facilitating access, not only by providing services but also by schemes such as voucher systems and subsidies which make basic services affordable by all. Another piece of World Bank advice is to 'price higher-level facilities realistically' (for example, universities and hospitals). Such interventions as scholarship schemes and health insurance allegedly will provide equitable access. Finally, pluralistic supply systems giving choice to consumers will increase overall quality and efficiency.

Such collaborative initiatives involving both public and private institutions, and non-governmental organizations, appear to present governments with opportunities to give their citizens improved access to services. Also, the competition in such service provision arrangements should work to encourage quality institutions. However, familiar problems of institutional capture by élites and middle classes could emerge with persons from these groups utilizing their power, knowledge and networks to reap the greatest benefits from the collaborative public–private arrangements.

Conclusion

All developing countries have programmes of administrative reform. Governments provide various reasons relating to improvements in efficiency and effectiveness to justify these initiatives: value for money, better quality services, increased productivity and faster delivery. A variety of techniques have been employed as means to these ends. We have examined some of these techniques in this chapter but our coverage has been by no means exhaustive.

There are other approaches available. Some move in and out of fashion. For example, management by objectives (MBO) was once extremely popular. Under an MBO regime, all activities had to be explained and legitimated in terms of their objectives. The idea was to focus attention on output rather than simply accounting for expenditure. However, in some instances the means (that is the writing of objectives) became the ends while the existence of objectives did not necessarily lead to their evaluation. Some objectives defied evaluation. In such cases, little improvement was registered.

At present, the urge to emulate the private sector has led to the search for market or competition surrogates in government organizations (Israel, 1987). The underlying assumption is that competition generates better performance. Thus, where privatization is not feasible it may still be possible for government organizations to be subject to competitive pressures from clients, the political authorities or between internal units. Getting public schools to compete with each other and with private schools for students and budgets would be an example of such policy. Another can be found in the former centrally planned economies of China, Vietnam and Laos where state-owned enterprises are being forced into market competition although remaining in government hands and retaining bureaucratic-type structures.

Governments will always employ a variety of administrative reform techniques at any one time. Some will be packaged together to achieve the desired changes. For example, a restructuring exercise might involve reducing the number of levels in public organizations and changing job specifications, especially the degree of formalization. Training will undoubtedly be necessary while a participatory initiative might accompany the other activities. Many of the techniques we have described in this chapter are not only grouped together in such packages in actual practice but particular techniques overlap. They are not necessarily discrete. For example, responding to pressure from clients might be described in terms of market surrogates, restructuring, accountability or participation.

If such an armoury of techniques is available the question arises as to why the results of administrative reform have frequently disappointed governments, the public and multilateral development agencies. A major reason has been the underestimation of the political opposition to such reforms among staff and other stakeholders who resist in all manner of ways from strikes to simple non-cooperation. A second factor has been the actual lack of importance attached to reform initiatives by governments. There have been significant gaps between initial rhetoric and reality. Experience tells us that for successful reforms there must be strong and consistent leadership from important figures in politics and the public service – prime ministers, cabinet ministers and secretaries of department. If their interest and commitment wanes then implementation suffers, schedules are not met, aims are not achieved and accountability lapses.

Despite results which have often failed to match expectations there is still great enthusiasm for administrative reform and considerable resources are made available to support it. The reformer's task is to identify correctly the problems and supply answers which are feasible both technically and politically. The reforms need to address the fit between organizations and environment. Also, it must be remembered that organizational environments in the developing world are uncertain and turbulent. This means that reform will be permanently on the agenda but varying in intensity according to the degree of turbulence, the funding available and the level of faith in this form of organizational engineering.

6
Planning for Development: The Solution or the Problem?

> All right, you want miracles. I can't produce them but I certainly can produce a plan. In that beautiful eighteen-volume document is a rosy future: day by day it curls at the edges, but the charts and the graphs stay resplendent.   (Caiden and Wildavsky, 1990, p. ii)

Planning, according to Albert Waterston (1965, p. 26), is 'an organized, conscious and continual attempt to select the best available alternatives to achieve specific goals'. This definition provides a basis for identifying the topics that will be the focus of this chapter, though it must be observed that there are many alternative definitions (Conyers, 1982, pp. 1–2). At the heart of definitional debates are competing concepts about the nature of planning. On one side are ideal models that envision plans as technical products crafted by impartial experts with access to all necessary data and almost infinite analytical capacity. On the other side are the descriptive models of political science, that see planning as a political process involving the interaction of numerous individuals and organizations that bargain and negotiate, from varying power bases, to achieve objectives that, at least partially, reflect their self-interest (Schaffer, 1984). As we shall see in this chapter, in the 'real world' planning is usually a complex mixture involving elements of both of these differing viewpoints.

Planning in developing countries: a short history

During the era in which most Asian and African nations came to independence, belief in the efficacy of development planning knew no bounds: 'the national plan appears to have joined the national anthem and the national flag as a symbol of sovereignty and modernity' (Waterston, 1965, p. 28). Plans would ensure that poor, agricultural countries would become rich, industrialized nations within a few decades. Such faith emanated from a number of sources.

First, there was past experience. Newly independent countries pursuing a socialist path saw the contemporary strength of the Soviet Union as clear evidence of the fruits of central planning. Those more attuned to the capitalist West heard of the miracles achieved by the Marshall Plan for European reconstruction and the efficiency of war-time planning in Britain and the USA. Secondly, there was theory. Socialist development theory entailed state control of the economy and consequently state planning of the economy. Contemporary liberal development theory (which was not so closely wedded to the free market at that time) in both its leading sector and big push variants relied on comprehensive planning to kick-start economies into economic take off (Rondinelli, 1993, p. 34). Thirdly, access to international financial resources was usually dependent on having a plan as a basis for negotiation with aid agencies and bankers. Finally, there were the domestic political pressures on national leaders to remain popular, and bolster their legitimacy. Plans were used to explain how rapid economic growth and national unity would be achieved. These arguments and pressures were persuasive and led at times to an almost blind faith in the necessity and efficacy of planning. Characteristic of this was the statement of Prime Minister Nehru of India that '[planning] and development have become a sort of mathematical problem which can be worked out scientifically . . . [men] of science, planners, experts who approach our problems from a purely scientific point of view . . . agree, broadly, that given certain preconditions of development, industrialization and all that, certain exact conclusions follow almost as a matter of course' (Johnston and Clark, 1982, p. 24).

National planning, as we shall see below, rarely achieved its ambitious goals, and although it continued in most countries its significance declined over the 1960s and 1970s. It was during this period that international development agencies shifted their focus and began to emphasize project planning based on micro-economic analytical principles. The heyday of project planning came in the 1970s and although remaining an important activity, it came under severe critical scrutiny during the early 1980s as projects failed to match expectations and methodological flaws became increasingly evident.

The aggressive anti-planning arguments of the free-market theorists and practitioners of the 1980s have tempered in the 1990s. Rather than suggesting that planning should be abandoned, contemporary critics are concerned about redefining the nature and quality of development planning (Chowdhury and Kirkpatrick, 1994; Killick, 1989). In the following sections we first examine the experience of national planning and then proceed to a review of project planning. Regional planning, district planning and decentralized planning are referred to in Chapter 7.

National development planning

National development planning is:

> . . . a deliberate governmental attempt to coordinate economic decision making over the long run and to influence, direct, and in some cases even control the level and growth of a nation's principal economic variables (income, consumption, employment, investment, saving, exports, imports, etc.) to achieve a predetermined set of development objectives. (Todaro, 1994, p. 566)

In centrally planned economies the emphasis is on state direction and control whereas in mixed economies it involves the programming of state resources to carry out public investment alongside economic policies that seek to stimulate and direct private sector activity. Arguments of *market failure* (that private sector activity is uncompetitive, non-existent or based on incorrect interpretation of economic signals), *resource allocation* (that there is a wide divergence between private and social valuations of what an investment will produce), and *attitudinal change* (that factionalized and traditionally-oriented populations can be energized and united) supported the case for development planning. A mystique grew around the activity which 'was widely believed to offer the essential and perhaps the only institutional and organizational mechanism for overcoming the major obstacles to development and for ensuring a sustained high rate of economic growth' (*ibid*).

Tony Killick (1976) has identified six main characteristics for national development plans:

1. Development plans present the policy objectives of the government, usually with a strong emphasis on economic development.
2. A strategy for achieving these objectives is identified. This varies between cases from the very specific to the very general.
3. The plan seeks to set out a set of internally consistent principles for optimal implementation that can guide day-to-day decision-making.
4. The plan attempts to understand, and influence, the whole of the economy.
5. The plan utilizes a macroeconomic model (ranging from very simple to very sophisticated) to forecast the anticipated performance of the economy.
6. While a development plan is a medium-term document, typically of five years, it commonly involves supplementary annual plans and also presents a longer-term view of national development.

An example of a national development plan, India's, is presented in Box 6.1.

Despite common characteristics different development plans have taken very different forms, varying considerably in the degree of detail and the nature of the analytical tools that have been used. While some plans, especially the early ones, were basically a mixture of descriptions and optimistic projections, others integrate aggregate economic analysis with complex inter-sectoral input-output modelling and subsequently cost–benefit analysis to identify specific investment projects.

Promise and performance

The miraculous expectations invested in national development planning were not realized. Waterston (1965, p. 293) found 'that there have been many more failures than successes in the implementation of development plans . . . the great majority of countries have failed to realize even modest income and output targets'. In a similar vein, Killick (1976, p. 161) concluded that 'medium term development planning has in most LDCs almost entirely failed to deliver the advantages expected of it.' Some commentators have taken the argument a stage further, claiming it is not simply that planning

---

BOX 6.1
India's five-year plans

In March 1950 the Government of India set up the Planning Commission charged with the formulation of 'a Plan for the most effective and balanced utilization of the country's resources'. The Commission set in motion a large number of discussions with federal departments and state governments and in 1951 produced a draft Five-Year Plan, heavily influenced by the types of plan produced in the Soviet Union. After further negotiations, and decisions to increase planned public expenditure by a third more than the draft plan, the First Five-Year Plan was published in December 1952, to cover 1951–6.

The First Plan, like later plans, covered virtually all aspects of the economy and social welfare in its 671 pages. It estimated the resources that would be available and set targets for production and service provision through to 1956. These targets covered central government, state governments and the private sector. For example, the private sector was set the target of increasing bicycle production from 99 000 units in 1951 to 530 000 in 1956. Each state government produced a corresponding plan document setting targets within the state.

The early Five-Year Plans were taken very seriously, but by the late 1960s the plans came to be seen as a routine activity, partly because of the arbitrary nature of much of the target formulation and partly because the Second, Third and Fourth Plans' targets were not achieved. Some commentators believe that the plans helped to contribute to the mass of regulations that have discouraged industralization. The recent moves to liberalize the Indian economy indicate that the country will soon have to modify its approach to planning.

---

has failed to deliver, rather national planning is in itself an obstacle to development. For example, Caiden and Wildavsky (1990, p. 293) lambasted comprehensive multi-sectoral planning as a mechanism for decisions which maximized every known disability and minimized any possible advantage for poor countries. According to this view national development planning has retarded rates of economic growth and discouraged the evolution of institutions and procedures that could lead to more effective decision-making.

What has gone wrong with development planning? The lists produced by analysts (Caiden and Wildavsky, 1990; Killick, 1976; Rondinelli, 1993; Waterston, 1965) are long but can be summarized in six main points. First, the majority of plans were wildly over-ambitious in terms of the rates at which development could be achieved, assumptions about resource availability and in their assumptions about the degree of control that a government could exert on the private sector in a mixed economy. Such optimistic miscalculation was fuelled by the pressures on politicians and the unfounded faith of technocrats in their scientific tools. Secondly, the data on which such plans were based were poor and at times not available, so that rough guesses and intuition (Marzouk quoted in Rondinelli, 1993, p. 43) often provided the key parameters. Thirdly, there were shortcomings in the analytical methods used in plans. While these were often sophisticated and intellectually demanding they could not model the full complexity and adaptability of the economy. They were often totally inappropriate for low data contexts. As Killick (1976, p. 181) warned, 'returns from our [economists] "investment in calculus" are dependent on a level of abstraction from the real world . . . which threatens the social usefulness of our profession'.

The fourth major problem was that such plans were incapable of dealing with unanticipated shocks, whether external (for example changes in prices) or internal (for example civil war requiring a massive reallocation of public expenditure into defence). In particular, the 1974 and 1979 increases in oil prices made the content of virtually all plans operating at those times redundant overnight. Fifthly, there were a number of institutional weaknesses. Some related to the positioning of planners in isolated national planning units remote from the line ministries that would have to implement plans. This led to poor communications and friction between planning agencies and other parts of government. More broadly, the low capacity of the public and private sector to implement plans in many countries hampered plan achievement. Last, but by no means least, comes politics. Much of the theory of national development planning assumed the activity to be done by technocrats pursuing policies that would optimize some non-contestable social good. In practice, the activity was largely determined by political forces and especially by politicians. National leaders were never lacking in rhetoric about how development would be achieved, but they frequently demonstrated a lack of commitment to planning and plan implementation. This situation is well illustrated by Sri Lanka, where national plans were prepared largely for show but had minimal influence on actual decision-making (Bruton *et al.*, 1992, p. 85). Given such a long list of ailments one might well pose the question 'should we abandon development planning?'

The end of development planning?

The criticisms of development planning in the 1970s led to a growing consensus that comprehensive economic planning was infeasible and undesirable. The opening up of former Soviet republics and Eastern European socialist economies in the 1980s and 1990s means that such planning is now only practised in a handful of countries. However, for some critics reducing the scope and ambition of planning was not sufficient. Throughout the 1980s, neo-liberals at agencies such as the World Bank and IMF argued strongly for the almost complete rolling back of the state and for the abandonment of planning. Planning was seen as an invitation for government to distort markets which, once distorted, could not achieve the allocative efficiency of which they were capable. In the last few years, this position has been modified with the recognition by the Washington institutions that 'it is not a question of state or market: each has a large and irreplaceable role' (World Bank, 1991, p. 1). As Chowdhury and Kirkpatrick (1994, p. 3) note, the current academic and professional literature takes a 'middle-ground position' and sees a continuing role for more limited forms of development planning. There is also evidence that in a small number of states, such as Botswana, Indonesia and Malaysia (Wallis, 1990a, pp. 52–5), development plans have been at least partially successful.

In most countries there is now agreement that planning techniques need to be used on a continuous basis as a part of a process of 'development policy management' attempting to provide a stable macroeconomy, coordinate public policy, use public expenditure efficiently, anticipate problems and changes in the external and internal environments, ensure competitive markets and stimulate market development. Government intervention is deemed necessary in sectors where markets alone cannot be relied on then. According to the World Bank (1991, p. 9), these include 'education, health, nutrition, family planning, and poverty-alleviation; building social, physical, administrative, regulatory and legal infrastructure of better quality; [and] mobilizing the resources to finance public expenditures'. Such a prescription entails the continuance of public sector planning, often by new approaches and, importantly, with a focus on the development of human capital and institutions as well as the physical infrastructure that was the focus of the plans from the 1950s to the 1970s.

Greater attention is also being paid to the most fundamental and routine of national development planning activities: the preparation of the annual budget for public expenditure . More than 20 years ago, Caiden and Wildavsky (1990) pointed out the potential contribution that improved budgeting and management of public finance could make to development. Many countries now link their annual budgets to modest, medium-term rolling plans for capital expenditure and

---

BOX 6.2
Sri Lanka's rolling Public Investment Programme

In 1979, the newly-elected Government of Sri Lanka introduced a rolling, 5-year Public Investment Programme (PIP) to replace the failed comprehensive national plans that had been attempted by its socialist predecessor.

The PIP is produced annually by the Department of National Planning in the Ministry of Policy Planning and Implementation. It summarises the country's recent economic performance and prospects; examines trends in key sectors; reports on the implementation of existing projects; and, identifies new projects for funding. In an appendix, reviewed each year to take account of changes in resource availability and national priorities and objectives, the planned capital expenditure for each on-going and new project is listed by sector for the next five years. Total costs and costs to be met by foreign assistance are also specified. Before new projects are permitted to enter the PIP they are carefully screened by ministries, donors, a committee of Department Heads and the Cabinet.

Inclusion in the PIP does not guarantee funding, as it is only an indicative plan, but as the PIP sets the capital expenditure priorities for the annual budgets it is of great significance. The PIP provides an important link between the annual budget and the medium-term goals of the government.

Source: Research by the authors. For a fuller discussion see Hulme, D. and Sanderatne, N. (1995) 'Sri Lanka: Democracy and Accountability in Decline', in J. Healey and W. Tordoff (eds) *Votes and Budgets* (London: Macmillan).

---

new recurrent expenditures. This helps to ensure that public investment in capital and development works remains a significant budgetary item, and that development projects are carefully screened and analysed. Sri Lanka's rolling, five-year programme for public investment provides an example of such attempts to link annual budgeting to medium-term frameworks (see Box 6.2). Such partial plans are vastly different from the comprehensive blueprints of the 1950s and 1960s. National development planning has changed in its ambitions, objectives and approaches but it remains an important state activity. At the very least such planning can contribute to the more effective programming of publicly financed development projects. It is to these that we now turn our attention.

Project planning

'During the 1960s and 1970s projects became the primary means through which governments of developing countries translated their plans and policies into programmes of action' (Rondinelli, 1993,

p. 5). Projects were seen as the 'cutting edge of development' (Gittinger, 1982, p. 1), where resources were converted into improved livelihoods and economic growth. Individual projects had always required some form of planning – at the very least some objectives, a rough budget and a schedule of activities – but in the 1960s and 1970s a number of methodological breakthroughs occurred, and these encouraged a belief, particularly amongst donors, that projects could be selected and planned in ways that almost guaranteed results.

At the heart of such methodologies is the project cycle (see Box 6.3). This conceptualizes projects as a logical sequence of activities in pursuit of known objectives. The planning of projects is seen as rational in that information is gathered and analysed in relation to defined objectives; alternative courses of action are generated; the results and risks of different alternatives are assessed; the optimal course of action (in terms of stated objectives) is selected and subsequently implemented; projects are evaluated, and information from these exercises is fed back into later phases of the project and to policy in more general terms.

Much project activity, and virtually all new projects in low-income countries, involve assistance from foreign aid agencies. As a consequence negotiation and supervision need to be fitted into the cycle. Complex project 'spirals' now describe the process (see Box 6.4). Donor involvement has led to a concentration on the preparation and appraisal stages of the cycle to ensure that investment is justified. Virtually all externally financed projects require very detailed plans before approval, and a cost–benefit analysis to estimate the likely social return on the project (for a simple discussion of cost–benefit analysis and worked examples see OXFAM, 1988). These requirements have meant that most projects involving external finance are designed by specialist planners (commonly expatriates) using sophisticated techniques. The alternative project plans are appraised in terms of likely costs, benefits and risks. The best project is selected and, if approved, is implemented.

Unfortunately, the rigour that such techniques bring to project analysis has not always revealed itself in terms of project results. The World Bank (1988, p. 25) has found that some 51 per cent of its rural development area projects, over the period 1965 to 1985, failed to achieve the Bank's minimum acceptable rate of return of 10 per cent. While there have been many successful projects in developing countries (for example see World Bank, 1987 on land settlement projects

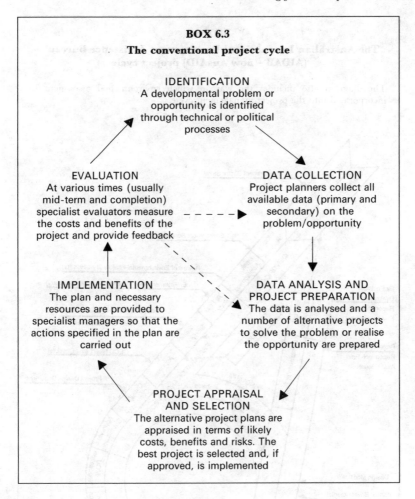

BOX 6.3

The conventional project cycle

IDENTIFICATION
A developmental problem or
opportunity is identified
through technical or political
processes

EVALUATION
At various times (usually
mid-term and completion)
specialist evaluators measure
the costs and benefits of the
project and provide feedback

DATA COLLECTION
Project planners collect all
available data (primary and
secondary) on the
problem/opportunity

IMPLEMENTATION
The plan and necessary
resources are provided to
specialist managers so that the
actions specified in the plan are
carried out

DATA ANALYSIS AND
PROJECT PREPARATION
The data is analysed and a
number of alternative projects
to solve the problem or realise
the opportunity are prepared

PROJECT APPRAISAL
AND SELECTION
The alternative project plans are
appraised in terms of likely
costs, benefits and risks. The
best project is selected and, if
approved, is implemented

in Malaysia, Cairncross *et al.*, 1980 on village water supply in
Malawi, or Chowdhury and Cash 1996 on oral rehydration in
Bangladesh) there are many examples of white elephants such as
the well-documented Magarini project in Kenya (Porter *et al.*, 1991)
and the integrated rural development projects (IRDPs) that litter
Asia and Africa (see World Bank, 1988 and *Manchester Papers on
Development*, 1988). A set of problems within the project planning
process has been identified as making it likely that projects commonly
underperform in terms of their stated objectives. These have been
examined in detail by several writers (Chambers, 1983; Johnston and

BOX 6.4

**The Australian International Development Assistance Bureau's
(AIDAB – now AusAID) project cycle**

The diagram also includes the way in which environmental assessment is
incorporated into the project management cycle.

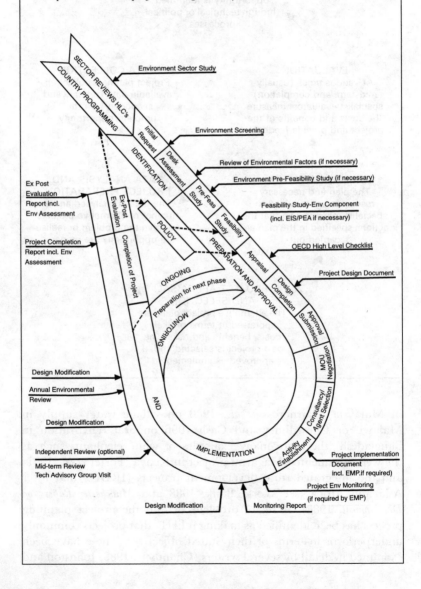

Clark, 1982; Hulme, 1994a; Rondinelli, 1993), and are summarized below.

The nature of development problems
Johnston and Clark (1982, pp. 23–8) make a powerful case that the challenges of development, particularly in rural areas, are not 'well structured' problems, as project planning methodologies assume, but are 'ill structured' or simply 'a mess'. Such problems cannot be 'thought through' by bright technocrats: rather they have to be 'acted out' by processes of social experimentation and interaction. No amount of *ex ante* expert analysis can identify a solution to such complex problems.

Poor data
Orthodox project planning methodologies demand large amounts of reliable data. In most developing countries such data is not available and so planners have to make assumptions. There is a widespread tendency for such assumptions, about yields, costs, the rates at which people will change their behaviour, to be over-optimistic (see Porter *et al.*, 1991, for numerous examples). Commonly project planners have compounded the problems of data non-availability by ignoring the indigenous knowledge of intended beneficiaries (Chambers, 1983).

Uncertainty
A central feature of project environments in developing countries is uncertainty and instability. However, conventional methodologies make little allowance for the impact that a sudden change in physical factors (for example rainfall), economic factors (for example prices) or social factors (for example the level of lawlessness) will have on a project's effectiveness. The methodologies have pursued sophistication and complexity whilst frequently minimizing flexibility and opportunities for experimentation (Chambers, 1993, pp. 27–39).

Separation of planning from management
Project planning methodologies have distinguished the planners of projects from the managers. The former have been seen as high-powered analysts, technocrats whose 'tools became their power' (Rondinelli, 1993, p. 8). The latter have been classified as mere implementors who only need to follow the plan. This has led to project management being accorded a relatively low status and at

times has contributed to morale problems. More importantly it has led to an underestimation of the contribution of good management to project performance and of the complexity of creating management capacity. Rather belatedly, in the 1980s, project planners have begun to recognize the problems of implementation (Gow and Morss, 1988).

Lack of beneficiary participation
The failure of conventional project planning approaches to involve beneficiaries in project identification, data gathering, design and selection has fostered beneficiary dependency, discouraged feelings of local ownership of project activities and sometimes alienated the intended beneficiaries of projects.

Projects and politics
Conventional project planning methodologies are based on normative analytical frameworks that ignore political factors (Hulme, 1994a). This is a considerable weakness given the large body of empirical evidence which indicates that project identification, planning, selection and implementation are highly political processes in which aid agencies, political parties, local élites, politicians, bureaucrats and others seek to achieve outcomes that meet their individual, group, organizational or class interests (*ibid.*). By avoiding political analysis, conventional methodologies facilitate the concealment of partisan behaviour and reduce the opportunity for the powerless (i.e. the intended beneficiaries) to gain influence over the project process.

Alternative approaches to project planning

The array of problems identified above has fostered the generation of a vast critical literature but as Cernea (1991, p. 8) argues, 'despite the recurrent debates on the merits and disadvantages of projects as instruments of development intervention, no effective alternatives have emerged, and projects are likely to remain a basic means for translating policies into action programmes'. The search is on for approaches that make projects more effective, and two fundamentally different responses can be distinguished.

The first has been to refine existing methodologies so that as gaps are revealed they are plugged by additional methods and disciplines. This has been the approach of most international financial agencies and donors. They have upgraded the project cycle to a complex project spiral, as mentioned earlier (see Box 6.4); they have adopted logical framework analysis (LFA) for design and monitoring of projects (Gosling and Edwards, 1995, pp. 178–92); and they have expanded the content of project planning by the creation of a number of additional sub-disciplines – social development appraisal (see ODA, 1995), environmental impact assessment, gender planning (see Moser, 1993) and institutional analysis. Keeping up with these constant changes poses difficulties for both observer and practitioner.

The second response has been more radical and proposes the replacement of the conventional approach to project planning. Two different conceptual bases underlie such proposals. One (adaptive administration) highlights the role of project management and implementation *vis-à-vis* project planning (Rondinelli, 1993). The other (participatory rural appraisal) emphasizes the role of community participation at all stages of the project cycle (Chambers, 1993 and 1994; Mascharenhas, 1991). To explore these we examine the work of Dennis Rondinelli and researchers at the International Institute for the Environment and Development (IIED) in the following paragraphs.

Adaptive administration

Rondinelli (1993) has made an impassioned plea for development projects to be conceptualized as 'policy experiments' requiring 'adaptive administration'. He argues that an experimental approach which places elements of planning, implementation and monitoring in the hands of project managers, is essential. This is because of the environments in which development projects operate (limited information, high risk, uncertainty and political manipulation) and the capacities that are required to become effective in such environments (learning, experimentation, creativity, organizational flexibility and access to local knowledge).

Development interventions should commence as small-scale 'experimental projects' searching for solutions to local problems that are appropriate to available levels of resources and technological capacity and that can be replicated elsewhere. It may take many years of experiment before such projects begin to produce results. In many cases they may fail and need to be closed down. However, successful experimental projects can be converted into 'pilot projects' that expand the scale of operations or test the applicability of the project in different environments. Significant further innovation and adaptation will be needed at this stage. Successful pilot projects can form the basis for 'demonstration projects . . . to show that new technologies, methods, or programmes are better than traditional ones because they increase productivity, lower production costs, raise income or deliver social services more efficiently' (*ibid.*, p. 139). Such projects are still very risky and selective redesign and adaptation will continue. Finally, for that small proportion of experiments that become fully-fledged, comes the process of project 'replication and dissemination'. Simple blueprints are inappropriate as there must be careful consideration of how to develop administrative capacity for service delivery, which institutions should be involved (bureaucratic or private sector), and how to ensure financial sustainability.

Rondinelli's ideas are summarized in Table 6.1. They demand that actors in the project process, particularly donors and financiers, shift their focus from 3 or 5-year plans into flexible, open-ended experiments that combine planning and management and emphasize administrative capacity-building. This is difficult for politicians and aid agencies to accept as they are more used to promising 'magic bullets' that will solve development problems rapidly. Nevertheless, it has received some acceptance in areas such as rural development planning (Hulme and Limcaoco, 1991) and by aid agencies, such as Norway's NORAD.

Participatory rural appraisal

For the other radical critics of conventional approaches to project planning, the key themes of adaptive administration – experimentation, flexibility, learning and creativity – are crucial, but there remains too great an emphasis on the role of external experts, bureaucrats and aid agencies. Instead, what is required is an approach that permits much greater beneficiary involvement in project identification, selection, design, implementation and evaluation. This ensures that local knowledge is utilized, activities are consistent with local resource endowments (human, organizational, material and financial) and that the project process contributes to the 'empowerment' of disadvantaged groups. Such approaches have been spearheaded by the work of a large number of local, national and international NGOs as described by Robert Chambers (1993, p. 97, and 1994). The International Institute for the Environment and Development (IIED) has played a key role in promoting the most

TABLE 6.1

Rondinelli's framework for adaptive administration of development projects

Project type or stage			
Experimental	**Pilot**	**Demonstration**	**Replication or production**

	Experimental	Pilot	Demonstration	Replication or production
Unknowns or design problems	Problem or objective			
	Possible alternative solutions			
	Methods of analysis or implementation	Methods of analysis or implementation		
	Appropriate technology	Appropriate technology		
	Required inputs or resources			
	Adaptability to local conditions	Adaptability		
	Transferability or replicability	Transferability		
			Replicability	
	Acceptability by local populations	Acceptability	Acceptability	
	Dissemination or delivery systems	Dissemination or delivery systems	Dissemination or delivery systems	Dissemination or delivery systems
				Large-scale production technology

Higher   Lower

Characteristics

_ _ _ _	Uncertainty, and risk _ _ _ _ _ _ _ _ _ _ _ _ _ _ _ _ _ _ _
_ _ _ _	Political vulnerability _ _ _ _ _ _ _ _ _ _ _ _ _ _ _ _ _ _
_ _ _ _	Innovativenesss _
_ _ _ _	Addition to existing knowledge _ _ _ _ _ _ _ _ _ _ _ _ _
_ _ _ _	Need for creative knowledge _ _ _ _ _ _ _ _ _ _ _ _ _ _
_ _ _ _	Need for flexibility or organizational structure _ _ _ _ _ _ _
_ _ _ _	Need for rare or specialized technical skills _ _ _ _ _ _ _ _

Source: Rondinelli, D. A. (1993) *Development Projects as Policy Experiments: an Adaptive Approach to Development Administration,* 2nd edition (London: Routledge), p. 120.

widely known approach, participatory rural appraisal (PRA), through its training activities and its Participatory Learning and Action Notes (PLA Notes) bulletins. Debates about how PRA should be properly done are manifold. Here we can provide only a simple illustration of the key elements.

Usually a PRA exercise is initiated by a trained NGO worker who has been in a village for some time. S/he arranges with villagers for a 2- or 3-day period to be devoted to the exercise. There is an initial briefing in which it is emphasized that PRA is a means by which villagers can systematically analyse their problems, explore possible solutions and draw up a plan of action. Then, villagers (sometimes as a full group sometimes in small sub-groups) produce a map of their village and its resources based on their knowledge. They usually draw it in sand or dirt with symbols (seeds, old cans, sticks and pebbles) representing local features. During this phase, villagers discuss issues such as which of their resources are over-exploited or under-utilized. On the map, villagers identify individual households (by number, letter or symbol).

The next stage is wealth ranking, where the villagers' first task is to agree on a categorization for wealth (e.g. very wealthy, secure, poor, vulnerable). They continue by debating which category is appropriate for which households. During this stage they identify those families that are in greatest need of additional income or welfare services. Probably on the second day, they establish (again through village-led discussions) what are the main priorities for the village in terms of problems to be tackled or opportunities seized. A matrix of agreed problems/opportunities is drawn up and then, by a simple technique known as pair-wise ranking (Mascharenhas, 1991), villagers compare problems/opportunities and through discussion reach a consensus on their prioritization.

In the final stage, usually the third day, villagers agree on a plan of action to tackle priority problems/opportunities. If the process is successful then they will have identified possible local projects, appraised them and agreed on the initial phase of an adaptive implementation. The plan of action will be 'owned' by the villagers. The NGO worker will have encouraged discussion and explained simple techniques but will not have intervened by providing advice or opinions (for a critical discussion of 'who' participates in PRA see Mosse, 1994).

Major attempts are presently underway to train public servants in the use of PRA in countries such as India, Kenya and Sri Lanka. The number of agencies claiming to have adopted PRA is rapidly expanding but opinions remain mixed about whether local-level bureaucrats can take on the dramatic behavioural changes entailed in such a strategy.

While debate about the relative strengths and weaknesses of conventional project planning, adaptive administration, participatory appraisal and other methods remains heated, a number of lacunae around which agreement is occurring can be identified. Most planners will now agree that there is no optimal approach to project planning. The approach that is most appropriate in a specific case will depend on the objectives and the context. Increasingly, project planning is recognized as requiring a 'menu' of methodologies in which the very earliest stage of the project cycle involves the selection of the specific approach (or mix of approaches) that is to be utilized. For high specificity objectives in stable environments (such as building a road in a politically stable middle-income country), a conventional approach may be best. However, for low specificity objectives in unstable, low information environments (such as poverty-alleviation in a semi-arid area of a low-income country), more experimental and participatory approaches are most likely to achieve developmental goals.

Conclusion: planning in the real world

The great faith that was placed in national and project planning in earlier times has collapsed. But this does not mean that planning needs to be thrown on the scrap-heap. Rather it calls for new and more effective ways to plan that fully recognize that planning is a real-world, and not an ideal-world, practice. The approaches used for planning must recognize that knowledge is often limited, information only partially available, uncertainty and risk considerable, analytical capacity is a scarce resource and that planning is inherently a political process.

For national planning this means that attempts to control the national economy, as though it was a well-understood machine, must be put aside. Instead, the focus should be on managing a limited number of macroeconomic policies effectively; programming public investment on a medium-term view to ensure that the essential physical and social infrastructure (on which private-sector activity is dependent) is developed; and, strengthening the annual budgetary process.

For project planning it entails the recognition that there is a menu of methodologies (for details see Gosling and Edwards, 1995) from which a choice appropriate to specific objectives and contexts must be made. A greater concern with implementation and intended beneficiary participation is likely to yield dividends well beyond those that will be produced by increasingly sophisticated but irrelevant quantitative analysis. In an uncertain and rapidly changing world 'acting out' approaches to societal problem-solving have much to recommend them despite the intellectual appeal of pretending that groups of technical specialists can 'think through' such problems.

7

Decentralization within The State: Good Theory but Poor Practice?

A major obstacle to the effective performance of public bureaucracies in most developing countries is the excessive concentration of decision-making and authority within central government. Public sector institutions are commonly perceived to be geographically and socially remote from 'the people' and to take decisions without knowledge or concern about actual problems and preferences. The popular remedy for such centralization is decentralization, a term which is imbued with many positive connotations – proximity, relevance, autonomy, participation, accountability and even democracy. So great is the appeal of decentralization that it is difficult to locate a government that has not claimed to pursue a policy of decentralization in recent years. It has currency across the ideological spectrum, and leaders from Khartoum to Kathmandu have made many declarations of their intent to promote decentralization. They receive support, and sometimes technical assistance from multilateral and bilateral aid agencies.

In reality, all national leaders have no choice but to decentralize some decision-making and authority. Total centralization (all authority being vested in a single individual who takes all decisions) is infeasible even for the most efficient autocrat in a micro-state. The needs of the modern state to provide some services to at least part of its citizenry, to exercise political control over its territory and to bolster its legitimacy require that a degree of authority is delegated and some decisions are made outside of the political and administrative centre. In consequence, all systems of government involve a combination of centralized and decentralized authority. However, finding a combination of central control and local autonomy that satisfies regime needs and popular demands is a persistent dilemma for governments. Centralization and decentralization are not attributes that can be dichotomized: rather they represent hypothetical poles on a continuum that can be calibrated by many different indices. The potential number of indices and difficulties of gathering relevant data and aggregating it have meant that the objective 'measuring' of decentralization has eluded analysts (Smith, 1985). Can we even provide an adequate definition for the term?

The meaning of decentralization

Various writers have proposed very different meanings for the term decentralization and much ambiguity surrounds the concept. Our purpose here is not to proclaim the superiority of one meaning over others but to ensure that the reader is fully aware of the different usages that may be encountered and of the definition that is adopted in this chapter.

Most authors are agreed that decentralization within the state involves a transfer of authority to perform some service to the public from an individual or an agency in central government to some other individual or agency which is 'closer' to the public to be served. The basis for such transfers is most often *territorial*, that is grounded in the desire to place authority at a lower level in a territorial hierarchy and thus geographically closer to service providers and clients. However, transfers can also be made *functionally*, that is by transferring authority to an agency that is functionally specialized. Such transfers of authority are of three main types. The first is when the delegation is within formal political structures (for example when the central government delegates additional authority to local government); the second is transfer within public administrative or parastatal structures (for example from the headquarters of a ministry to its district offices); and the third is when the transfer is from an institution of the state to a non-state agency (for example when a parastatal national airline is sold off to private shareholders).

If these distinctions are accepted then we can combine them to recognize six main forms that policies of decentralization might pursue (see Table 7.1). This helps us to explore the major concepts that have been presented as decentralization. It should be noted that reality is often somewhat more complicated as hybrids and 'mixed authorities' can occur (for example when a council is established in which both elected representatives and public servants have voting rights).

If the transfer of authority from central government to a decentralized agency is to be effective then it must be matched by a transfer of responsibility; that is, the decentralized agency must provide the

TABLE 7.1

Forms of decentralization

Nature of Delegation	Basis for Delegation[1]	
	Territorial	Functional
Within formal political structures	Devolution (political decentralization, local government, democratic decentralization)	Interest group[2] representation
Within public administrative or parastatal structures	Deconcentration (administrative decentralization, field administration)	Establishment of parastatals and quangos[3]
From state sector to private sector	Privatization of devolved functions (deregulation, contracting out, voucher schemes)	Privatization of national functions (divestiture, deregulation, economic liberalization)

[1] In this study, geographical decentralization, such as the establishment of a new capital city or the transfer of parts of headquarters offices to locations outside of the capital city, is not included. This is because such activities merely involve relocation not delegation.
[2] This form has not received as much attention from writers on decentralization as other forms.
[3] Rondinelli and his associates (e.g. Rondinelli and Nellis, 1986) often call this form 'delegation'. However, this is somewhat confusing as all forms of decentralization are, at least in theory, delegations.
Source: This table has been developed from an idea presented in G. Hyden (1983) *No Shortcuts to Progress: African Development Management in Perspective* (London: Heinemann).

particular function(s) for which it now has authority. This will entail the creation of additional or new modes of accountability by which the decentralized agency accounts for its performance to a higher authority. When authority is delegated by devolution, a typical accountability mechanism is local elections in which the local popu- lation is ultimately the 'higher authority'. With deconcentration the additional accountability mechanisms are usually within the bureau- cracy, although ultimately a minister or national leader may be seen as being accountable to national political institutions for the decon- centrated actions and performance. When authority is transferred to parastatals and quangos, accountability mechanisms, although often specified in legal documents, become somewhat diffuse. For example, is it the parastatal's board which is ultimately responsible for performance or is it the minister who appoints the board?

It must be noted that decentralization does not imply that all authority should be delegated. The central government must retain a core of functions over essential national matters and ultimately has the authority to redesign the system of government and to discipline or suspend decentralized units that are not performing effectively. How extensive this core of central government functions should be remains a major ideological and intellectual debate of the late twentieth century. Many analysts believe that the six forms of decentralization identified in Table 7.1 have differing degrees of validity. Decentralization 'purists' regard devolution, the transfer of authority to sub-national governments electorally accountable to sub-national populations, as the only authentic form of decentraliza- tion. All other forms are held to involve more concentration of power than democratic local government and, when judged against this ideal, are interpreted as exhibiting degrees of centralization. Promi- nent amongst these 'purists' are Mawhood (1983) and Alderfer (1964) who argue that deconcentration, interest group representation and the establishment of parastatals may concentrate authority in the hands of a small group of bureaucrats and/or their political masters at the national level and do not enhance accountability in the way that devolution can.

For a much larger group of commentators (Bryant and White, 1982; Commonwealth Secretariat, 1985; Fesler, 1965; Maddick, 1963; Smith, 1985) decentralization is seen as referring to both devolution and deconcentration. Smith (1985, p. 1) characteristically defines the term as 'the delegation of power to lower levels in a territorial hierarchy, whether the hierarchy is one of governments within a state or offices within a large-scale organisation.' Thus, decentralization refers to territorially-based delegation and not to purely functionally-based delegation. It is this definition that is used in this chapter.

This definition would be too narrow for Rondinelli, a prolific writer on decentralization in the 1980s. In his early work Rondinelli (1981) included parastatals, and particularly regional development authorities, within the meaning of decentralization. The previous 25 years had witnessed the establishment of parastatal agencies with gay abandon in most developing countries. However, in the 1990s, with governments divesting themselves of parastatals as fast as they can, it makes greater sense to discuss such entities separately, and particularly in terms of privatization policies, in Chapter 8.

This finickiness would dismay Rondinelli, and his associates, for as the 1980s have progressed he has extended and reprioritized the institutional forms that he recognizes as decentralization. By the mid-1980s, his meaning of decentralization also incorporated the replacement of state agencies by private businesses and non-profit organizations (Rondinelli and Nellis, 1986); by 1989, privatization was presented as the first option amongst forms of decentralization (Rondinelli, McCullogh and Johnson, 1989); and by 1990, a discussion of decentralization policy in Senegal dealt with deregulation and privatization, or what economists more commonly term economic liberalization (Rondinelli and Minis, 1990). Devolution and deconcentration are discussed basically in terms of their contribution to facilitating liberalization, and the central feature of decentralization policy appears to be defining a minimalist role for the state, rather than reassigning authority within the state. This led Slater (1989, p. 519) to argue that the promotion of decentralization is currently a means of pushing forward 'the angel of privatization' under the guise of a pre-existing policy label.

Conyers (1990) has become so confused by the differing usages of the terms decentralization, deconcentration, devolution and local government, and the extraordinary diversity of decentralization practices between countries, that she suggests the abandonment of these labels. Instead analysts should provide a detailed specification of the case they are studying, or the normative model they are advancing, in terms of five dimensions (see Conyers, 1990, p. 20, for details). This permits the recognition of a much wider variety of forms of decentralization, making it more feasible to explore the relationships between variables and judge whether comparisons are appropriate. It is a cumbersome prescription, but may be wise advice. Serious scholars have long recognized that 'generalisations are particularly treacherous in this field' (Bird, 1990, p. 280) and that attempts to directly compare one decentralization with another can often be superficial and have little social scientific validity and produce little of practical value.

Why decentralize?

A formidable battery of theoretical arguments can be deployed to make the case that greater decentralization within the state will assist poorer countries to develop more rapidly. Rondinelli (1981) cites 14 specific benefits that may accrue from decentralization. Third World politicians have used a combination of these factors at times to present decentralization as a panacea for all manner of problems. These claims have their foundations in normative theories of politics, management and economics.

A primary source of support for decentralization comes from classical liberal democratic political theory, such as the work of John Stuart Mill, and sees both national and local level benefits arising from devolution and mass participation in formal political structures at a local level. Smith (1985, pp. 18–30) categorizes the benefits of democratic decentralization into six main forms (Table 7.2).

The first two of these arguments, political education and training political leaders, were significant elements of the former colonial powers' swan song, but they are now rarely heard. The third and fourth, relating to political stability and political participation, are the most commonly cited political benefits that contemporary national leaders claim for decentralization. The latter two, accountability and responsiveness, are also often cited, though they overlap with justifications deriving from theories of public administration and management that see decentralization primarily in terms of enhancing the technical efficiency of service delivery.

The public administration and management frameworks are much less concerned with devolution and political participation and focus more on delegation within organizations and coordination between organizations. They argue that decentralization will lead to better decision-making and hence greater efficiency and effectiveness on the following grounds:

TABLE 7.2

The benefits of democratic decentralization

1. *Political education* teaches the mass of the population about the role of political debate, the selection of representatives and the nature of policies, plans and budgets, in a democracy.

2. *Training in political leadership* creates a seedbed for prospective political leaders to develop skills in policy-making, political party operations and budgeting with the result that the quality of national politicians is enhanced.

3. *Political stability* is secured by participation in formal politics, through voting and perhaps other practices (for example active support of a party) which strengthen trust in government so that 'social harmony, community spirit and political stability' are achieved. In addition, a mechanism is created to prepare the masses for the profound social and economic changes associated with development.

4. *Political equality* from greater political participation will reduce the likelihood of the concentration of power. Political power will be more broadly distributed thus making decentralization a mechanism that can meet the needs of the poor and disadvantaged.

5. *Accountability* is enhanced because local representatives are more accessible to the populace and can thus be held more closely accountable for their policies and outcomes than distant national political leaders (or public servants). A vote at local elections is a unique mechanism for the populace to register its satisfaction or dissatisfaction with the performance of representatives.

6. *Responsiveness* of government is improved because local representatives are best placed to know the exact nature of local needs and how they can be met in a cost-effective way.

Source: A summary of the writing of B. C. Smith (1985) *Decentralization: the Territorial Diversion of the State* (London: George Allen & Unwin), pp. 18–30.

1. *Locally specific plans* can be tailor-made for local areas using detailed and up-to-date information that is only locally available.

2. *Inter-organizational coordination* can be achieved at the local level.

3. *Experimentation and innovation*, fostered by decentralization increases the chances of more effective development strategies being generated, and subsequently diffused.

4. *Motivation of field-level personnel* is enhanced when they have greater responsibility for the programmes they manage.

5. *Workload reduction* at agencies at the centre of government will relieve them from routine decision-making and give them more time to consider strategic issues so that the quality of policy should improve.

Using public choice theory, economists have reached similar conclusions about the potential of decentralization. Sophisticated analytical frameworks have been developed to make this case but the basic contention is that 'under conditions of reasonably free choice, the provision of some public goods is more economically efficient when a large number of local institutions are involved than when only the central government is the provider . . . a large number of providers offer citizens more options and choices' (Rondinelli, McCullogh and Johnson, 1989, p. 59). Such competition promotes efficiency. Both supply-side and demand-side benefits are held to arise from institutional pluralism (Smith, 1985, pp. 30–7). While these propositions are held to have broad applicability, most empirical work has focused on municipal systems in the sophisticated and relatively wealthy context of North America.

Proponents of decentralization policies can justify their position in terms of political, administrative and economic theories. Rarely, however, do they consider the counter-arguments that can be made against their case. For example, if we drop the assumptions of a benevolent state, reasonably dispersed political power and social harmony that underpin theories of liberal democracy, then it may be argued that decentralization could fuel regional identities, intensify forces for secession and create political instability; or, a local élite might capture decentralized structures and consequently use them to meet its own narrow interests rather than those of the mass of the local populace. The claims for increased technical efficiency by managerialists can be countered by arguments that locally-made plans may be inconsistent with resources and national policies; differences in local plans and provision will generate regional inequalities; a large number of local units means that more resources must be devoted to administrative coordination and auditing; shortages of trained manpower will lead to decentralized agencies being staffed by incompetents; poor areas and poor people may even get relatively poorer.

Similarly, the propositions of public choice theorists are open to attack over the issue of externalities between locales. For example, a council may tax local residents so that it can provide parks, but these may be used by non-residents from neighbouring areas who are not paying for this service. In addition the unit costs of tax collection by local authorities are far greater than those of central government (Bird, 1990, p. 280).

So far, we have looked at the reasons for decentralization from a normative stance. This permits the exploration of the potential benefits and disbenefits of decentralization but as such institutional choices are made 'neither to maximize democratic access to government nor to provide public services as efficiently as possible' (*ibid.*) they shed little light on the specific decisions taken by governments and national leaders. Commonly, these are seen as being taken in relation to pragmatic political concerns such as the need to respond to ethnic or religious separatism, to strengthen the incumbent regime's legitimacy or to serve the direct self-interest of those who hold political power. Such analyses have a variety of conceptual bases that are descriptive rather than normative. They include Marxist, neo-Marxist and élite theories as well as the more eclectic frameworks of public policy analysis. In such analyses decentralization policy is usually viewed as a tool that is cynically deployed by the holders of political power to maintain their control and achieve their narrow objectives.

Recognizing this gulf between normative theoretical propositions and empirical analyses grounded in descriptive conceptual frameworks aids the understanding of the many paradoxes that are encountered in the study of decentralization. For example, how policies that claim to provide greater local autonomy can give greater central control or how talk of improving managerial efficiency can be interpreted as a strategy for restructuring the polity. 'Such changes may be presented and debated in the technical language of administrative efficiency or constitutional principles, but they reflect the outcome of conflicts of interest between groups in society which feel they have something significant to gain or lose' (Smith, 1985, p. i).

Devolution and deconcentration

Having identified devolution and deconcentration as the main forms of territorial decentralization within the state it is necessary to consider some of their features in more detail before reviewing the recent practice of decentralization in developing countries.

Devolution

The devolution of power to sub-national units of government is seen by many as the ideal form of decentralization as it combines the promise of local democracy with technical efficiency. Sub-national governments include local governments, local authorities, district councils provincial governments and state governments. They vary enormously in size both between and within countries (from a few thousand people to tens of millions); they can be single-tier or multiple-tier; and, their responsibilities may range from a large number of important functions to a few minor functions.

The classical model of devolved local government was advocated in the 1950s and 1960s as the blueprint that newly-independent countries should pursue (Hicks, 1950; Maddick, 1963). It has five main features (Mawhood, 1987, p. 12).

1. It should be a local body that is constitutionally separate from central government and responsible for a range of significant local services.
2. It should have its own treasury, budget and accounts along with substantial authority to raise its own revenue.
3. It should employ its own competent staff who it can hire, fire and promote.
4. A majority-elected council, operating on party lines, should decide policy and determine internal procedures.
5. Central government administrators should serve purely as external advisors and inspectors and have no role within the local authority.

Proponents of the classical model appreciate that this is a long-term task. Thus, Maddick saw the need for the evolution of such systems. Initially, local services might be delivered by the bureaucracy according to central policies; subsequently, a local authority would manage these functions under strong guidance from central government administrators; finally, and following the build up of capacity, local government would be given more authority and a higher degree of autonomy. Serious attempts to implement the classical model have been few and far between, however, and most decentralizations have ensured that there is considerable central government influence and control over sub-national government (Ranis and Stewart, 1993).

Deconcentration

All developing countries operate administrative structures that delegate responsibilities for functions within specific territories to field-level civil servants. This is termed deconcentration. It is important to note that while such systems decentralize decision-making and power from the headquarters of the administrative system, the delegation of powers is to an official appointed by and accountable to central government rather than to a representative of the local community who is accountable to that community. Thus, deconcentration can pursue the objective of technical efficiency leading to greater effectiveness but not popular participation.

Although some writers on public administration give the impression that choices about field administration are made on the basis of managerial parameters and are apolitical, decisions to deconcentrate are, in fact, highly political. Firstly, the political interests of those who control state power are often the prime concerns when central governments opt to transfer authority to field administrators, rather than to local governments. Secondly, field administrators commonly perform political duties for the central government. These include the maintenance of political stability, the obstruction of opposition political groupings, ensuring that the decisions of sub-national authorities follow central policies and monitoring the political loyalties of field staff and others (Smith, 1985, pp. 147–51).

The design of field administration systems differs from country to country, but Smith (1985, pp. 151–5) provides a useful framework for considering specific systems. He recognizes three main options: functional systems, integrated prefectoral systems and unintegrated prefectoral systems.

Functional systems
In these 'the senior representatives of the state bureaucracy in the provinces are in charge of functionally specific state services, such as education, health, industrial development, or agricultural extension work' (*ibid.*, p. 152). Coordination is envisaged as occurring at central or regional levels and there is no general representative of central government at the field level. Functional systems emphasize vertical communications, technical expertise, specialization and uniformity of service provision.

Integrated prefectoral systems
These place considerable power in the hands of a general representative of the central government, for example the prefect or district governor. The prefect is responsible for good government within his (her is almost unknown) territory, is the superior of all other civil servants within the territory and the chief executive of the local authority. Such a design allocates political functions to the field administration thus limiting the autonomy of sub-national govern-

ment. It emphasizes coordination above specialization, and has been commonly associated with tensions between generalist and specialist administrative cadres.

Unintegrated prefectoral systems

These involve a prefect, but vest much less power in that individual. He/she is usually responsible for departmental coordination, but is not the administrative superior of the senior technical officers in the territory. Similarly, the prefect advises but does not direct the local authority. Such a model attempts to achieve a matrix management system involving both vertical and horizontal communication.

While developed countries, such as the UK and USA, have demonstrated a marked tendency for functional systems, developing countries have, with a few exceptions, adopted prefectoral systems. Former French colonies have commonly pursued the integrated prefectoral approach, whilst former British colonies have opted for unintegrated prefectoral systems (though often with a strong prefect). Although historical precedent may explain this in part, it also indicates a marked preference on the part of central governments and national leaders to pursue decentralization through deconcentration rather than devolution.

Decentralization in practice

In this section we review the practice of decentralization in developing countries. Practice turns out to be far more complicated than theory might suggest, and in many cases combinations of devolution and deconcentration are found in a variety of 'mixed authorities', that is bodies in which both public servants and elected representatives share authority. Determining who actually holds power in such instances is difficult, but it is evident that in most developing nations there are considerable forces (historical, ideological and class-based) that favour centralization whilst espousing decentralization.

Africa

In Africa, the colonial governments that carved states out of the indigenous political structures favoured central control. To assert this control and to introduce their policies both the British and French operated field administrations that concentrated decision-making power in the hands of a non-indigenous, centrally-appointed officer; the *chef de commune* or the district commissioner (DC). There was minimal interest in devolving power to local representatives as, at least during the, nineteenth century and early twentieth century, the colonial ideology defined Africans as lacking the intellectual apparatus for modern governance. The DC or *chef de commune* ensured that law and order were maintained and commonly performed a set of political, administrative and judicial roles.

The Second World War had a profound impact on the attitudes of colonial powers. For Britain, this is best illustrated by the Colonial Office's '1947 dispatch' which sought to introduce an 'efficient and democratic system of local government' to its possessions. In some territories, such as Kenya and Southern Nigeria, this meant building on earlier experiments. In others, such as Lesotho and Nyasaland (now Malawi), it meant starting from scratch. The policy envisaged the gradual evolution of local government and, at least during the initial phases, the DC would play a prime role in tempering local autonomy with central oversight by tutoring, advising and inspecting local authorities. The colonial power feared that too much autonomy would lead to inexperienced managements wasting resources and would generate undesirable political demands, such as calls for decolonization. As nationalist movements developed and identified local government processes as one arena for the pursuit of independence, then the evolutionary approach of the Colonial Office came increasingly under attack.

The attempt to establish local governments on the British model were curtailed in the 1960s as African nations became independent. The national leaders of these new states faced a quite different set of problems than had their colonial masters, and had a much more ambitious goal to pursue – development. Uppermost in many of their minds was the need to create a national identity and to introduce a national planning system (see Chapter 6 for a discussion). Popular participation in local authorities was perceived as having the potential to unleash micro-nationalist political forces, whilst decentralized planning ran counter to the notions of efficient planning structures peddled by aid agencies, academics and technocrats.

Hyden (1983), Wraith (1972) and Kasfir (1983) have analysed the African experience and argue that under the banner of decentralization, the 1960s and 1970s actually witnessed the clawing back of power by the centre with attempts to exert even greater central control over local decisions (for example, by state-controlled cooperative movements). In Kenya during the 1960s, District Development Committees (DDCs) were established and then were complemented by District Development Advisory Committees (DDACs) on which local representatives sat. This placed local authorities in the position of being advisory to an advisory board, as decision-making powers were not delegated to the DDC. 'The structures of field administration were expected to be clearly dominant' (Wallis, 1990b, p. 439). Later in the decade, the three major functions of local government (primary education, health and roads) were transferred to central government as was the council's major source of revenue. The switches to the Special Rural Development Programme (SRDP) in the 1970s and the District Focus for Rural Development (DFRD) in the 1980s have emphasized deconcentration. In the 1990s, it is evident that the power and influence of local government representatives are no greater than 30 years ago.

Although the degree of devolution to local authorities at the time of independence did differ, the extension of deconcentrated authority at the expense of devolved authority was a feature of the 1960s and 1970s. In Uganda, DCs were given powers to direct District Councils (Kasfir, 1983, p. 33) and central government took the power to appoint councillors. In Tanzania, the functions of primary education, road maintenance and health were taken over by central government, so that local government had 'no meaningful responsibilities' (Hyden, 1983, p. 89). Nigeria saw its local councils dissolved by the central government and the appointment of committees of management to run their affairs. In a similar fashion, devolved authorities withered or were dissolved in Senegal, Guinea, Ivory Coast, Zaire and Ghana (Kasfir, 1983, p. 32). In Lesotho, the parliament abolished local government in 1968 (Wallis, 1990a, p. 129).

Although the claim has been made that Africa experienced a second round of decentralization (Kasfir, 1983; Conyers, 1982) in the late 1970s and early 1980s, there is little evidence that recent policies have significantly reversed the post-independence trend. Zambia's 1980 decentralization initiative gives local authorities more powers but has restructured their memberships so that appointed members now dominate. Efforts to devolve power in the Sudan, and fend off civil war, have been superseded by a military government that is strongly centralist and that seems content to let the bulk of the country slide into chaos and immiserization. At times during the 1980s and 1990s, domestic and international NGOs have substituted for government across large areas of the country. In parts of Africa,

NGOs have become a *de facto* 'decentralization by default' (Davis, Hulme and Woodhouse, 1994). The weakness of the state in Africa, in terms of both legitimacy and capacity, has fostered three decades of attempts by regimes to control rural areas by deconcentration.

Asia

In Asia, there has been a tendency for independent governments to prefer delegating power within the public service rather than to locally elected authorities. There has been much rhetoric about participation and local autonomy but central governments have jealously guarded their power. However, the processes, contexts and chronology of these events have been very different from Africa. Municipal authorities, with elected representation, functioned in several major urban areas in South Asia by the late nineteenth century and the Ripon Mandate of 1882 showed an optimism about the feasibility of local self-governance. Decades before independence, nationwide village *panchayats* operated in India. The concept of self-government in local affairs, however poorly implemented, existed in colonial India long before independence. However, the Collector (the equivalent of Africa's DC) remained the dominant figure in local decision-making and held sway over village *panchayats* and district boards (Friedman, 1983).

This remained the *modus operandi* after independence, until the success of the Etawah project led to a new emphasis on local government through the Community Development Programme (CDP). However, as a national level programme the CDP failed to achieve its goals (Hulme and Turner, 1990) and when it was abandoned a three-tiered system of local government, the *panchayati raj*, was introduced across the country. This involves directly-elected village *panchayats*, an indirectly-elected *panchayat samiti* (block level) and an indirectly-chosen *zilla parishad* (district level) (Friedman, 1983, p. 37). Performance has varied considerably and although many have allegedly failed to carry out their delegated functions (Khanna and Bhatnagar, 1980) there have been some notable achievements in Karnataka (Crook and Manor, 1994) and also Gujerat and Maharashtra.

Pakistan shared a common colonial heritage with India, and President Ayub Khan's Basic Democracies had a number of features akin to the *panchayati raj*. The system was instigated under martial law, however, and the initially elected representatives had little public legitimacy. Subsequent military governments have favoured the centralization of power and the system 'has fallen into relative neglect . . . local government is essentially seen as an arm of the central ministries' (Friedman, 1983, p. 38). Bangladesh pursued the Basic Democracies system until it achieved independence from Pakistan in 1971. A series of decentralizations has followed, most notably the *Upazila* system introduced by the Ershad regime in 1982 (Siddiquee and Hulme, 1994). It was supposed to devolve power to local-level *Union Parishads* and *Upazila Parishads*, but its record is ambiguous. Although funding for these local councils improved, around 40 per cent of resources were stolen and local accountability did not improve as elected representatives found that patron-client links to central government were of most personal significance (Crook and Manor, 1994).

Sri Lanka continues to struggle with the question of how 'new' decentralization policies might give its Tamil population sufficient autonomy to placate secessionists. Having spent a decade building up its capacity to plan at the district level it recently switched to a provincial planning system and then a divisional (sub-district) approach. Thailand and Indonesia, both countries in which there is considerable military influence, have adopted the mixed authority approach that permits central controls whilst creating an impression of some local autonomy and participation. The Philippines is the only Southeast Asian country to promote any significant devolution. This is being pursued through the 1991 Local Government Code which allocates additional functions to locally elected bodies and provides for wide participation. Implementation is likely to be bedevilled by many problems.

Latin America

The fundamental contention of a 1980s review of decentralization in Latin America remains valid, that 'the concentration of decision-making within central government ministries, often referred to as overcentralization, is a fundamental characteristic of Latin American governments' (Harris, 1983, p. 183). Devolution to local authorities has been rare and typically there is a predominance of central government agencies operating at the local level. Dissatisfaction with the performance of central ministries led many Latin American nations, such as Brazil and Mexico, to spawn a vast number of decentralized agencies or parastatals, outside of direct ministry control, during the 1950s, 1960s and 1970s. These are now perceived to suffer from serious problems of control and coordination which are being addressed through policies which assume a sectoral or regional focus. Harris perceives these as further centralization. The redemocratization of Latin American nations may create new opportunities but there is an historical legacy of centralist attitudes and interests from both politicians and bureaucrats that must be overcome before devolution will become a serious option.

The South Pacific

Decentralization policies have played a significant role in South Pacific nations (Larmour *et al.*, 1985). This is partly for pragmatic political reasons such as geographic and ethnic fragmentation, but also reflects the fact that they were late to achieve independence. Most acquired this status in the 1970s when one of the lessons of African and Asian statehood was to avoid overcentralization of political and administrative power. Indeed, Papua New Guinea (Box 7.1) embarked on one of the developing world's most radical decentralization programmes soon after independence. The results of this experiment have however been mixed and between 1992–5 successive national governments have either tried to abolish provincial government or at least to recentralize certain functions. Is decentralization, as Michael Somare, the Prime Minister whose government introduced the policies stated, 'good theory but poor practice?' (quoted in Standish, 1983, p. 236).

The performance of decentralization policies

Previous sections have made passing reference to the performance of decentralization policies. In this section we look in more detail at the results that have been achieved. Two general points about the literature on this topic must be noted at the outset. First, many commentators refer to performance in terms of a limited set of indicators without explaining why other indicators are not selected. Particularly common is the managerialist perspective in which policies are evaluated in terms of the efficiency of service delivery. Clearly such measures are important, but consideration should also be afforded to political impacts such as the strengthening of national unity or greater public participation in decision-making.

BOX 7.1

A case study of devolution: decentralization in Papua New Guinea

The Australian colonial authorities governed Papua New Guinea in a centralized fashion in which the field administration played a pivotal role. Local governments were first introduced in the 1950s but as self-government drew near there was an accelerated attempt to establish and make effective, small-scale local governments. In most rural areas these performed poorly. The nation's indigenous leaders were sympathetic to notions of decentralization but vague about the form this might take and the timing, until the island province of Bougainville unilaterally declared its independence, two weeks before Australia relinquished control of Papua New Guinea in September 1975. After a tense period of negotiations and threats Bougainville rejoined Papua New Guinea, as the North Solomons Province, and a constitutional amendment provided for nationwide provincial government based on the concessions granted to the would-be secessionists.

Elected provincial governments were established in each of the country's 19 provinces by 1979. These had legislative powers over provincial and concurrent functions, drew up an annual provincial budget on the basis of local taxes and central grants, designed provincial plans and oversaw the operations of 70 per cent of the country's civil servants. Considerable administrative disruption was associated with the switch to devolved government. Rancorous petty-politicking rather than coherent policy, responsive administration and accountability often characterized provincial government. The impact of decentralization has varied from province to province, but its developmental performance has fallen well short of what proponents of the strategy had claimed and much disillusionment set in. Even the claim that decentralization had succeeded politically by maintaining the nation's territorial integrity is now highly questionable as a secessionist movement led to central government withdrawal from the North Solomons. Somare, the Prime Minister who took the decentralization bills through parliament, later proposed a national referendum to see whether the populace wished to abolish provincial government. Recent national governments have moved to abolish provincial governments or recentralize some functions.

Provincial government politicians have resisted and reduced the recentralizing content of a new Organic Law on decentralization which was passed by parliament in 1995. Under the new system, the province's member of the national parliament becomes the provincial premier while the members of the provincial assembly are drawn from local governments. These small bodies will also assume responsibilities for local planning although there are doubts about the administrative capacity of many local governments to perform basic management tasks.

In some circumstances a reduction in the effectiveness of service delivery might well be an acceptable trade-off for the achievement of a political goal. For example, the government of Sri Lanka would willingly adopt a technically deficient service delivery system to settle the civil war with Tamil factionalists.

Secondly, many of the commonly cited indicators are poorly defined. For some indicators, particularly those of a political nature (for example enhanced political participation), precise quantification may not be possible and 'an informed judgement' (Kasfir, 1976, p. 17) may be the best that can be achieved. For others, particularly those relating to service provision, quantification is possible. However, very few studies of decentralization in developing countries have taken the trouble to measure changes in characteristics such as access to health care or quality of feeder roads.

Aside from these problems of data coverage and quality two other difficulties arise. One is that when multiple criteria are used they may provide conflicting evidence: for example, that more participation in local decision-making has been achieved but that the quality of service delivery has declined. The other is the difficulty of determining whether an observed change is due to a decentralization policy or other factors. For example, was the decline in rural services in Zambia in the late 1980s caused by the new decentralization policies or did this result from structural adjustment programmes?

With these provisos in mind it is possible to group writers on the performance of decentralization policies in terms of two propositions. The first proposition is that decentralization policies have produced very limited or even negative results, often at a high cost. The second proposition is that although decentralization policies have not proved universally successful their achievements are significant and increase as time passes.

Smith (1985) typifies the first school of thought: 'Experience of decentralisation in less-developed countries has almost everywhere fallen short of expectations and the declared objectives of policy-makers' (*ibid.*, p. 188). The pronounced preference that governments have shown for deconcentration and converting locally elected bodies into mixed authorities has meant that 'the participative quality of decentralised institutions has been especially prone to erosion' (*ibid.*). Even where significant devolution has occurred, as in Papua New Guinea, the nature of political activities that has ensued has led to villagers becoming cynical and withdrawing from political involvement with the state (Standish, 1983, p. 231). Studies of local government expenditure have concluded that the greater part goes for staff costs and that much of this is unrelated to the provision of services (McCullough, 1983). A large number of writers have provided evidence of decentralization policies performing poorly (Bienen *et al.*, 1990; Chitere and Monya, 1989; Oberst, 1986; Hyden, 1983).

The alternative proposition, typified by Rondinelli and Nellis (1986), argues that despite 'widely varying results' recent experiences create a case for 'cautious optimism'. Amongst the examples cited are Morocco, where deconcentration has led to development funds going to more remote areas; Thailand, where deconcentration has led to the mounting of a successful rural employment generation programme; Pakistan, where deconcentrated integrated rural development projects seemed to benefit a large segment of the population; and Papua New Guinea, where devolution has led to 'increased participation in decision making' and has improved planning, management and coordination capacities at the provincial level. There is some sleight of hand, however, in the creation of this case for cautious optimism as a systematic analysis of comparable indicators is not presented. Rather, the case is based upon a limited set of examples and carefully selected sources of information.

Two rigorously structured and systematic attempts to measure and compare the achievements of decentralization policies stand out from the general literature. These are by Montgomery (1972 and summarized in 1988, pp. 1–26) and Crook and Manor (1994). Montgomery's study (Box 7.2) is now almost 25 years old and focused on the implementation of land reform policies. He concluded that the devolved implementation of such policies performed much better than deconcentrated implementation (which in turn performed better than centralized administration) in terms of peasant income, power and tenure security. Also, the devolved approach only strengthened the power of the bureaucracy in one case, whereas deconcentrated and centralized implementation always enhanced the position of the bureaucracy *vis-à-vis* the peasantry. Analysts of decentralization might well query whether land reform is atypical of local service functions, being a 'one-off' rather than a continuous service, and the definitions and measures that Montgomery adopts for the study are open to challenge. Nevertheless, this study provides the most rigorous evidence that we have to date to support the empirical generalization that 'decentralization works'.

Crook and Manor (1994) conducted a comparative study of devolution in Bangladesh, the Indian state of Karnataka, Ghana and Côte d'Ivoire. In each case they examined whether levels of popular participation and representation had been modified and then identified the 'institutional performance' of the reforms in terms of changes in effectiveness, responsiveness and institutional processes. The achievements of devolution policies were found to be very varied and they produce a far more complex picture than Montgomery's study (Table 7.3).

BOX 7.2
Decentralization and land reform

John Montgomery utilized data from USAID's 1970 Spring Review of land reform in 25 countries. He classified each of these cases in terms of the administrative process that was utilised for the implementation of reform.

(i)   Centralized processes that relied on a single agency within the central bureaucracy;

(ii) Decentralized processes involving deconcentration or bureaucratic pluralism (the division of responsibilities among several central agencies);

(iii) Devolution when less use was made of the professional bureaucracy and local political leaders took responsibility for at least one of the major administrative tasks involved in land reform implementation.

Each land reform was assessed in terms of whether there was evidence that it had increased peasant income, increased peasant power over decision-making, increased peasant security of tenure or increased the political power of the bureaucracy.

Administrative process	Number of cases	Peasants' increased income (%)	Peasants' increased power (%)	Peasants' increased tenure security (%)	Bureaucrats' increased political power (%)
Centralized	9	11	11	22	100
Decentralized	6	33	0	67	100
Devolved	10	80	80	100	10

The study demonstrated that the *devolved* implementation of land reform produced superior results to the *decentralized* (i.e. deconcentrated) or *centralized* processes in terms of peasant income, power and tenure security. The devolved processes only strengthened the power of the bureaucracy in one case. A series of other tabulations were used to check that this correlation did not simply reflect regime type, motives for reform and vulnerability to agrarian unrest.

Source: Abstracted from Montgomery, J.D. (1988) *Bureaucrats and People: Grassroots Participation in Third World Development* (Baltimore: Johns Hopkins University Press).

In Karnataka, the policies were very successful at producing better levels of service provision and a more responsive government. In Bangladesh, improvements in service provision were observed but the system remained biased towards the élite. The results in Cote d'Ivoire and Ghana were much less positive, as reflected in the responses of the recipients of local government services. The authors conclude that the results achieved by policies of devolution are as much a product of the wider social and political context as they are of the nature and features of the policy itself. Such a conclusion points to the difficulties of prescribing policies, the topic of the next section.

TABLE 7.3

Devolution in four countries

Country	Were services better than those provided previously?	Were local authorities more responsive than previously?	Percentage of sample of service receivers who believed the devolved system can meet their need (%)
India (Karnataka)	Yes	Good	69
Bangladesh	Yes	Medium	36
Cote d'Ivoire	Yes to 1989	Poor	36
Ghana	No	Poor	18

Note: For India the statistics refer to the District and in Bangladesh to the Upazila (now called Thana).
Source: Crook, R. and Manor, J. (1994) *Enhancing Participation and Institutional Performance: Democratic Decentralisation in South Asia and West Africa* (London: Overseas Development Administration), p. 210.

Prospects and prescriptions

Both proponents and critics of decentralization strategies recognize that intentional, as opposed to rhetorical, decentralization faces considerable problems because of 'the centralising tendencies which are such a ubiquitous feature of contemporary states' (Smith, 1985, p. 193). National politicians are reluctant to cede power; central bureaucracies resist the delegation of responsibilities; when responsibilities are transferred there is rarely a corresponding transfer of financial resources; and those resources that are available at the local level are often poorly deployed by inexperienced, ill-trained and underpaid field staff. Added to this is the catch-22, that the socio-economic structures of many developing countries entail that authentic decentralization policies (particularly devolutions) are likely to be manipulated by local élites that may use decentralized power to strengthen their position at the expense of lower-income groups:

> . . . it is conceivable, even likely in many countries, that power at the local level is more concentrated, more elitist and applied more ruthlessly against the poor than at the centre . . . greater decentralization does not necessarily imply greater democracy let alone 'power to the people' – it all depends on the circumstances under which decentralization occurs. (Griffin, 1981, p. 225)

In the light of such problems, what policies should be pursued? Much depends on the perspective that is adopted and the cases that are considered but it is possible to identify five main positions:

1. *Devolution*: Devolve power to local authorities along classic lines. This is the position of those who view poor performance as being a result of national leaders lacking the 'political will' to introduce policies that transfer decision-making responsibilities to locally elected bodies. For example, Chitere and Monya (1989, p. 50) argue that Kenya should eschew its mixed authority system, in which national parliamentarians and civil servants have a big say, for a 'comprehensive local government system'. However, such a belief in liberal democratic theory, without an analysis of economic and social structures, can be interpreted as taking a 'romantic view of decentralisation' and failing to recognize that 'it is not an absolute good in its own right' (Smith, 1985, p. 191).

2. *Incrementalism*: Proceed incrementally, learning from existing policies but continuing the emphasis on decentralization. This is the position of Rondinelli and Nellis (1986), USAID and the World Bank. It is based on the arguments that centralized planning has been discredited, that there is some empirical evidence that decentralization can achieve desirable results but that the complexity of the changes it requires in financial systems and human capacities mean it must be gradualist.

3. *Centralization*: In societies where there is pronounced rural socio-economic inequality, development goals might best be attained through centralization. Slater (1989, p. 502) in his critique of the incrementalist case points to the possibility of centralization being preferable in many peripheral states. Huque (1986, p. 91) is more direct and states that 'centralized administration has its merits and, in some cases, is more effective and economical than decentralized administration'. Such a position can be based partly on ideological grounds, but also on empirical evidence from a number of countries (Alavi, 1971; Bienen *et al.*, 1990; Ray and Kumptala, 1987).

4. *Irrelevance*: Related to the previous position, but perhaps more dramatic, is the argument that decentralization policies (or centralization policies) are really irrelevant. These merely reflect the status quo. Fundamental social change is required before decentralization/centralization policies will achieve developmental goals. Hyden (1983, pp. 106–7) illustrates this position in

claiming that 'improvements in government performance are dependent on the transformation of society' and that a particular type of dominant class must emerge in African states before decentralization initiatives (or any other public sector reforms) will yield benefits.

5. *Contingency*: The final position has its roots in the contingency theories that are popular in management literature. According to advocates of this position, generalizations about decentralization policies are nonsensical and that the appropriate choice must be determined by a careful consideration of the specific objectives and contexts. In many ways this is the conclusion that Smith (1985) reaches, but it is best illustrated by the work of Leonard (1982), and more recently Moris (1991). He outlines a methodology by which consideration of programme objectives and contexts could guide an institutional designer in the choice of organizations and types of linkages that are most likely to yield developmental results.

Conclusion

The decentralization policies that Third World nations have pursued have not proven to be a panacea for making state-sponsored interventions more effective in promoting development. While much of this shortcoming can be understood in terms of absurdly high expectations, an additional cause has been the cynical use of the term by many regimes. Under the banner of decentralization they have introduced policies that concentrate power and decision-making and weaken local arenas for political debate. Serious devolutions have been rare, and deconcentration or the establishment of mixed authorities have been the favoured modes for Third World leaders.

Throughout the period 1940 to 1980, decentralization has been a concept that focused on the delegation of power within the state. However, the 1980s saw the term extended beyond the state to refer to the market-oriented policies of the new right that dominate development policy. We examine these and their relation to public enterprises in the next chapter, but the serious student of government will give some thought to the question of whether including privatization within the remit of decentralization is a matter of definition or ideology.

8

Public Enterprise Reform: Private Sector Solutions

'Bureaucrats are still in business' lamented a 1995 review of public enterprises in developing countries (World Bank, 1995b). The reason for this pessimistic tone was that after a decade of public enterprise divestiture and a growing consensus that governments performed less well than the private sector in many business-type activities, the size of the public enterprise sector remained the same – too large. The number of such enterprises and their share of the GDP vary between countries but as we have already noted, they provide a far greater percentage of public sector employment than in the OECD economies and generally account for a larger percentage of GDP (see Box 8.1). They are engaged in a diverse range of activities such as steel manufacture, tractor-making, grain milling, bakeries, crop marketing, the provision of public utilities, banking, airlines, hotels, oil refining, chemicals, textiles and any other business venture in which government has decided to become involved. While the profile of the public enterprise sector is different for each country, the impulse to reform is common for all countries.

In this chapter we will briefly examine the origin of public enterprises and then identify their many problems which have led to the current push for reform. Examination of the various methods of public enterprise reform will follow, with special attention being paid to the feasibility and the desirability of these methods.

Before commencing our discussion it is necessary to establish a working definition of what public enterprises or state-owned enterprises (SOEs) actually are. They can be broadly described as state-

---

BOX 8.1

The role of public enterprises in developing countries

1. *Value added*
   In developing countries the share of value added from public enterprise stayed constant throughout the 1980s at about 11 per cent of GDP although in many countries the share of public enterprises in manufacturing value added has exceeded 50 per cent of national totals.

2. *Total investment*
   In a representative sample of 14 developing countries, public enterprises accounted for an average of 25 per cent of total investment.

3. *Credit systems*
   It has been roughly estimated that public enterprises account for 30 per cent of domestic debt and 20 per cent of foreign debt.

4. *Non-agricultural employment*
   Public enterprises account for about 15 per cent of such employment in developing countries as compared to 4 per cent in OECD countries

5. *Regional variations*
   These can be considerable. At the extreme, in Algeria, Egypt and Zambia at various times in the 1980s, public enterprises accounted for between 40 and 60 per cent of GDP. In 1991, public enterprises provided 23 per cent of formal employment in Africa as compared to 3 per cent in Asia.

6. *The poorest countries*
   Available evidence suggests that the poorer the country the larger the relative size of the public enterprise sector in the economy.

Source: Nellis, M. and Kikeri, S. (1989) 'Public Enterprise Reform: Privatization and the World Bank', *World Development*, vol. 17(5), pp. 659–72; and World Bank (1995) *Bureaucrats in Business: The Economics and Politics of Government Ownership* (New York: Oxford University Press).

---

owned production units which sell their output and are thus directly involved in the market process. This contrasts with other state activities and responsibilities such as national defence and the provision of law and order which are not marketed. Although state enterprises assume various forms the following standard check-list is a useful guide:

A public enterprise is an organization which,
- is owned by public authorities . . . to the extent of 50 per cent or more;
- is under the top managerial control of the owning public authorities . . . including the right to appoint top management and to formulate critical policy decisions;

- is established for the achievement of a defined set of public purposes, which may be multi-dimensional in character;
- is engaged in activities of a business character;
- is consequently placed under a system of public accountability;
- involves the basic idea of investment and returns and service.

(Praxy and Sicherl, 1981, p. 24)

The origins of public enterprises

Public enterprises were first established by the colonial powers, usually to facilitate economic development. For example, in Nigeria the British started to set up marketing boards in 1936 and converted certain government departments into public enterprises after 1945, such as the Nigerian Railway Corporation and the Nigerian Ports Authority (Adamolekun, 1983). In Papua New Guinea, the Electricity Commission and the Harbours Board were established in the 1960s while Air Niugini, the national airline, was formed in 1973, two years before independence. When India became independent the country possessed more public enterprises than Britain, the former colonial power. But the massive expansion of public enterprises in the developing world came after independence in the 1960s and 1970s – and it occurred in all types of economies from communist through to capitalist (see Box 8.2). Several interrelated factors explain this growth.

For socialist or communist countries there was a necessary ideological commitment to the public ownership of the means of production. Private ownership was seen to lead to exploitation and underdevelopment whereas public ownership would ensure that the evils of capitalism were avoided. Nationalism often backed up such views and provided a potent political justification for government intervention in market activities. Such action would ensure that foreign nationals and multinational corporations would not secure control of the economy. These nationalist sentiments were not confined to socialist and communist countries but could be used as justification for the nationalization of foreign enterprises and the creation of new public enterprises in market-oriented economies.

Further justification and encouragement of public enterprise formation came from economic theory and the perceived role of central planning (see Chapter 6). Development was identified as something which did not occur automatically. It had to be engineered by

---

BOX 8.2

The origin of public enterprises in Bangladesh

Bangladesh became independent in December 1971 after 9 months of bloody war which took a heavy toll on life and property. The immediate imperatives at independence were to establish a civil administration and to rehabilitate the economy. The political leadership did not design a comprehensive strategy to manage the economy after independence, but it was soon faced with no alternative but to take over the management of industrial units and financial institutions. This included 725 industrial units (47 per cent of the country's fixed assets in the industrial sector) which had been abandoned by their non-local owners who had left the country. Within three months the government had decided in favour of a much broader nationalization which included the entire jute, sugar and textile industries. This increased the state's ownership of modern industry from 34 per cent to 92 per cent. The government created 10 sector corporations to control, supervise, manage and coordinate different groups of industries. Further, all banks were nationalized and reconstituted into six banks.

This expansion of state ownership took place under a political leadership that had traditionally followed a middle-of-the-road economic philosophy. It had neither the ideological conviction nor the organizational capacity to oversee the implementation politically. However, the Constitution subsequently strengthened the ideological base for state ownership since it incorporated socialism as one of its basic principles. The outcome of state ownership and management of industrial enterprises was in general unsuccessful. In the period up to 1975, capacity utilization was low, state-owned industries suffered losses in successive years, and the index of industrial production did not show much improvement.

Source: Modified from Chowdhury, T. E. (1992) 'Privatization of State Enterprises in Bangladesh, 1975-84', in G. Lamb and R. Weaving (eds), *Managing Policy Reforms in the Real World* (Washington DC: World Bank, EDI Seminar Series), pp. 57–70.

---

governments using centralized planning. The examples of the Soviet Union (then seen as a great economic success) and the Marshall Plan for rehabilitating post-war Europe were employed to provide practical demonstrations of the efficacy of central planning. A component of such engineered change was that government would need to intervene in areas of the economy which might be thought to belong to the private sector. The need to control the direction of economic development, the absence of domestic capital or the reluctance of private sector to invest, mistrust of private sector motivations, strategic requirements and the shortage of indigenous entrepreneurial skills were utilized as justifications for government participation in market activities. The new public enterprises would not only fill gaps in the economy but would also generate profits which could be used for new investment. Such thinking spawned numerous public enterprises in countries with diverse political philosophies and regimes.

A commitment to big government complemented this outlook. Governments were seen as the only organizations with the capacity to engineer the necessary changes which would produce development; and if governments needed to get involved in producing steel, marketing crops or providing banking services then this was justified. Getting the prices right was of secondary importance. The state was assumed to be a beneficient entity oriented to promoting the welfare of all with central planning as a technical, rather than a highly political, affair. There was no question of rolling back the state. Rather, the growing number of public enterprises in the 1960s and 1970s indicated a concerted effort to extend the frontiers of the state.

Local political factors have also contributed to the growth in numbers of public enterprises and the particular configurations of public enterprises in different countries. For some governments, there might have been implicit objectives of providing employment and even generating political support through establishing public enterprises. A drive to nationalize foreign businesses by conversion to public enterprises could distract public attention from poor government performance. Alternatively, there can be quite explicit politically-motivated policies relating to public enterprises. For example, following the major racial conflicts in 1969 in Malaysia the ascendant Malay political élite instituted policies to incorporate and expand the economic role of the Malay upper and middle classes. State intervention in the economy, often through public enterprises, was used as a vehicle to achieve these policy objectives (Woon, 1991). Similarly, in Thailand and Indonesia there are examples of public enterprises being used to take over control of various economic sectors from local Chinese business classes.

Public enterprise performance

Public enterprises have not made the positive impact on development performance that was initially anticipated. While there are success stories there are considerably more examples of public enterprises failing to achieve both their economic and welfare objectives. In this section we will review some of the many problems that have beset public enterprises across the developing world.

The leading issue is that public enterprises have not made the expected profits and thus have not been sources of investment capital. In fact, they have often been drains on scarce government financial resources and have contributed to spiralling levels of national debt. One study involving seventeen developing nations revealed that all but one suffered deficits in the public enterprise sector in the second half of the 1970s (Gillis *et al.*, 1987). Between 1981–87, the Philippine government would have run budget surpluses were it not for the financial haemorrhaging caused by the need to support public enterprises. By mid-1988, state enterprises in the Philippines had incurred US$12.02 billion in debt, almost 50 per cent of the country's total external debt (Woon, 1991). In 1985–86, 93 of 211 production units in the central state sector in India were losing money (Naya, 1990). Excluding the petroleum assets, the public sector made a financial loss. In West Bengal some of the National Textile Corporation mills were spending twice as much in labour costs as they earned in revenue for each metre of cloth produced. Reports of sub-Saharan Africa have consistently emphasized almost universally poor performance with cash flows failing to cover running costs (for example World Bank, 1983; Nellis, 1986). A more vivid account notes the following:

In good times and bad times, public enterprises have on the whole been a waste of money. The overwhelming evidence from across Africa – from government's own reports, World Bank missions and scholarly studies – clearly demonstrates that they have consumed far more resources than they have generated. Rather than contributing, they have depleted national resources. All too many public enterprises sit like huge white elephants over the African landscape, voraciously consuming what has been produced by others. (Wilson, 1986 as quoted by Haile-Mariam and Mengistu, 1988, p. 1572)

But profitability is neither a complete nor an accurate measure of public enterprise performance (Nellis and Kikeri, 1989) (see Box 8.3 for the relation between public enterprises and pollution). Public enterprises may fulfil non-commercial objectives and even efficient operations can run at a loss because products are priced at below market rates. Even if public enterprises do appear to be making money this may be due to monopoly position and/or government pricing policy which makes consumers pay above market rates for inefficiently produced items. Estimating the non-financial social contribution of public enterprises to development is a far trickier

---

BOX 8.3
Public enterprises and pollution

Some World Bank research indicates that divesting state-owned enterprises, especially older ones, may help the environment since state-owned plants tend to be more polluting than their private sector counterparts. For example, in a study of private pulp and paper plants in four countries (Bangladesh, India, Indonesia and Thailand) it was found that private plants, whether foreign or domestically owned, controlled pollution much better than state-owned plants operating at similar scale and efficiency. State-owned plants polluted over five times as much per unit of output as comparable plants in the private sector. The major explanation appears to be that state-owned plants are better placed to evade pollution controls than their private counterparts.

Cubatão, in Sao Paulo State, Brazil, used to be known as 'the Valley of Death' because of extreme pollution problems. The state's pollution control agency, Companhia de Technologia de Saneamento Ambiental (CETSEB), had some success in cleaning up the valley but found two state-owned factories to be the major polluters of water and air and the major regulatory headache. The steel (COSIPA) and petroleum (PETROBRAS) plants were able to use their bureaucratic connections to escape pollution regulation. A veteran pollution inspector observed: 'To a public enterprise we are just another government bureau. They feel that we have no right to tell them what to do, and they have enough clout in the government to keep us away'. Officials of CETSEB were eagerly anticipating the privatization of COSIPA, since they have far fewer problems with private firms. For the people of Cubatão, privatization of COSIPA should literally bring a breath of fresh air.

Source: Adapted from World Bank (1995) *Bureaucrats in Business: The Economics and Politics of Government Ownership* (New York: Oxford University Press), pp. 38–41.

---

business. Public enterprises have been the vanguard of industrialization in some countries. Entrepreneurial and management skills have been developed in public enterprises and diffused to the wider economy. Substantial employment has been created while regional development has been encouraged through the deliberate decentralization of public enterprises. Some actions by state enterprises, such as the building of a road, may generate external benefits to the economy which are not recorded in the organization's accounts. While all this may be true, such gains may have been made at a high cost. Critics argue that even greater gains could have been made if resources had been utilized differently or more efficiently.

Leaving aside the question of whether such large-scale investment in public enterprises was an ill-informed and mistaken strategy from the start, we can identify a range of management problems which have beset public enterprises. You can note many similarities with the criticisms of non-market state bureaucracies encountered in Chapters 4 and 5.

A fundamental problem has been the vagueness and/or multiplicity of goals. This leads to a lack of concern with strategy and the ways in which organizations might adapt to changing environmental conditions. Weak structures of accountability have exacerbated the situation and frequently have meant that public enterprise managers have not been held responsible for the performance of their operations. The absence of appropriate performance evaluation criteria or the unsuitability of those that exist has contributed to the relative disinterest in performance – how it should be measured and improved. The attitude that government can bail you out of difficulty has been a common conception in the public enterprise sector.

The organizational structures of public enterprises have been characteristically bureaucratic, not surprising since they are the progeny and wards of other bureaucratic agencies of government. These structures emphasize routine, rules, control and hierarchy. They are frequently unable to cope with changing environments and lack proactive orientation. Rigidity rather than flexibility has been the norm. The managers themselves may be poorly schooled in management techniques and contemporary management practices in the private sector. For example, skills in marketing, product development and in the management of growth and diversification have been poorly represented and possibly little valued as they have no place in the prevailing model of bureaucratic management.

Managers may also have to cope with overstaffing. Public enterprises have proved to be ideal vehicles for the disbursement of political patronage, and political appointments have swelled the ranks of public enterprises in many countries. Even when managers are experienced and able they may be prevented from implementing policies and processes which could enhance performance as political decisions rather than business decisions determine what the public enterprise does. There are many masters including ministries, planning agencies, monitoring bodies and politicians. All have an interest and claim a right to tell public enterprises how to run their businesses.

There are other problems such as wrong initial choices of technology and plant size. Subsequent failure to modernize or adapt technology may create further difficulties. There have been many reports of financial malpractices in such areas as purchases, sales and capital construction. Poor accountability mechanisms explain why such things go undetected or unpunished but it is the politicization of enterprises and organizational cultures of uncommitment which actually encourage such corrupt practices in the first place.

A combination of the above managerial shortcomings have contributed to what Khandwalla (1987) describes as 'public enterprise sickness'. It is not found in all public enterprises but some or all of the features outlined above have characterized the operation of many public enterprises in developing countries and have been identified as prime reasons why public enterprise reform is so vital. 'Rethinking' the state has provided even greater impetus to this task (World Bank, 1991).

Rethinking the state

By the early 1980s expansion of the public enterprise sector ceased to be a policy preference in most developing countries. Not only was there widespread recognition of the debilitating management problems discussed above but there was a more fundamental questioning of the role of the state in economic development. An emerging consensus was that the state was overextended, inefficient and needed to be 'rolled back'.

The ideological impulse came from the election of conservative governments in the United States, the UK and other parts of Europe. They pushed for placing tighter limits on state activities, and in the case of the UK provided a radical practical demonstration of how this could be achieved especially through the privatization of public enterprises. Multilateral agencies such as the World Bank added their support to the argument that 'governments need to do less in those areas where markets work, or can be made to work reasonably well. In many countries it would help to privatise many of the state-owned enterprises' (World Bank, 1991, p. 9).

Development planning was judged largely to have failed. There had been repeated inability to achieve planning targets; macroeconomic crises associated with mushrooming foreign debt and budget deficits became endemic; and state intervention in the economy through import substitution industrialization was strongly associated with inefficency and resource misallocation (Cook and Kirkpatrick, 1988; Van de Walle, 1989). The collapse of communism in the former Soviet Union and Eastern Europe and their rush into creating market economies merely furnished the epitaph for central planning and heavy state involvement in productive economic activities.

The dominant paradigm has become a neo-classical market-oriented view of the development process which seeks to realign the roles of the state and the market. Emphasis has shifted in favour of the private sector and away from state intervention. The new paradigm has found expression in policies of economic liberalization. Removing price distortions in product, labour and capital markets, reducing government expenditure, privatization of public enterprises, and creating a legislative-constitutional environment conducive to the private sector have been key components of this economic liberalization (Cook and Hulme, 1988).

Few, if any, would disagree with the idea that the role of the state in economic development needs recasting but there are many shades of opinion around this new orthodoxy. At one extreme there are those who have almost uncritical belief in the allocative efficiency of the 'invisible hand' of the market. They regard the state as predatory and all politicians, bureaucrats and organizations in civil society as exclusively driven by self-interest. They advocate the minimalist state and *laissez-faire* capitalism where the market is supreme. In this model, public enterprises are perceived as market distorting devices which must be privatised.

Others find such faith in the efficiency and equity of the 'invisible hand' alarming. As Joan Robinson has observed, it can also work by strangulation (Streeten, 1993). Streeten has argued for the continuation of an 'activist' state which sets prices, is engaged with civil society and intervenes more effectively than in the past to facilitate an improvement in living for the poor. To him the fundamental structural change that is required is a redistribution of assets and an access to power. This view still entails reform of the public enterprise sector as such action will facilitate improvements in productivity and in the redistribution of income and wealth.

The pragmatic view of the role of government in economic development does not classify the state as malevolent and simply reduce policy and action to the articulation of aggregated individual interests. It is admitted that governments seek to maintain the support of key constituencies or even extend their political base, but it is also held that the same governments can adopt efficient economic policies which can help to realise visions of their societies' futures. Naya (1990) provides a useful list of such functions that define the new 'direct' role of the state:

- Provision of public goods (for example enforcement of contracts, defence);
- Provision of some merit goods (for example education and health);
- Development of transportation, communication and power systems;
- Dissemination of economic information
- Institution of a 'transparent' and flexible regulatory framework;
- Promotion of scientific and technological research;
- Provision of a safety net for low-income groups.

He notes there are economic functions which the state alone can perform and there are those which it can perform better than other sectors under particular circumstances. The state must relate the social and economic goals it has set for itself to consideration of whether the private sector has comparative advantage in activities which would facilitate the achievement of these goals. Continuous evaluation of government's role in the economy is essential as environmental conditions are subject to change and policy will need to respond to such changes.

Such a position appears to fit with our view that public enterprises have the potential to play an important role in development, but not in all circumstances and not at all times. Experience has shown that many problems have beset individual enterprises and the sector in general in all countries. Thus, reform is essential for development but the appropriate policy will differ between countries as environmental circumstances such as GDP per capita, level of industrialization, human resource profile and size of the private sector vary so much. In the next section we examine a range of public enterprise reform options which policy-makers and administrators have at their disposal.

Strategies for public enterprise reform

There is no shortage of advice and case studies on public enterprise reform for policy-makers and administrators in developing countries. An enormous volume of literature has been written on the subject and numerous consultants have made good livings from it. The problem is to avoid information overload and to clearly delineate the major issues and options. To accomplish this we have drawn heavily from the work of Mary Shirley and John Nellis (1991), long-time researchers and commentators on the subject.

The policy framework

The most fundamental step in public enterprise reform is to establish the appropriate policy framework. Policies concerning trade, finance, pricing and labour are the most important for the development of an efficient public enterprise sector. If the appropriate policy platform in these areas is lacking, then changes in management structures and processes are unlikely to work.

A major incentive to efficiency is the competitive market as 'it pushes firms to develop their marketing skills, pay close attention to service, keep up technologically, and control costs' (*ibid.*, p. 7). However, this assumes that managers are allowed to act as businessmen not bureaucrats. The policy stimulus comes from opening up international trade and through restructuring the domestic market. Once such actions are taken the public enterprise managers would no longer enjoy highly protected markets, favoured status or monopoly position but would need to take business decisions such as cost-cutting measures and demonstrate the business skills required for the competitive market.

Financial policy also requires attention as governments have often provided public enterprise with financial guarantees, shouldered their debts and funded their deficits. This security has led to resource misallocation, growing indebtedness and a tendency to expand enterprises. For pure economic efficiency, the state should cease subsidizing public enterprises and force them onto private capital markets where they will be subject to the same financial criteria as private firms. However, an incremental strategy is advisable as public enterprises may be unable to cope with the shock of sudden and full exposure to the financial markets. Box 8.4 shows how weak financial regulation can similarly undermine privatization initiatives. Also, debt reduction is often necessary while the fulfilment of social or strategic objectives may make reduction of subsidy preferable to its total removal.

With the orientation to competition comes the necessity to introduce pricing policies which militate against monopoly tariffs that are either too high or too low and are thus not related to 'efficiency prices'. One possible policy action is to set unit cost targets in reference to benchmark indicators from other countries. The bodies that make such decisions and monitor performance should be competent and able to respond fairly and rapidly to requests for price changes.

BOX 8.4
Financial regulation and privatization in Chile

Chile twice privatized a large number of state-owned enterprises. Problems encountered during the first attempt (1974–82) illustrate the importance of establishing adequate financial sector regulation and supervision. Chile began the first period with deregulation: the government abolished interest rate ceilings, eliminated credit allocation controls, reduced banks' reserve requirements, freed capital controls and allowed new entry. The authorities also privatized state banks. Many were purchased by business conglomerates, with a mere 20 per cent down payment. The conglomerates then used loans from the banks to finance the purchase of nonfinancial firms with down payments of only 10 to 40 per cent. These highly leveraged purchases concentrated financial and industrial power in the same hands. Under such circumstances, the ineffective, understaffed and underfunded bank supervisory system was unable to prevent insider lending. When domestic economic problems, external shocks and an overvalued exchange rate caused a depression in 1992, the conglomerates used their banks to prop up their failing firms so that banks and firms alike were quickly in serious trouble. During the resulting financial crisis, the government took back control of some fifty previously privatized enterprises, including banks that accounted for 60 per cent of total bank deposits.

Following the 1992 crisis, Chile strengthened the role, staffing and funding of its bank supervisory system; it then recapitalized and reprivatized the banks and sold off the nonfinancial enterprises for a second time. Regulations prohibited the sort of highly concentrated, highly leveraged purchases and insider lending that had characterized the first reform effort. Today, Chile's private financial system is well developed, with a large number of nonbank intermediaries, and supports a booming private industrial sector. Chile's experience suggests that countries undertaking bank privatization and liberalization of interest rates and credit controls should make sure that sound supervision and regulation mechanisms are in place first.

Source: World Bank (1995) *Bureaucrats in Business: The Economics and Politics of Government Ownership* (New York: Oxford University Press), p. 93

Labour policies are also critical to efficient operations. Public enterprises are typically governed by the rigid bureaucratic rules of the public service. Such regulations have frequently permitted excess numbers of workers, strong upward pressure on wages at lower levels and wage compression between top and bottom grades. This can reduce the incentive of management to promote efficiency and to assume greater accountability. Introducing labour policies which match the private sector should lead to greater efficiency but may involve great social costs especially through labour reduction. Such policies may also be expensive as increased managerial salaries and redundancy payments could be considerable.

Policy-makers may also need to attend to legal changes by removing the privileges or disadvantages of public enterprises and putting

---

BOX 8.5

Participation as regulation: an initial step in Bangalore

A serious handicap facing the individual dealing with a public utility is the lack of knowledge of the 'rules of the game' and the right to service. Expectations are often low and incentives for collective action are often limited.

A random sample of 800 households in the industrial city of Bangalore, India, highlighted dissatisfaction with the quality of service supplied by the telephone, electricity and water utilities. Only 9 per cent of those sampled were satisfied with their telephone service. Even fewer people were satisfied with electricity and water services. Problems cited included supply shortages, excess billing, inability to get errors corrected and a general lack of communication with the service agency.

The conclusion of a broader study of quality of service were clear: more competition and better information are needed. The two groups of agencies that performed relatively well in consumer assessment – banks and hospitals – operate in a relatively competitive environment. Another conclusion was that consumer 'voice' mobilized through groups such as consumer associations, can be an important force in sectoral reform and reorganization. These associations can provide critical monitoring and feedback to minimise abuses and hold public officials accountable. Well-publicized inter-city comparisons of service quality would create an information base on which consumer associations could act.

Source: World Bank (1994) *World Development Report 1994* (New York: Oxford University Press), p. 71.

---

them on a more even footing with private sector organizations. The regulatory framework instituted and operated by government should place emphasis on the requirements for competition and accountability both for the public and private sectors. However, the task of legal reform may be immense in some transitional economies where legal frameworks for the private sector are in their infancy.

The policy and regulatory frameworks might also be improved by participation from those who utilize the products of public enterprises. Such democratization could be a useful means of improving public enterprises to provide products and services more efficiently and effectively to the consumers they are supposed to serve. The example in Box 8.5 from Bangalore shows how one can take a first step in promoting popular participation in defining policy and regulation.

Management reforms

Creating the appropriate policy framework changes the environment in which public enterprises operate. This provides the opportunity, perhaps necessity, for public enterprises to respond with management reforms which are oriented to performance improvement.

The first task is to establish the role and scope of the public enterprise sector. This requires scrutiny of why the state owns enterprises, that is, what objectives it hopes to achieve through the enterprises – strategic, revenue-raising, national ownership or non-commercial. Classifying enterprises as 'strategic' or 'essential' and 'nonessential' and 'nonstrategic' will assist in deciding what actions to take – for example to retain or divest. The addition of economic criteria such as 'viable', 'potentially viable' and 'non-viable' will give further guidance – for example to improve or liquidate. The cluster of non-commercial objectives presents problems for governments wishing to turn their public enterprises into profit maximizers as the noncommercial objectives usually detract from profit maximization. This does not mean, however, that such objectives should be jettisoned in the name of the market. Rather, governments can encourage economic efficiency while still accommodating non-commercial objectives. They must simply expect lower profits.

Having decided the role and scope of the public enterprise sector, governments need to turn their attention to the individual enterprises. Shirley and Nellis (1991, p. 21) suggest that four essential actions must be taken to define the relationship between government and public enterprise:

- Set clear and obtainable objectives compatible with the commercial operation of the firm.
- Give management greater autonomy over the operation of the firm and select managers capable of operating independently.
- Establish clear rules, procedures and limits for government involvement in decision-making.
- Hold managers accountable by negotiating targets, monitoring and evaluating results, and rewarding managers and staff on the basis of performance.

Some governments have attempted to address these action areas by making public enterprises formulate corporate plans which contain objectives, strategy, targets and benchmarks for monitoring their achievement, and an investment plan. However such plans have often been thwarted by a public enterprise environment of price controls, subsidies and assured loans to pay for mistakes.

An alternative is the performance contract drawn up between governments and public enterprises. The former agree to meet certain financial and other obligations and to cease meddling in public enterprise business, while the latter accept negotiated performance targets. Islam (1993) sees performance contracts as 'theoretically sound' by defining the limits within which both parties operate, providing a results-oriented evaluation system and making mangers accountable. But, in a review of experiences in Senegal, India and Pakistan he notes that the boundaries between government and public enterprises have often been unclearly demarcated and even where they have, they were not enforced. The World Bank (1995b) is even less enamoured of performance contracts noting that they can exacerbate poor incentive structures facing managers.

The performance contract highlights the central issue in the reform of public sector management, that is how to increase the responsibilities of enterprise managers while altering government actions from control of financial transactions to the stimulation and evaluation of results. If managers are to assume such responsibilities then they must be both professional and entrepreneurial: 'dynamic, resourceful, and adaptable in managing growth, expansion and diversification, and they need to use various techniques of professional management in their routine operations' (Khandwalla, 1987, p. 7). This is a tall order which will require investment in skilled personnel, training, introduction of a culture of 'innovative professionalism', restructuring of organizations away from dysfunctional machine bureaucracies and attention to motivation via such means as financial incentives and participative decision-making. However, examples of such organizations can be found.

Privatization

For more than a decade the most prominent mode of public enterprise reform has been privatization. Between 1988 and 1993, over 2700 public enterprises in more than 60 developing countries were transferred to private hands bringing governments a revenue of US$96 billion (World Bank, 1995b; IFC, 1995). This divestiture of public enterprises fulfils the multiple function of reducing public expenditure, raising revenue and promoting the development of the private sector. In pursuit of these objectives various modes of privatization have been employed. They include denationalization, contracting-out, self-management/cooperatives and deregulation (ODI, 1986).

Denationalization is the most common method of privatization and involves selling public enterprises back to the former owners or through a new share flotation on the stock market, or by closing down the public enterprises altogether. Simply changing the ownership does not ensure economic efficiency. This is achieved through restructuring, altering culture, adopting other forms of organizational change and creating a competitive or regulatory environment that promotes efficiency. It is also desirable that the state has commenced these actions before sale takes place. At worst, however, denationalization can be a transfer of monopoly from one inefficient owner to another with no gain for the economy and its consumers.

Contracting-out or leasing enables the state to finance an enterprise using a private firm to run it. Public works, urban development and water supply schemes have been the most frequent users of this mode of privatization (see Box 8.6). It can encourage smaller more flexible enterprise units which can adapt their structures and activities to meet changing environmental conditions.

Self-management provides another privatization alternative. This involves transferring ownership and management of public enterprises to their workforces. In the agricultural sector, cooperatives or farmer associations may be used to take over the functions of former state corporations. There may be problems of management capacity or of management authority to institute reforms to make enterprises more efficient. Lack of capital and inadequate back-up services are other reported problems. Earlier promotion of cooperatives resulted in highly bureaucratic regulatory systems and in the capture of cooperatives by local élites (Hulme and Turner, 1990). Both factors discouraged participation and stifled professional innovative management.

The final mode of privatization is the 'market-loosening' strategy of deregulation. This involves the abolition of statutory barriers preventing private operators from competing with state enterprises. For example, monopolistic crop marketing boards have been abolished or forced to compete with private companies. This usually results in higher prices for farmers and increased output for the market. This changed environment makes it no longer worthwhile for farmers to engage in illegal trading across porous national borders to avoid the low prices of the crop marketing boards in their own countries. Governments may also use deregulation to encourage private sector participation in infrastructure provision. In Malaysia, Thailand and the Philippines, the private sector has constructed highways and

---

BOX 8.6

Privatizing water and improving service in Buenos Aires

Obras Sanitarias de la Nacion was the state-owned operator of the greater Buenos Aires water and sewerage network. Its ground-breaking privatization was developed with World Bank assistance and involved competitive bidding for a 30-year concession to operate the entire system. The bids had to satisfy minimum technical and financial criteria, after which the key determinant was the lowest proposed tariff. Aguas Argentinas proposed a 27 per cent reduction from the existing tariff and won.

The tender also required Aguas to commit to an investment in rehabilitation and expansion of approximately US$4 billion in six five-year plans over the life of the concession, allowing the connection of all residents currently without water or sanitation services. Government and company voluntary redundancy programs reduced the company's workforce from 7800 employees in May 1993 to about 3500 currently. The International Finance Corporation (IFC) helped finance the initial two-year investment programme, which included essential repairs, rehabilitation, acquisition of new equipment and a portion of the voluntary retirement plan and pre-operational expenses. Proper classification of users combined with metering is expected to contribute to improved demand management and to lead to a reduction in per capita consumption. Aguas also expects to reduce water wastage through the reduction of physical losses. The use of poor quality sources of ground water will be eliminated and the city's wastewater will be treated, resulting in benefits to the health of the population.

Since May 1993, when Aguas Argentinas was awarded the 30-year exclusive concession, it has expanded the water network to 600 000 new residents, eliminated water shortages, increased potable water production by 26 per cent and improved the reliability of service. Annual revenues have increased by 35 per cent from US$216 million in 1993 to US$293 million in 1994. As Aguas has the right to charge fines for late payments and finally to suspend services for non-payment, the collection rate has increased from 81 per cent during the first quarter of operation to 93 per cent by December 1994. Net income has improved from a loss of US$23 million for the first eight months of 1993 to a profit of US$25 million for 1994. This has made Aguas a model for water privatization in other developing countries. IFC is proposing to help further with the post privatization investment programme by arranging financing for the 1996 and 1997 investment programme from non-traditional lenders including domestic and foreign pension funds and insurance companies.

Source: IFC (1995) *Privatization: Principles and Practice* (Washington D.C.: World Bank), p. 44.

---

power plants on schemes such as build-operate-transfer (BOT) where the private company builds the infrastructure, runs it, charges and collects the tariffs, and after an agreed period hands over the infrastructure to the government (see Box 8.7).

Shirley and Nellis (1991) warn against judging privatization by the number of transactions, or the price paid or whether the enterprise survives. They advise that the test of privatization is whether the

---

BOX 8.7

Privatizing infrastructure in the Philippines

In the late 1980s, economic development in the Philippines was adversely affected by infrastructure bottlenecks particularly in power generation and transport. The government, the traditional supplier of infrastructure, was unable to meet the huge costs of building the urgently required power plants and roads. To address the problem the government abandoned tradition and inaugurated an innovative scheme for private sector provision of infrastructure.

In 1990, a law was enacted which allowed private sector corporations to build and operate public sector projects before transferring the asset back to government, usually after 20–25 years. Through this BOT law, the government hoped to encourage private sector participation in infrastructure development, reduce its fiscal burden and encourage the inflow of foreign capital, expertise and technology.

The law has been successful in the most critical area of shortage – power generation. In four years, the National Power Corporation has completed 17 privately funded electricity power projects while another 15 projects are under implementation. These projects will amount to 3367 megawatts and represent investment of approximately US$5–6 billion.

In other sectors, the BOT arrangement has not proved so attractive. For example, in mass transit, the US$350 million Manila Light Rail Transit is the only privatized project. A number of other projects earmarked for BOT operations have remained without takers such as expressways, an airport cargo terminal and water supply projects. This has led the government to review the BOT law in order to make it more flexible for potential investors. In addition to BOT (Build-Operate-Transfer), there are now options such as BT (Build-Transfer), BOO (Build-Own-Operate), BLT (Build-Lease-Transfer), and ROO (Rehabilitate-Own-Operate). In each case the project company follows strict government specifications but is offered a 'security package' involving limited guarantees for the project's probable risks. Also, the government has increased the percentage ceiling that it is willing to invest from 20 to 50 per cent. Efforts to reduce red-tape in the approval process have been introduced. With these amendments to the original BOT law, the government is responding to the environment in its efforts to bring private sector investment and efficiency into the spectrum of Philippine infrastructure.

---

transaction yields a net benefit to the economy as a whole. It is a relatively new strategy and some developing countries may not have all the necessary conditions for success. For example, there may be a shortage of the sophisticated and specialized skills needed to manage a privatization programme; a stock market may not exist; inadequate attention may be given to placing privatization in the context of a broader programme of economic reform; and the political environment may reveal powerful opponents or, conversely, foster rapid privatizations that give national élites ownership of assets at give-away prices.

Politics and feasibility

Although all developing countries have some form of public enterprise reform programme the pace of change has most often been slow.
Economic factors, such as those given in the previous section, are
frequently cited as explanation. But they are only part of the story.
Non-economic factors of a political and administrative nature will
also affect the content and implementation of public enterprise
reform programmes (Cook and Minogue, 1990). Thus, the World
Bank has emphasized that 'privatization is always political' (IFC,
1995, p. 1) and that successful reform must be: *politically desirable* to
leaders and constituencies; *politically feasible* for leaders to implement;
and *politically credible* to investors and other affected constituencies
(World Bank, 1995b).

   Political transparency is also identified as a factor which will assist
in addressing political impediments thus facilitating the reform
process. Privatization programmes may be held up or even deemed
unnecessary if governments wish to keep public enterprises out of the
hands of those who appear to be the likely buyers. Such undesirables
may include particular business groups which are out of favour with
the administration or which may be seen as gobbling up too much of
the market. Sometimes, nationalist sentiments persuade governments
from divesting what are perceived to be strategic industries to overseas buyers. Such transfers of ownership can be interpreted as highly
undesirable losses of sovereignty. National minorities may be the
groups which have the necessary capital, but selling state enterprises
to them could produce a political backlash. For example, in Indonesia there has been little privatization. The dominant Chinese
business class would be the likely purchaser of public enterprises
but this would be most unpopular with the numerically and politically dominant groups. Past violence against the Chinese and continuing undercurrents of popular hostility would make privatization a
politically dangerous economic strategy.

   The bureaucracies charged with formulating and implementing
public enterprise reforms may demonstrate reactions ranging from
reluctant support to downright opposition and recalcitrance' (*ibid.*,
p. 392). In 1991, there were allegations that bureaucrats were trying
to stall Pakistan's ambitious privatization plans for 115 state-owned
companies (*Far Eastern Economic Review*, 29 August 1991). Businessmen complained that bureaucrats were loath to surrender their

power over large areas of the economy and had deliberately over-priced the public enterprises. The senior public servants were accused of 'condescending, almost paternalistic attitudes' towards politicians whom they knew they would survive. The bureaucrats were also opposed to politicians gaining commercial advantages through close ties to big business.

Resistance to public enterprise reform also comes from trade unions. These can be well organized, numerically strong and have good political connections. The opposition of unions will derive from a fear of job loss, weakened collective bargaining powers, and a perceived worsening of terms and conditions of work. Even if privatization is pushed through there can still be considerable labour unrest as the example of the Bangladeshi textile industry shows (Lorch, 1991). A one-year ban on dismissals from the divested enterprises was imposed by the government. But even after that, powerful unions and high severance pay discouraged lay-offs while government enforced public enterprise pay rises on private mills. Employee relations were strained in both public and private sectors where militant unions, affiliated with political parties, fought to gain control of workforces and mills. Mill directors were sometimes beaten and locked in their offices or denied access to them. Labour discipline and motivation were affected. While some private enterprises allowed unions to dominate, in others, management attempted to weaken them by offering generous benefits. If that did not work, some owners set up large security forces (up to one guard for every ten workers) to control workers. A few owners simply closed their factories.

Further political considerations include, in some countries, the persistence of the value that 'the state must retain a clear responsibility for economic management and an associated competence in management and administration' (Cook and Minogue, 1990, p. 393). This situation is likely to occur where a strong commitment to centralized planning is retained. A tension will then exist between the impulse to reform public enterprises to secure accelerated economic growth, and the desire to control that growth and the state institutions that are seen to play a major role in securing it. While countries with a tradition of central planning, such as India, invariably encounter this problem to some degree, it is far more pronounced in the transitional economies such as Vietnam, Laos or China where the entire economies are undergoing transformation to 'market economics'.

There are inevitable political qualms about releasing central state control. For example, in Vietnam there has been a range of initiatives to reform the public enterprise sector. However, they have largely been administrative responses to fiscal difficulties. Some smaller and unprofitable enterprises have been closed down but critics argue that 'most of the behemoths continue to lumber forward on their money-burning paths' (*Far Eastern Economic Review*, 4 May 1995). Control of public enterprises by line ministries has been retained while current laws reduce government flexibility in privatization and commercialization. The lack of a clear vision of where the sector should be going suggests government reluctance to abandon its traditional mode of control in favour of the market.

In addition to privatization and commercialization of public enterprises in transitional economies there have been novel experiments to encourage other state organizations to participate in entrepreneurial activities – sometimes for their very survival. These initiatives often result in a loosening of central control. For example, in China there has been official encouragement of school enterprises to supplement meagre teacher income and to fund school renovation (Shih, 1994). The small school enterprises produce inputs for large, urban state-owned enterprises and encounter no effective regulation.

On a much larger scale, the People's Liberation Army (PLA) in China has been developing a reputation for business rather than for warfare over the past 15 years. In 1994, the PLA was known to have over 10 000 enterprises and 700 000 employees with an estimated production valued at US$6 billion. The size of the sector may even be greater as some enterprises, especially at the military unit level, go undeclared (Bickford, 1994). In addition to traditional business activities such as arms manufacture, the PLA is involved in a wide diversity of commercial activities such as shipping, foreign trade, hotels, property development and even currency futures. Much of the profit is needed to pay for such basic items as food because of government under-funding of the PLA. There are problems, such as corruption, poor coordination and diversion from military preparedness, but the PLA has been drawn into the market economy with 'an entire generation of officers and enlisted men . . . being socialized into the workings of the market' (*ibid.*, p. 472). Box 8.8 shows another Chinese experiment in 'public ownership' involving township and village enterprises (TVEs) whose novel structure and management account for their superior performance when compared to the standard Chinese state-owned enterprises.

BOX 8.8

**How China's township and village enterprises
differ from state enterprises**

China's township and village enterprises (TVEs) are an anomaly. Publicly
owned, usually by a township or village government, they are nonetheless similar
in some ways to private enterprises. China's state enterprises, on the other hand,
more closely resemble the state-owned enterprises of other countries in that they
are run by central bureaus and ministries. For these reasons, the term state-
owned enterprise (SOE), as generally understood and as defined in this book,
includes China's state enterprises but not the TVEs. The following differences
between TVEs and state enterprises are held to explain why TVEs perform
better.

Better governance: TVEs are locally owned, supervised and managed instead of
being supervised by far-off central bureaus and ministries. As much as 90 to 95
per cent of local revenues as well as the incomes, perks, and de facto pay of local
officials come from TVE earnings. As a result local governments, which
themselves face a hard budget constraint, have a direct stake in their
performance. TVEs' goals are clear: maximize post-tax returns to capital
investments and employ the local labour force (as distinct from migrant casual
labour).

Hard budget constraint: TVEs do not receive subsidized bank credits or centrally
allocated materials; they buy and sell inputs and outputs at market prices. TVEs
must rely mostly on capital generated from their own earnings or local and
household resources. (Only 8 per cent of all banking loans go to TVEs, while
SOEs capture at least 80 per cent.)

Greater autonomy with fewer social obligations: Compared to SOEs, TVEs are more
free to hire and fire labour, link wages to performance, rent and buy land locally,
construct, and transact business with buyers and sellers of their own choice.
Unlike state enterprises, TVEs are not obligated to provide such services as
housing, health care, education, and lifetime employment and pensions to their
employees and their dependents.

Greater competition: The number and smaller average size of TVEs, coupled with
the growth of domestic demand and reduction of barriers to internal trade,
ensure growing and ever fiercer domestic competition. Each year thousands of
new TVEs enter the market, while thousands of old and failing ones exit from it.
The greater concentration of TVEs in coastal provinces (though by no means
confined to them) and the strong links to investors from Hong Kong and Taiwan
(China) increase competitive pressures by bringing new technologies, new
management methods, export markets, and a kindred model to emulate.

Source: World Bank (1995) *Bureaucrats in Business: The Economics and Politics of
Government Ownership* (New York: Oxford University Press), p. 74, from original
work by Singh, I. and Jeferson, G. (1993) 'State Enterprises in China: Down
from the Commanding Heights', *Transition*, vol. 4(8).

Conclusion

In this chapter, we have seen that public enterprises are present in all developing countries. They have been established by colonial and post-colonial governments, by communist and capitalist regimes, in one-party states and plural democracies. Everybody has at some stage had a reason for establishing these state business concerns. The major motivation has been the desire to accelerate the economic development process by getting the state to set up and run the missing business enterprises which will produce goods and services which are seen as essential to development. This has resulted in a bewildering array of state business activity. But the theory which justified and encouraged such intervention into ostensibly market activities has run into disrepute while the public enterprises have been widely criticized for inefficiency, ineffectiveness and placing massive strain on scarce government resources.

Such 'public enterprise sickness' has been treated with a variety of medicines. Privatization, a radical treatment, has captured much of the publicity, but its popularity does not mean that public enterprises are doomed to extinction. There are other measures available which do not focus on the change of ownership. For example, policy reforms can introduce the disciplines and demands of competition to public enterprises while new management regimes can orient the businesses to efficiency and effectiveness. All treatments share the common objective of dismantling the dysfunctional bureaucratic structures and processes which have handicapped public enterprises throughout the developing world.

But public enterprise reform is not simply a technical matter of introducing private sector medicine to the ailing public sector patient. The interplay of political forces must be taken into account in designing and implementing public enterprise reforms. Care must be taken to attempt what is feasible and not simply shoot for impossible goals. Strategies must incorporate consideration of the attitudes and actions of interested parties. What is technically possible is not necessarily what is politically feasible.

The economies that are making the transition from socialist central planning to the market economy face enormous difficulties. They suffer from a combination of severe technical shortcomings and the political reluctance to relinquish the strong grip of state control. But such economies can surprise as we have seen with the encouragement of TVEs in China and the massive growth of military-owned business concerns in the same country. Thus, we have both privatization and new public enterprises occurring simultaneously. This could be in line with Pereira's (1993) contention that we will not reach the 'minimal' state of neoliberal theorizing. His long view reveals cyclical patterns of state intervention in the economy but each new cycle brings a new mode of state intervention. The question this begs is what form of intervention comes next?

9

Beyond the Market, Beyond the State: The Rise of Non-Governmental Organizations

Earlier chapters have concentrated on the roles and actions of organizations that are either part of the state apparatus or are market-based. This reflects the dominant orientations of development policy, with an emphasis on state-led development from the 1950s until the 1970s being followed by a 'counter-revolution' highlighting the private sector. But there are a vast number of organizations that are 'neither prince [state] nor merchant [market]' (Nerfin, 1986). These are associations formed within civil society bringing together individuals who share some common purpose. This 'third sector', as it is sometimes called, has a wide array of members – formally registered national non-governmental organizations, community groups, professional associations, residential committees, trade unions, kinship groups and cooperatives.

Such organizations pursue a wide variety of objectives – welfare, economic advancement, recreational, spiritual upliftment, professional identification and cultural promotion. Although such organizations generally have a wholesome image it should be noted that not all can be regarded as progressive. In particular, some 'third sector' organizations are strongly chauvinist in terms of gender, religion, culture, race and ethnicity. In this chapter we focus particularly on those organizations in which the common value that members and trustees claim is the pursuit of development (for the definition of this term see Chapter 1). We shall refer to these organizations as development non-governmental organizations (NGOs).

The origins of NGOs vary. Many of them, especially those that function exclusively at the local level, have deep historical roots within indigenous society and have operated, and evolved, over centuries (for example water-user societies, revolving savings and credit associations). Other NGOs have their origins in the colonial period. This is particularly the case for those with missionary bases that provide health and education services and often promote local economic development (for example Caritas). Finally, there are a growing number of formally registered NGOs in developing and developed countries that have been created in the last two decades to pursue a developmental mission. Despite differences in origin, specific objectives, philosophy, scale (of operations, staff and budget), location and structures a perception has arisen that such organizations may represent a development alternative that makes the achievement of progress more likely than in the past.

Types of NGO

Many differing typologies have been drawn up for NGOs or, as they are commonly termed in the USA, private voluntary organizations (PVOs). In this section attention is drawn to a number of the main criteria that have been used for classification to help the reader appreciate the range of agencies included in this chapter and their heterogeneity in terms of scale, location, objectives, relationships and strategies.

A primary distinction can be made between organizations that are based in one country (or several countries) and seek to assist in the development of other countries. These are international NGOs (INGOs). Most of these are based in OECD members states, although a number of Third World networks based in the South are evolving (for example World Rainforest Movement). Below these, in terms of geographical coverage, are what Carroll (1992) has called 'intermediate NGOs' which operate across a developing country or a region of a country. In this chapter these are termed Southern NGOs (SNGOs). Closest to the practice of development are grassroots organizations (GROs) that operate within only a limited area, such as in a group of villages or in part of a city. In general, higher levels of this NGO continuum (for example INGOs) seek to provide assistance, in terms of finance, resources or technical assistance to those at lower levels (for example GROs).

At all levels a fundamental distinction can be drawn between NGOs that seek to provide mutual benefits (benefits to members only) and those that seek to provide public benefits (that is to people who are neither members nor workers of the NGO, or to society at large). This distinction is significant as while the accountability structures for mutual benefit agencies are relatively straightforward (with leaders accounting to members, at least in principle), those of the public-benefit NGOs are often much less clear. This has led Uphoff (1995) to argue that public-benefit NGOs are not part of a 'third sector', but are part of the private sector.

Clark (1991, pp. 40–1) has suggested a useful alternative categorization. He distinguishes between NGOs in terms of their strategic orientation, differentiating between those that focus on relief provision; those that follow the aid market (public service contractors); mutual benefit and public benefit NGOs; and, those that concentrate on advocacy, policy-lobbying and empowerment (see Box 9.1). Although many NGOs blend a mix of these positions, or change their position over time, the typology gives the reader an idea of the very different objectives and methods that NGOs may utilize.

The rise and rise of NGOs

Until the late 1970s, there was little appreciation of the potential role of NGOs in implementing development projects and influencing policy. Southern and international NGOs were perceived as bit players providing services and with some expertise in short-term relief and emergency work. GROs were seen as interesting – artefacts for anthropologists to study – but irrelevant to mainstream development. The two major attempts by governments to create networks of grassroots organizations in rural areas – cooperatives and community development groups – had produced disappointing results at high cost (Korten, 1980; Hulme and Turner, 1990, pp. 184–90).

However, the 1980s have witnessed a remarkable change in the scale and significance of NGOs. They have now moved to centre-stage in terms of both development practice and debate (Farrington

---

BOX 9.1
The main types of NGO

1. *Relief and Welfare Agencies* (RWAs) such as Catholic Relief Services, various missionary societies, and so on.
2. *Technical Innovation Organizations* (TIOs). NGOs which operate their own projects to pioneer new or improved approaches to problems, and which tend to remain specialised in their chosen field. Examples include the British Intermediate Technology Development Group, the international Aga Khan Foundation and 6-S in the Sahel.
3. *Public Service Contractors* (PSCs). NGOs which are mostly funded by Northern governments and which work closely with Southern governments and official aid agencies. These NGOs are contracted to implement components of official programs because it is felt that their size and flexibility would help them perform the tasks more effectively than government departments. Examples include CARE and the Emergency Social Fund in Bolivia.
4. *Popular Development Agencies* (PDAs). Northern NGOs and their Southern intermediary counterparts which concentrate on self-help, social development, and grassroots democracy. Examples include the seven independent OXFAMs (in different fundraising countries), Bangladesh Rural Advancement Committee (BRAC), and Centro Ecumenico de Documentacao e Informacao (CEDI) and Federacao de Orgaos para Assistencia Social e Educacional (FASE) of Brazil.
5. *Grassroots Development Organizations* (GDOs). Locally based Southern NGOs whose members are the poor and oppressed, and which attempt to shape a popular development process. They often receive support from PDAs, though many receive no external funding at all. Examples include the rural workers' unions of Brazil, the Self Employed Women's Association of Ahmedabad, credit and savings groups in the Indian sub-continent, and movements of the landless in many countries.
6. *Advocacy Groups and Networks* (AGNs). Organizations which have no field projects but which exist primarily for education and lobbying. Examples include the Freedom from Debt Coalition in the Philippines, the Third World Network based in Penang, environmental pressure groups in the North and South, and Health Action International (campaigning for reforms in the marketing of pharmaceuticals).

Source: Clark, J. (1991) *Democratising Development: The Role of Voluntary Organisations* (London: Earthscan), pp. 40–1.

---

and Bebbington, 1993, p. 1) and have a high profile in the popular media (no television 'crisis' story from the Third World is complete without an interview with the field staff of Médecin Sans Frontières, Concern or OXFAM).

In 1989, they disbursed US$6.4 billion to developing countries, some 12 per cent of total Western aid. In terms of net transfers (grants and loans less repayments), NGOs channelled more resources into the Third World that year than the World Bank (Clark, 1991, p. 47). In many countries, NGOs work with members or beneficiaries on an enormous scale. For example, in Sri Lanka the Thrift and Credit Cooperative Movement has more than 700 000 members (Hulme, Montgomery and Bhattacharya, 1996) while the *Sarvodaya Shramadana Movement* operates 9500 community groups with a membership of the same order of magnitude. In Bangladesh, it is estimated that around 10 per cent of the population (that is 11 million people) receive some form of service from NGOs, whilst in India the government can barely keep up with the registration of newly formed NGOs. In Rio de Janeiro more than 1500 spontaneous associations operate (Fuentes and Frank, 1989). An expanding number of INGOs – more than 4000 in OECD countries by the late 1980s (OECD, 1988) – channel funds and assistance to SNGOs and local organizations. Van der Heijden (quoted in Clark, 1991, p. 51) estimates that INGOs, through their relationships with SNGOs, assist some 60 million people in Asia, 25 million in Latin America and 12 million in Africa.

Not only are NGOs operating on a larger scale, but they are extending their role to take on more responsibilities. In Somalia, Northern Uganda and Southern Sudan, NGOs have operated as local administrations, co-ordinating and planning operations across entire districts at times of turmoil. The case has been made that NGOs have been 'displacing the Mozambican government' in the health sector (Hanlon, 1991, p. 216) while it is estimated that 40 per cent of health care in Kenya is provided by NGOs. In Bangladesh, the government has ceded responsibility for the allocation of newly formed lands in some parts of the Bay of Bengal to OXFAM. The growing influence of NGOs was highlighted at the United Nations Conference on the Environment and Development (UNCED) at Rio in 1992, when NGOs sat alongside the representatives of sovereign states and at times were cast as presenting the authentic 'voice of the poor'.

These changes in the role and status of NGOs should not mask the diversity of what is happening in different countries and regions. In Asia there has been a rapid growth in the numbers of SNGOs, often headed by charismatic leaders. Although financially dependent on external funds, these organizations have grown out of indigenous initiatives and have a significant degree of autonomy from their sponsors. The Bangladesh Rural Advancement Committee (BRAC) is a good example (see Box 9.2). The strategy of such organizations is often unclear to the outside observer and can appear Janus-faced (Hulme, 1994); telling the government that they are non-political (as required for registration purposes and to avoid unfavourable

---

BOX 9.2

The Bangladesh Rural Advancement Committee (BRAC)

BRAC was set up in 1972 by a group of Bangladeshi social activists seeking to provide relief and welfare services to people in the Sylhet area following the traumas of the war of liberation. In 1973, it began to experiment with integrated development projects – agriculture, fisheries, rural crafts, local organization, literacy, health and family planning – in the Sulla area. It found it difficult to succeed with a community-based approach and in 1976 decided to work exclusively with the landless poor, and not permit other villagers to become programme members. In the late 1970s it also undertook research into the socioeconomic processes of village life and produced influential reports such as 'The Net' describing how more affluent villagers and bureaucrats 'net' resources targeted for the poor.

During the 1980s, BRAC has expanded its programmes across Bangladesh. Its Oral Therapy Extension Program reached 13 million women, it runs more than 10 000 non-formal primary schools and its Rural Credit Program has almost a million members. A BRAC Bank, lending only to poor women and men, is to be established. Recently it has abandoned its Freirian-inspired Functional Education Programme for consciousness-raising and started a large-scale Human Rights and Legal Education Programme (HRLE) that gives members specific information about their rights according to the laws of Bangladesh.

BRAC is directed by one of its founders, Fazle Abed who was originally employed in the private sector. It now employs 16 000 people full-time, has a 20 storey high head office and has achieved international recognition for its work.

---

treatment) while claiming to sponsor empowerment processes (that is political change) at the local level. The Philippines is a notable exception to this generalization.

In Latin America, NGOs have been much less circumspect, and have commonly taken overtly political, and often anti-government, positions. They have openly espoused the need for political change and some have worked closely with political parties. Strategic orientations of Latin American NGOs have more commonly emphasized lobbying, advocacy, confrontation and challenge than in Asia.

The situation in Africa is complex. Certainly NGOs have become more prominent but it is the INGOs that have held the limelight. Although intermediary NGOs are increasing their numbers rapidly they remain heavily influenced by foreign agencies and funding. In part, the early emphasis on emergency work may explain this, but it must also be noted that in many African countries indigenous NGOs have evolved in unfavourable environments where any indication of being 'political' would produce a strong state backlash (Bratton, 1989). There are great contrasts between nations such as Kenya, where a well-developed network of INGOs, SNGOs and GROs exists, and Somalia, where NGOs were actively discouraged until the recent collapse of the state.

The increasing scale, profile and capacities of NGOs have led to changes in their roles and relationships. In terms of strategy Korten (1990, p. 117) has conceptualized this as a generational shift from a focus on relief and welfare, to community development, to advocacy and finally people's movements. Within the third sector relationships are changing rapidly at the present time. INGOs are having to rethink their role as SNGOs have raised technical capacities, have questioned the legitimacy of INGOs to act as advocates for people in developing countries and can access funds directly from donors (Hulme and Edwards, 1997). Increasingly larger and more assertive SNGOs are proposing that they should take the lead in field operations and advocacy.

A mix of forces has fuelled the rapid rise to prominence of NGOs. In particular, the ideological ascendancy of neo-liberalism in the late twentieth century has created a global environment conducive to the 'third sector' (Salamon, 1993). The perceived poor performance of the public sector in developing countries has led to a search for more effective and efficient organizational forms for the delivery of goods and services, especially amongst aid donors. The latter have reappraised their programmes and have placed greater emphasis on linkages with NGOs. For example, in the UK the fastest growing part of the official aid programme in the early 1990s was the Joint Funding Scheme with NGOs, and the Government's Overseas Development Administration (ODA) is now keen to work directly with SNGOs.

It must be noted, however, that a doctrine of assumed effectiveness has grown around NGOs much of which is either erroneous or unsubstantiated. There is very little evidence that NGOs are more cost-effective than government agencies (Robinson, 1992; Riddell and Robinson 1995) as is often believed, and the data available on performance are very limited (Edwards and Hulme, 1995 and Hulme and Edwards, 1997). NGOs are often able to work with the poor, but their capacity to assist the poorest of the poor is limited (Farrington and Bebbington, 1993, p. 120). Aid agencies have been reluctant to observe the limitations of NGOs: 'small size, restricted impact, distance from policy decisions, professional and technical limitations, poor coordination, problems of representativeness and accountability' (*ibid.*, p. 25).

Since 1989, neo-liberal economics have been harnessed alongside western notions of liberal democracy into what has been called the New Policy Agenda (Robinson, 1993). NGOs and GROs have been viewed by donor nations as vehicles for democratization and the strengthening of civil society. Indeed, they have been rechristened civil society organizations (CSOs) that may act as a counterweight to the state, opening up channels for communication and participation, providing a training ground for activists promoting pluralism and protecting human rights (Blair, 1997). Thus, Western donors have pushed for a greater role for NGOs not merely to improve developing country economies but also to improve their polities.

Macroeconomic forces have also been important in encouraging the increase in NGO numbers and activities. IMF and World Bank conditionalities on structural adjustment loans, national indebtedness and further adverse movements in the terms of trade have meant that many countries, and particularly those in Africa, have seen vast reductions in public expenditure. This has led to the withdrawal of state-provided services. Local organizations and higher level NGOs have stepped into these vacuums in an attempt to maintain basic levels of service.

The comparative advantage of NGOs: competing concepts

Alongside the influences described above one can also discern a set of micro level arguments that have been developed to explain the comparative advantage of NGOs. Why might NGOs be able to succeed in circumstances where other forms of organization, and particularly public services, have floundered?

Students of organizational behaviour and management have identified a range of features that differentiate NGOs from government agencies pursuing similar goals. These include flexibility, responsiveness, the capacity to experiment and learn from experience, linking processes to outcomes and the NGO ability to enlist the energies and commitment of intended beneficiaries. Fowler (1988, p. 11) attributes these features to two distinctive characteristics of NGOs:

1. NGO relationships with intended beneficiaries are based upon principles of voluntarism, rather than those of control which typify government agencies.

2. NGOs have a task-oriented approach that permits them to achieve 'appropriate organization . . . [as] development, change and diversity, rather than maintenance, control and uniformity, can be their guiding image and organizational design'.

The first of these has been elaborated on in great detail by many writers, under the label of 'participation' (Korten, 1980; Oakley and Marsden, 1984). It is argued that when beneficiaries are involved in programme design and management, then programmes are more relevant and attractive to beneficiaries who take a much greater interest in them. The latter principle has only recently become a major topic for analysis, but is receiving a great deal of attention as even mainstream management theorists search for the secrets of NGO effectiveness (Drucker, 1989).

If one accepts the explanatory power of these two factors (and there is by no means a consensus on this), then an immediate and fundamental problem for NGOs becomes apparent: the dilemma of 'scaling-up' (Edwards and Hulme, 1992). The qualities associated with these two characteristics may be incompatible with organizational growth (Tendler, 1987) as they may be lost if growth occurs. They may also lead to NGOs managing their growth poorly (Dichter, 1989; Hodson, 1992) with a consequent reduction in efficiency. Views as to whether NGOs can grow and remain operationally effective differ markedly. David Korten (1990), whose work has been very influential, has recently revised his earlier ideas and now argues that the organizational expansion of NGOs will mean they become unresponsive bureaucracies.

A second set of concepts that seeks to explain why voluntary organizations perform well has been derived from work on the sociology and politics of local organizations. Empirical work by Esman and Uphoff (1984) on the ways in which environmental factors and internal variables influenced the performance of GROs indicated that, at least at the local level, there was no optimal organizational model for a GRO and that some form of contingency theory was required to relate objectives, environment and organization to outcomes. A set of complex findings emerged (summarized in Hulme and Turner, 1990, pp. 194–7) including evidence that GRO performance was positively correlated with (i) a participatory orientation; (ii) horizontal linkages with other GROs; and (iii) vertical linkages with intermediary NGOs or unions of GROs.

Uphoff (1992) has subsequently used ideas from this inductive work and other studies to propose a 'post-Newtonian social science' that, amongst other things, seeks to explain the operations of voluntary organizations. This interpretation 'see[s] people's behaviour as variable . . . rather than as something fixed . . . what matters is not which values one has – we all have many – but which values are activated and applied in a given situation' (*ibid.*, p. 337). Thus, in some contexts, GROs can help to orient individual behaviour towards cooperative and other-regarding values. When this happens then it may influence the pre-dispositions of a wider group of individuals and make it more likely that collective action will be considered as a strategy and, if acted upon, that individuals will strive to make it succeed.

The idea of collective action and the expectations it creates – especially when presented by GRO leaders – generates 'social energy' in which new mental and physical resources become available, and as local-level organizations proliferate 'social relations become more caring and less private' (Hirschman, 1984). GROs can network, horizontally and vertically, adding to these processes of social energization. This posits the concept of socioeconomic man: an individual capable of acting in terms of both self-interest and in the interests of others.

However, for the last 15 years it is notions of economic man that have been in the ascendant. For the committed ideologue of the new right, the voluntary and non-profit based actions of NGOs are a theoretical impossibility except in the rare cases when collective action maximizes private gains. Who would do anything if not paid the market rate and who would not be a free-rider whenever the opportunity presents itself? In this conception, NGOs are brief and temporary aberrations, and behaviour will rapidly return to a private interest form. However, a less radical interpretation of neo-liberal economic theory recognizes a role for NGOs in the economy as part of the 'non-profit private sector': organizations that provide a service without making a profit. NGOs innovate and compete, thus improving the functioning of the market for the particular goods or services they provide and contributing to an environment fostering the evolution of more efficient and effective organizations.

The World Bank, along with USAID, has been a strong adherent to this school of thought. Its position is illustrated by a quote from a major report on how to promote development in Africa.

Recognising the drawbacks of relying too heavily on public bureaucracies, future development strategy could make greater use of the private sector. . . At the grassroots level this means village and ward associations; at the intermediate level, various local non-governmental and cooperative unions and other organizations; and at the national level, chambers of commerce and industry, trade associations, umbrella NGO organisations . . . and professional associations of bankers, doctors, lawyers, accountants and the like. Such groups and communal actions can build on the African traditions of self-help. (World Bank, 1989, p. 59)

NGOs are thus seen as having comparative advantages over government, especially in the provision of safety nets for vulnerable groups as economies undergo the strains of liberalization. But, what types of relationship do NGOs have with government agencies? We now turn to this question.

NGOs and the state

As can be seen from the previous section much of the interest in and support for NGOs has arisen because of severe problems in the delivery of services by state agencies. Notions of the comparative advantage of NGOs, especially in poverty-alleviation, have a corollary of state failure. In such circumstances one might well anticipate that relationships between NGOs and government organizations (GOs) would be antipathetic. This is often the case, but NGO–GO relationships are diverse and complex. The influence of specific contextual factors – such as the nature of an NGO's objectives and strategies, the sector it works in, donor behaviour and the nature of the state – all shape relationships in a variety of ways. At times some GOs may be on favourable terms with NGOs, while others are antagonistic. For example, in Ethiopia INGOs commonly have good relationships with central government agencies but are greatly resented by local authorities (Teka, 1994).

Of key importance in determining NGO–state relationships is the disposition of the regime. Bratton (1989) has argued that in Latin America 'deep estrangement' has been characteristic with regimes feeling threatened because NGOs have adopted an adversarial stance. In South Asia, he reports that relationships have been 'far happier', with governments such as those in India providing direct

support for NGOs. The links between NGOs and African governments are seen as being somewhere in the middle of these two
extremes: 'although uncomfortable bedfellows . . . they are destined
to cohabit' (*ibid.*, p. 585). African governments are suspicious of
NGOs but like the additional resources that they can bring in. But
circumstances can change. For example, the Kenyan government's
originally favourable attitude to NGOs has transformed dramatically
over the last decade (see Box 9.3).

Another major determinant of NGO–GO relationships is the
strategic orientation of an NGO. NGOs that adopt a conflictual
approach, either by arguing that government policy is wrong or that
government is not legitimate, are treated as adversaries. In some
circumstances this may mean that they are ignored, while in others it
may mean that internal security forces and the military take action
(ranging from harassment to liquidation). In situations where NGOs
compete directly with GOs, or appear to offer the possibility
of replacing GOs, then tense relationships are characteristic. For

---

BOX 9.3

NGO–government relationships in Kenya

Following the attempted coup in 1982, the Kenya government's previously open
and accommodating attitude towards NGOs gradually hardened to the extent
that in 1989, for instance, the national women's organization (*Maendeleo ya
Wanawake*) was affiliated to the national President's party by decree. Similar
threats have been made against the National Council of Churches, and the more
radically empowering NGOs, particularly those affiliated to the Catholic
Church. They have come under close scrutiny from the internal security services.

In 1991, after only cursory consultation with NGOs themselves, a new
framework was established for compulsory registration of NGOs with a statutory
board accountable to the Office of the President. Efforts to ensure compatibility
of NGOs' operations with local development plans include the requirement that
NGOs should submit proposals for expatriate recruitment and for imports to the
relevant District Coordinating Committee for approval. Additionally, NGOs are
required to coordinate their activities at district level with those of government
under the District Focus for Rural Development strategy established in 1985.
However, the coordinating performance of this strategy has been highly uneven.

Actions such as these have led to views (*Kenya Daily Nation*, 26 June 1992) that
the Coordination Board created under the NGO Act will continue to be treated
with suspicion by NGOs.

Source: Farrington, J. and Bebbington, A. (1993) *Non-Governmental Organizations,
the State and Sustainable Agricultural Development* (London: Routledge), p. 52, from
original work by Wellard, K. and Copestake, J. G.

example, in Bangladesh many civil servants complain of NGOs being unfairly favoured by donors because they are fashionable and they invest heavily in public relations. They argue that NGOs have inflated costs because of the salaries they pay and the resources, particularly vehicles, they utilize. Privately, the country's ministers say that donors 'make' the government use NGOs – in effect NGO involvement is an aid conditionality!

Detailed studies of NGO–state relationships provide ample evidence of their diversity but tentative generalizations are emerging. Farrington and Bebbington (1993 and its companion volumes) conclude that NGOs and GOs are 'reluctant partners', but argue strongly that there could be considerable developmental benefits if NGOs and GOs collaborated. Commonly, the weaknesses of GOs are matched by corresponding strengths in NGOs, and vice versa. For example, NGOs can often be effective in communicating with poorer farmers and helping them to adapt new technologies to their needs, but NGOs lack the technical capacity to make significant advances in agricultural technology. GOs have much greater capacity for technology development but find it difficult to adapt technologies to the specific needs of poorer farmers and to communicate innovations to farmers. By working together, each can help the other overcome its weaknesses. A specific example of NGO–GO collaboration in Indonesia is provided in Box 9.4.

Hulme and Edwards (1997) are concerned that NGOs are paying so much attention to managing their relationships with states and donors that they are 'losing their roots' with the poor and powerless. If they do not seize the present opportunity for strategic reorientation, which might entail scaling-down and pursuing fewer objectives, then they will drift into cooption or irrelevance (Pearce, 1997).

While NGOs often assert their right to know what governments are doing, governments have at least four legitimate reasons for wanting to know what NGOs are doing. The first of these is to ensure that NGOs are pursuing activities that merit their special treatment, such as being non-taxable and having import duties waived in many countries, because of their charitable status. The second is to ensure that NGOs, and especially non-membership NGOs, properly account for the resources that they utilize. There is now widespread concern in Asian and African countries that large numbers of NGOs are being set up largely for the benefit of their directors and staff. Unfortunately most governments have a very limited capacity to identify such fraud and punish its perpetrators. Interestingly, although many NGOs

---

BOX 9.4

NGO–government relationships in Indonesia: the case of the Institute for Social and Economic Research, Education and Information (LP3ES)

Formed by activist intellectuals in 1971, LP3ES conducts socioeconomic research, education and information exchange in the pursuit of integral development of human resources. It works extensively with government, seeking to change its centralised top-down modes of operation into approaches which allow local people more say in their future.

Government-sponsored expansion of irrigation in the 1970s and early 1980s increasingly spread into areas which already had some irrigation infrastructure of their own. However, the top-down character of new irrigation design meant that farmers had little interest in maintaining it. At the government's request LP3ES began research on social and technical aspects of irrigation development in the mid-1980s, bringing in 'community organisers' on the Philippines model and experimenting with different forms of water users' associations. Information collected during these three years of action research later proved invaluable when LP3ES was asked to assist the government in designing procedures for handing over to farmers the maintenance of all irrigation schemes under 500 ha (totalling some 1 million in all) to farmers. To work successfully with the government of Indonesia required the prior building up of trust between NGO and GO staff, NGO willingness to pursue incrementalist approaches, and measured amounts of opportunism, advocacy and constructive criticism.

Source: Farrington, J. and Bebbington, A. (1993) *Non-Governmental Organizations, the State and Sustainable Agricultural Development* (London: Routledge), p. 164, from original work by Bruns, B. and Soelaiman, I.

---

push for government transparency and accountability, very few are prepared to be transparent about their own activities (Edwards and Hulme, 1995).

The third reason for government concern with NGO activities is to try to ensure that different NGOs coordinate their activities with government agencies. This requirement often leads to conflict, with NGOs claiming that coordination actually means control and greatly reduces their efficiency, as has been the case in Nepal (see Box 9.5). Governments point out that failures in coordination lead to villagers receiving different messages from different agencies. This causes confusion and leads to unnecessary duplication of services in some areas when other areas have no services at all. The final reason that governments have to oversee NGO activities relate to internal security. Many governments are concerned that NGOs create ideal vehicles for hiding types of political activity which, rightly or wrongly, the government has defined as unlawful. In Central and South America, NGOs have at times been used as cover to help

---

BOX 9.5

Government mechanisms for NGO coordination in Nepal

Voluntary action at the local level has a long history in Nepal, and continues to be an important means of providing facilities (bridges, trails, canals, schools, temples) where communities remain isolated. From the 1950s to the 1970s, government was hostile to the establishment of new, larger NGOs unless they could serve to draw in foreign funds and provide employment opportunities for the élites who supported the political system. Compulsory registration of NGOs with the newly established Social Service National Coordination Council (SSNCC) under the patronage of the Queen was introduced in 1975, with strengthened procedures in 1978, but a number of NGOs are still able to operate without registering.

The new constitution of 1990 removed some of the SSNCC's powers of patronage and control, but a recently drafted government directive envisages a new range of financial controls over NGOs and visa restrictions for expatriate NGO staff, to be implemented through a re-strengthened SSNCC. Recently approved local government bills envisage NGO representation on Advisory Committees to be set up by each Municipality and Village Development Committee. NGOs will also participate in the design and implementation of local development activities, with funds both from increased local government budgets and from their own resources.

Local government bodies are given the powers to ensure that the activities of NGOs are consistent with the agreed local development framework, to insist on coordination of activities among NGOs and to audit their accounts. Although the extent to which this legislation will be implemented remains to be seen, it is clear that closer coordination of NGOs' activities with government development plans is anticipated.

Source: Farrington, J. and Bebbington, A. (1993) *Non-Governmental Organizations, the State and Sustainable Agricultural Development* (London: Routledge), p. 54, from original work by Shrestha, N. and Farrington, J.

---

resource insurgents of both the left and the right. There is much evidence that the USA's Peace Corps was utilized by the CIA for gathering intelligence in the 1960s and 1970s. Concern for regime security remains a central issue in many countries. This partly explains the continuing reluctance of many governments to whole-heartedly embrace NGO activity.

We have already seen, in the case of LP3ES (see Box 9.4), that NGOs can consciously try to influence public sector activity and make it more effective and efficient through innovations in structures and procedures (for further examples see Edwards and Hulme, 1992, pp. 49–97). However, NGOs may also impact on GOs in unintended ways and often for the worse. The most obvious situation in which this happens is when NGOs (offering more fulfilling work, better pay and conditions, opportunities for overseas travel or whatever) attract key staff out of GOs. This situation is particularly serious in small countries where replacements are difficult to find. In the Gambia, both the Ministries of Agriculture and Health have reported increased operational problems because of the loss of key personnel to NGOs (Davis, Hulme and Woodhouse, 1994). Such losses may not only hamper field activities but, ultimately, may reduce the capacity of GOs to formulate policy and undertake internal reforms.

In other cases, NGOs can contribute to a more generalized loss of motivation in GOs. In both Bangladesh and Sri Lanka, the authors have frequently been told by public sector field staff that results can only be achieved if they are resourced (vehicles, salaries, allowances, telephones and so forth) at the levels of locally-operating NGOs. But such a situation is impossible as these NGOs are resource-intensive organizations, despite their image, and their programmes are rarely replicable on a regional or national scale with only domestic funding. This is usually not evident to the government field-worker, who shakes his or her head and may assume that nothing can be achieved until everyone has a four-wheel drive or motor-bicycle, 'like NGO people'.

NGOs, empowerment and politics

The earlier sections have largely treated NGOs in terms of their operational activities such as providing credit or health care. However, many NGOs claim to be redistributing power at the local level and influencing policy so that it is more favourable to the poor. They describe their objective as 'empowerment'. This term is most often used in a rather loose sense but Friedmann (1992, p. 33) has attempted to be more specific. He proposes that we see empowerment as the extension of the social power (access to bases of productive wealth), political power (access to and influence over the processes by which decisions are made) and psychological power (the sense of personal potency and self-confidence) of poor individuals and households. It has political implications for the relationships that such people have with the state and its agencies, with private firms and individual traders, and with those in civil society who wield power.

Empowerment is a grand objective – but can NGOs attain it? For proponents of NGOs, empowerment is seen as a difficult, but potentially realizable goal if appropriate strategies are selected. The writings of Friedmann (1992), Clark (1991), Gran (1983), Max-Neef

(1991) and many others have made this case but it is Korten's (1990) influential analysis that is discussed here. Korten's vision is of a 'people-centred development' operating in a democratic society with a mixed economy and a large and dynamic NGO movement. The myriad of organizations which comprises the movement demands the accountability of the state and of market-based organizations. This is seen as lacking at present in all countries but particularly in developing countries.

The NGO movement also lobbies for policies that more effectively meet the needs of civil society, and serves as a catalyst for the creation of new NGOs. However, only certain forms of NGO can contribute to such a vision: these are voluntary organizations driven by a commitment to shared values or a mission (Clark's PDAs in Box 9.1) and people's organizations (mutual benefit grassroots organizations). Public service contractors, those non-profit organizations that are state or donor funded to deliver services or goods and that feature so prominently in neo-liberal theory, are judged to be ineffective. They follow the market created by governments and/or donors which reflects the interests of those who are already powerful. From this perspective, one of the greatest challenges for NGOs today is to resist the temptation of cashing in (metaphorically and literally) on their present popularity by contracting to implement donor-designed projects. A switch to such activities will change the fundamental characteristics of an organization (see Table 9.1) and move it away from an empowerment approach.

In essence, Korten's prescription is grounded in a pluralist political framework. This makes it vulnerable to a set of questions about the nature of social and political change. Why would those who hold state power permit a plethora of NGOs demanding accountability and empowerment of the poor to evolve? Within the community, how would such organizations avoid capture or annihilation by local élites? And amongst themselves, are NGOs likely to network, coalesce and cooperate or are competition, suspicion and conflict more likely relationships?

For Paulo Freire (1972), a Brazilian priest who helped to inspire liberation theology and whose ideas are held in great respect by many NGO personnel, this pluralist image of life in developing countries is fundamentally flawed. He proposes a much more radical analysis that encompasses the conflictual nature of class relationships and the active role that oppression plays in perpetuating poverty. What is needed is not individual or group empowerment, but 'social class

TABLE 9.1

Key characteristics of organizations pursuing a mission and public service contractors

Characteristic	Mission-based < - -*Continuum* - > Public service organization		contractors
Resources	Voluntary donations < - - - - - - - - > Contracts		
Goals	Social change < - - - - - - - - - - - > New contracts		
Accountability	Downward < - - - - - - - - - - - - - > Upward		
Staff orientation	Mission < - - - - - - - - - - - - - - > Job		
Staff status	Volunteer/member < - - - - - - - - > Employee		
Definition of targets	By members < - - - - - - - - - - - - > By government and donor		
HQ costs	Low < - - - - - - - - - - - - - - - - > High		
Planning	Incrementalist < - - - - - - - - - - - > Blueprint		
Capacity-building	For members < - - - - - - - - - - - > For agency		
Activity timescale	indefinite < - - - - - - - - - - - - - > 2–5 years		

Source: Hulme, D. (1994) 'Social Development Research and the Third Sector: NGOs as Users and Subjects of Social Enquiry', in D. Booth (ed.), *Rethinking Social Development* (London: Longman), pp. 251–7.

empowerment' (Freire and Shor, 1978). This entails that social activists (that is the members of mutual benefit organizations and the staff of public benefit organizations) adopt a 'dialogical and problem-solving' educational approach which leads poor people into analysing for themselves why they are poor and how they can change things. Such consciousness-raising will lead them out of their passivity and they will then work together to change the social, economic and political structures that oppress them. This strategy will almost inevitably yield a set of adversarial actions against existing structures and relationships. These may become violent and even revolutionary if those who hold power do not accede to the changes that the newly-conscious poor demand. The weakening of left-wing political ideas since the late 1970s has meant that while some NGOs continue to talk of 'conscientization', their framework for action has become pluralist not radical (see Box 9.2 for an example).

Strategic choices for NGOs

The earlier sections have identified the major forces that shape NGO activity. At one extreme is the temptation to adopt a service-delivery approach; at the other is the challenge to take on a radical political identity and directly confront local élites, the state and the international system. Many NGOs are currently examining their strategic options, aware of the passing nature of donor fads and the danger of co-optation. Edwards and Hulme (1992) have identified four main strategies that NGOs might pursue to enhance their contribution to development and poverty-alleviation. These are expanding their operational programmes, working with government, advocacy and policy-lobbying and supporting community-level initiatives. These strategies are not mutually exclusive and many NGOs practice a mix.

Deciding which strategy(ies) to emphasize and ensuring that strategy mixes are complementary and not contradictory is the central task for NGO managers. Some strategy mixes have significant potential synergies: for example when local-level operational activities provide a data source for policy-lobbying exercises (Edwards and Hulme, 1992, p. 215). Other mixes are likely to generate conflict within an agency: for example, when an agency that operates service provision gets involved in advocacy work that may threaten the financial sources that permit field operations. The study by Edwards and Hulme reveals that any notion of an optimal NGO strategy is specious. Strategies must be selected in terms of objectives and need to be appropriate for specific contexts. However, in common with Korten (1990) and Clark (1991), they argue that the consequences of scaling-up service delivery activities need to be very carefully analysed. For many NGO objectives, small may still be beautiful.

Conclusion

This chapter has illustrated the heterogeneity of NGOs and the differing concepts that inform their actions. In the last decade, NGOs have experienced a wave of popularity, fuelled by the generosity of aid donors and perceptions of state failure. But NGOs are no panacea for poverty-reduction and a number of their limitations have been identified. While they have some comparative advantages over the public sector it would be an illusion to imagine that the patchwork of services that NGOs provide could substitute for state provision of basic education, primary health care, welfare services and essential infrastructure. While some NGOs might justifiably claim to be helping the socially and economically excluded to integrate into society, others have distinctly sectional interests that could be seen as weakening social cohesion by fuelling religious and ethnic identities.

In the future, NGOs must look to the ways in which their activities can help shape the state and their role within civil society. A growing body of opinion argues that they need to pursue two main tasks. The first is the strengthening of civil society in ways that make it more cohesive and more effective in articulating its needs and demanding public accountability from the bureaucracy and political leaders. The second is reforming the state and its policies (by adversarial or collaborative tactics depending on circumstances) so that it is better able to meet the demands of the poorer sections of civil society.

10

The International
Environment:
External Influences
and Governance

Throughout this book, and particularly in Chapters Two and Five, reference has been made to the ways in which international factors shape and influence the nature of public administration and policy-making in developing countries. These international factors have included the activities of colonial powers in the nineteenth and twentieth centuries, the operations of international development agencies – such as the World Bank and UN agencies – and the current promotion of 'market forces' and privatization. This chapter explores the international environment in detail. Initially it describes the historical background of the colonial and post-war eras and identifies their administrative legacy. Subsequently it explores the contemporary scene and in particular the implications of the end of the Cold War and the increasing globalization of production, exchange, media and ideas. During the 1990s the choices open to the governments of developing countries about the reorientation of public sector activities have narrowed and an increasingly powerful orthodoxy, arguing that all countries should practice the 'new public management', has emerged.

The colonial era and its legacy

Colonial administrations have been caricatured as the 'night watch-man state', focusing on law and order, the extraction of taxes and the export of primary commodities. Policy-making was a responsibility for authorities back in London, Paris, Brussels, Lisbon and Canberra. The social and economic needs and desires of the 'native' population attracted minimal concern (other than occasional demonstrations of paternalism and the oversight of church and charitable organiza-tions); and power was vested in the hands of a small, and usually white, élite. The catharsis of independence was inevitably associated with hasty attempts at localization of positions in the state, with the establishment of administrative colleges and large-scale training initiatives supposedly supplying the qualified human resources. How-ever, such activities rarely created the capacity for indigenes to take over the limited functions of the colonial administration effectively, let alone work out how to meet the escalating public expectations and demands associated with independence.

Although the colonial legacy varied from power to power, and from ex-colony to ex-colony, a common set of features can be identified in many countries:

- A tendency towards the centralization of power;
- Ambiguity about the roles and relationships of public adminis-trators and politicians (as domestic politicians were latecomers);
- A tradition that senior civil service appointments should be allocated to generalist administrators, rather than to those with technical or specialist backgrounds;
- A reluctance to provide information to those outside of the administration;
- An emphasis on following statutes, rules and procedures (role not task);
- Limited consultation with the public and little recognition of a role for the media;
- An emphasis on written communication and the processing of paper;
- Relatively high levels of non-salary compensation for middle and senior level officers (for example free or highly subsidized housing).

While the colonial era ended more than 25 years ago in most developing countries – and almost 50 years ago for the Indian sub-continent – much of this legacy remains. Indeed, in countries such as Bangladesh, the current administrative laws are usually those introduced by the British 50 to 100 years ago. South Asian civil servants commonly claim that 'their system' follows 'the British system': such claims are made with pride and are to demonstrate the pedigree and quality of their civil services. They fail, though, to note that they are based on a British colonial model (rather than the British domestic model) and that, 50 years on, modifications might well be desirable.

The Cold War era

During the 1950s, 1960s and 1970s the influence of the Cold War – the tussle for the maintenance or expansion of spheres of influence between the USA (and its liberal democratic allies) and the USSR (and its communist allies) – heavily influenced events in developing countries. By providing both development and military aid the two superpowers sought to win the support of poorer countries. While both West (the USA) and East (USSR) had common perspectives on some administrative issues – such as the central role of state agencies in public service delivery, the desirability of national planning and the need of poorer countries for aid-financed technical assistance – there were vast differences about the role of the private sector and the nature of governance.

The influences of development aid on public administration and policy-making during this period are numerous (see Riddell, 1987) but here we shall mention only four that are of particular significance. First, despite the rhetoric of helping the neediest countries, aid-flows have tended to follow the foreign policy and commercial interest needs of donor countries. Notoriously, US aid has focused on middle-income countries, particularly Israel, Egypt and Turkey. In 1991, the world's biggest bilateral donors (the US and Japan) spent only 17 per cent of their aid budgets on the least developed countries while only two OECD countries allocated more than 40 per cent of their aid to the least developed countries (Randel and German, 1993, p. 65). Thus, aid was not targeted on improving the performance of bureaucracies in those countries most in need of assistance.

Secondly, as described in Chapter 6, up to the 1980s donors focused almost exclusively on disbursing aid through public sector projects. The consequences of this, allied to donor proliferation and weak donor coordination, were to divert policy-makers and senior bureaucrats from overall policy formulation to simply responding to the demands of consultancy missions about individual projects. Morss (1984) describes this process as institutional destruction in sub-Saharan Africa, and other writers (Cohen, Grindle and Walker, 1985) have shown how pervasive it has been.

Thirdly, much of the aid that donors disbursed promoted the transfer of models that subsequently proved inappropriate (but which created vested interests that made withdrawal difficult) or followed fashions that were later abandoned. The former situation can be illustrated by the donor predilection for building hospitals and training doctors in sophisticated curative medicine in the 1960s. Such investments hampered development of the primary health care and preventive medicine approaches that were most appropriate for low-income countries. The latter situation is illustrated by the 'community development' fad of the 1950s and early 1960s (Hulme and Turner, 1990). Although donors pulled out of funding this activity in the mid-1960s the ministries and departments of community development they established limped through the 1970s and 1980s absorbing public funds while searching for a new mission.

Finally, there is much evidence that the tens of billions of dollars that donors put into technical assistance, largely for the public sector, have contributed little to improved organizational performance or policy formulation. Berg (1993) has made a damning case of this outcome in Africa, where there is now a greater dependence in government on expatriate experts than at the time of decolonization. While some think that Berg's work has focused on the poorest example of aid effectiveness – sub-Saharan Africa – and is over-pessimistic, there is still a strong argument that development aid in the 1950–80 period did little to enhance management performance in the public sector.

The pressures of the Cold War not only led to development aid being allocated on the basis of the strategic interests of donors: they also fostered increasing levels of military assistance. Both superpowers rewarded friendly governments with arms and expertise for use in retaining power in the event of internal or external threats. Such dependent allies often engaged in corrupt and oppressive activities which the donors chose to ignore. The effects of these activities continue through to the present day in terms of the political importance of the military in many countries. This relates to the military's command over public resources and its influence over public policy. Between 1960 and 1987, developing country military expenditure increased three times faster than in industrialized countries from US$24 billion to US$145 billion, at constant prices (UNDP, 1994, pp. 51–7).

Even more alarmingly, the least-developed countries increased the military's share of GDP from 2.1 per cent to 3.5 per cent over this period (*ibid.*, pp. 170–1): for every physician they financed 88 military personnel. The military's influence over public policy has ranged from a capacity to ensure that 'defence' budgets are safe from cuts, to high proportions of 'retired' military personnel directing public enterprises, to the complete control of policy when military regimes seize power. Military coups have been a recurrent feature of political life in Africa, Asia and Latin America. Despite the recent wave of global 'redemocratization' the military remains standing in the wings, a contender for power, in a large number of developing countries.

Around 1980 a new set of issues began to emerge as many low-income and middle-income countries found themselves in a deepening financial crisis with increasing oil prices, rising interest rates, adverse shifts in the terms of trade and spiralling national debt. The short-lived attempt by developing countries to obtain a direct international political solution to their problems drained away after the Cancun Summit of 1981, and most countries found it necessary to negotiate with the international financial institutions (IFIs) for resources to keep their economies functioning. They sought economic stabilization loans from the IMF and structural adjustment loans from the World Bank (see Box 10.1).

These requests for IFI support coincided with the rise of neo-liberal thought in the West and the elections, and re-elections of Reagan and Thatcher. The IMF and World Bank were heavily influenced by neo-liberal and monetarist theories and made their loans conditional on recipient governments agreeing to economic targets (see Mosley, Harrigan and Toye, 1995 for a detailed analysis of structural adjustment). Central amongst such conditions were targets for lower levels of public expenditure, parastatal divestiture and reduced government intervention in economic, financial and industrial policy. The focus of these early structural adjustment programmes was basically economic, and although they had profound implications for the public sector (and social welfare) such second order effects were not given much attention. While many developing countries signed up for such loans – they had little choice – very few honoured all of the loan conditions

---

BOX 10.1

The World Bank, IMF and structural adjustment

The World Bank (officially called the International Bank for Reconstruction and Development) and the International Monetary Fund (IMF), sometimes known as the Bretton Woods institutions, were established in 1944 to ensure a cooperative approach among nations to international monetary issues and to financial reconstruction after the Second World War. Both have their headquarters in Washington DC in the USA and both have been very heavily influenced by US governments over the years.

The IMF focuses on providing credits to countries to help them stabilize their economies when they encounter balance-of-payment difficulties or problems associated with cyclical economic events. Although these loans are intended for short-term stabilization (one to three years), in the 1980s the IMF began to set conditionalities on countries wishing to draw down funds. These were similar to the conditionalities that the World Bank negotiates, in having a neo-liberal thrust (cutting subsidies, freeing trade, promoting exports, opening the banking system, floating the exchange rate), although the IMF and Bank often differ on detail, sequencing and emphases.

The World Bank's role is to provide developing countries and transitional economies with grants and loans for long-term development. By the early 1990s it was disbursing US$20 billion per annum for agricultural, industrial, infra-structural, educational, health and structural adjustment loans (SALs). The latter have become increasingly important since the mid-1980s: they support changes in policy. While most people agree that economic structural change is necessary in developing countries the Bank's SALs have been widely blamed for intensifying poverty and their contribution to economic growth is highly contested.

The Bank's influence extends far beyond its direct lending activities as it sets the international agenda for development; chairs the donor groups that provide aid to the major developing countries; and, is a focal point for aid activities in many countries.

(*ibid*). Commitments to privatization slipped and, where reductions in the number of public servants occurred, these were arbitrary or based on the award of 'golden handshakes' rather than a systematic review of priorities.

From the mid-1980s, Gorbachev's rise to power in the USSR led to reduced superpower military competition, although embarrassing hot spots such as Afghanistan remained. The fundamental turning point came in 1989 with the fall of the Berlin Wall, the collapse of communist regimes in Eastern Europe and the recognition that Russia's economy could not support its superpower status any longer. The end of the Cold War provides the context for the contemporary set of international influences on public administration and policy in developing countries.

The contemporary international environment: context

While the collapse of the Soviet Union as a superpower has not led to Fukuyama's (1992) proclaimed 'end of history', it has produced a situation in which capitalism, as an economic system, and democracy, as a form of governance, have no conceptual rivals of comparative stature. With only a few exceptions the contemporary agenda for national policies are economic and political liberalization. China, Vietnam, Laos and Cambodia are examples of economies that have opened up to the market and are in 'transition' to capitalism. India is moving towards economic liberalization while its neighbour, Sri Lanka, has swept away barriers to import and export. In Africa, multi-party political systems have replaced one-party states in Kenya, Malawi, Tanzania and Zambia. The Mexican economy has been integrated with those of its North American neighbours and a credible opposition has evolved to challenge the Institutional Revolutionary Party (PRI) which has held power for more than 60 years.

The conclusion of the Uruguay Round of the General Agreement on Trade and Tariffs (GATT) has created the legal and institutional framework for a deepening of the globalization of the world economy. This is evident on the supply side as commodities, capital, technology and organizational expertise move rapidly from country to country as transnational corporations search out lower cost bases for production and distribution. It is evident on the demand side as consumerism spreads into Africa, Asia, Latin America and the former Iron Curtain states: if you have the money, then 'Black Label', 'Marlboro', 'Levi', 'McDonald's' and 'Mercedes' can now be openly purchased in most parts of the world. The capacities of different nations to adapt to the rapid economic changes of a globalized economy vary enormously and, to date, it appears that the poorest countries will bear the highest costs.

Globalization is not merely an economic process: it also has social and political dimensions. Increasingly, non-Westerners are entertained by foreign television programmes, play rock-and-roll music, search out discotheques and practice behaviours that would have been strongly discouraged only a few years ago. The media are globalizing, with satellites beaming entertainment, news and advertisements into parts of the world that were formerly isolated. Increasingly, a handful of corporations determine what is and is not newsworthy (Smith, 1980). While many lament that globalization means Westernization, and thus Western hegemony, these criticisms have little impact because of the lack of any clearly articulated alternative (though one may be evolving in the Islamic world).

The end of ideological hostility between the 'capitalist' and the 'communist' blocs has not yielded the global peace dividend that many expected. While the large number of nuclear weapons that the USA and USSR had trained on each other have been drastically reduced the number and frequency of major conflicts has increased. Indeed, the 'new world order' proclaimed in 1990 has turned out to be the 'new world disorder' (Edwards and Hulme, 1994). The weakening of states formerly supported by the Soviet Union, the promises of democracy and choice, a resurgence in micro-nationalisms and the opportunistic behaviour of nations as different as Iraq and France (what really did happen in Rwanda?) has fuelled this disorder.

The conflicts of the late twentieth century are, however, quite distinct from those of earlier decades. First, they are largely within nations, rather than between nations: during the 1989–92 period only three of the world's 82 conflicts involving significant numbers of deaths were across national boundaries (UNDP, 1994). Secondly, most of these conflicts are outside of industrialized nations. In 1993, 65 of the 79 countries in which major conflicts or significant violence occurred were in developing countries (*ibid.*): these ranged across the developing world from Somalia to Iraq to Sri Lanka to Cambodia to Peru and El Salvador. Thirdly, most of the death and suffering created by conflict is now imposed upon non-military personnel. 'At the beginning of this century, around 90 per cent of war casualties were military. Today about 90 per cent are civilian' (*ibid.*, p. 47). The consequences of this are all too apparent as the number of refugees fleeing conflict has passed 20 million and continues to grow. If Duffield (1993) is correct then the escalation of conflict is not a temporary phenomenon but a trend which will continue.

While Western nations express their anguish about conflict, the USA, UK, France, Germany, Spain and the Netherlands continue to actively promote arms sales to developing countries. Some developing countries with significant arms manufacturing capacity, such as China, also vigorously exploit market opportunities in the arms trade. On both the demand and the supply side the stage seems set to guarantee the military a major role in developing countries. It has also had knock-on effects for the military in industrialized countries. In the UK, for example, the military increasingly sees its role as peace-keeping and emergency relief work overseas rather than defending Britain.

Finally in this section, mention must be made of changes in aid flows and the international agencies that plan and manage development grants and loans. Recession in the early 1990s and governments' plans to reduce public expenditure have led OECD countries to reduce aid volumes. In 1993, OECD aid fell to US$56 billion against US$61 billion in 1992 with 17 of its 21 members cutting their allocations (German and Randel, 1995, p. 3). The UK, US, Canada, Italy and Sweden have all cut flows significantly while Germany seems set, at best, to freeze expenditure at present levels. Only Japan is increasing its aid budget, but at much lower rates than in the 1980s. Given that many developing countries have substantial debts to service it seems likely that the resources available for development will decline in many countries.

Although it is difficult to distinguish 'policy dialogue' from 'donor conditionality', that is donors insisting that recipient nations agree to certain policy changes in order to access funds (Cassen, 1994, p. 59), there is much evidence that the setting of conditions will remain a significant aspect of aid in coming years. In the macroeconomic sphere most of the responsibility for this lies with the IMF and World Bank for their stabilization and structural adjustment loans (see Box 10.1). Commonly these conditions include economic policy conditions – devaluing the currency, floating interest rates, reducing public expenditure – and institutional changes such as public enterprise divestiture and the opening up of the banking system. Post-Cold War conditionality has spread to include political matters, such as human rights, election and media freedom, and Western advocacy groups have pushed for conditions to be set in terms of gender, environmental management and military expenditure. The application of sanctions in relation to non-compliance with conditions has been inconsistent and reveals the continuing importance of domestic economic and political considerations in donor behaviour. While sanctions may be applied to the small fry of Kenya and Malawi donors appear unwilling to risk their trade relations with countries such as China or Indonesia.

The future role of the multilateral development agencies is increasingly unclear. The UN system has lost credibility over the last decade with mounting public evidence of under-performance and incompetence in the FAO (Abbott, 1992), UNESCO and WHO (whose accounts the UK National Audit Office has refused to approve), and its peace-keeping and humanitarian activities. Its role in shaping technical cooperation has been withering away and the main 'think-tank' for how to improve policies and institutional capacities in developing countries in virtually all sectors has become the World Bank. The Bank has importance not simply in terms of the loans and grants it disburses but also in terms of the way that its actions shape the behaviour of other donors and of domestic policy-makers (George and Sabelli, 1994). Its position is far from secure. While it can absorb 'Bank-bashing' from left-wing critics, it is also confronted with growing threats from the Republican Party in the USA and from the wider American electorate, who question the need for the Bank now that the USSR has collapsed. In response, it has latched on to poverty-alleviation, environmental conservation and good governance as goals for its activities. The last of these, good governance, and its bed-fellow the new public management, have considerable implications for public administration in developing countries, and it is to these that we now turn.

The contemporary international environment: key concepts

Two concepts currently set the intellectual agenda for change in the public sector of developing countries – 'good government' and 'the new public management'. The notion of good government (also referred to as good governance) arose in 1990 as the dust settled over the Berlin Wall and international development agencies adjusted their policies. Western bilateral donors seized the opportunity to extend their activities beyond mere projects and policies to press for the reformulation of the framework for government in recipient countries. Fundamental changes in political and administrative structures, it was argued, were a prerequisite for development. The multilateral agencies (World Bank, IMF and UN agencies) concurred with this. They carefully skirted around pronouncements about formal political structures, as required by their articles of association, and have highlighted technical issues such as accountability and transparency.

Although there are a variety of interpretations of the exact nature of good governance (see IDS, 1993, pp. 7–8, for a list of statements) 'there has emerged a common core of ideas . . . there is a new orthodoxy which is likely to be with us for the foreseeable future' (Moore, 1993a, p. 1). This orthodoxy is promoted by the focusing of intellectual and political activity around the issue of good governance and, less subtly, by agencies attaching political conditionalities to loans and grants (Robinson, 1993).

Typical of bilateral donors is the UK's Overseas Development Administration (ODA), for whom the promotion of good government is a prime objective. ODA has identified four main elements that underpin the concept: the legitimacy of government, the accountability of government, the competence of government, and respect for human rights and the rule of law (see Box 10.2). The World Bank also identifies four key dimensions to governance, but avoids direct comments on political structures. These are public sector management, accountability, the legal framework for development, and information and transparency (see Box 10.2).

Of the many issues deriving from the good governance agenda there are two that are particularly relevant to our discussions. The first is that in both its political and technical forms, good governance places improved public sector management as a key developmental goal for donors: across Africa, Asia, Latin America and the former Iron Curtain, aid agency personnel are placing public sector management on their agenda and are hunting out projects in this field. Secondly, although there are some differences in the detail, the major donors are agreed that what developing countries must do to improve public sector management is to sweep away the traditional public administration paradigm that underpins their bureaucracies and introduce the new public management (NPM). We now turn to this.

While there are a number of approaches by which public sector management might be improved, contemporary theory and practice has focused almost exclusively on the types of reform adopted in the USA, UK and New Zealand (see Box 10.3) in the last 15 years. The long-term benefits of such reforms still await empirical validation, but for development agencies and international consultants these changes – efficiency units, performance management, contracting-out, market-testing, agency status – commonly called the new public management, are a blueprint. Donors concur with Osborne and Gaebler's (1992) conclusions, from their influential book *Reinventing Government*, that a 'new paradigm' has emerged for the public sector based on an 'entrepreneurial revolution'. This is apparently part of the 'march of history', and a 'global revolution' has been unleashed to transform public sector performance (*ibid.*, pp. 321–31). Although, in their own countries the progress of public sector reform initiatives has taken many years and been an evolving rather than a comprehensively

---

BOX 10.2
Official views on good government

The UK's Overseas Development Administration (ODA) notes that good government is 'complex' and identifies four components:

1. The *legitimacy* of government: government, which depends on the existence of participatory processes and the consent of those who are governed;
2. The *accountability* of both the political and official elements of government for their actions, depending on the availability of information, freedom of the media, transparency of decision making and the existence of mechanisms to call individuals and institutions to account;
3. The *competence* of governments to formulate appropriate policies, make timely decisions, implement them effectively and deliver services;
4. Respect for *human rights and rule of law*, to guarantee individual and group rights and security, to provide a framework for economic and social activity and to allow and encourage all individuals to participate.

The World Bank identifies four major components in governance. While these partially overlap with ODA's usage of the term, pronouncements on political structures are avoided:

1. *Public sector management*: government must manage its financial and personnel resources effectively through appropriate budgeting, accounting and reporting systems and by rooting out inefficiency particularly in the parastatal sector.
2. *Accountability*: public officials must be held responsible for their actions. This involves effective accounting and auditing, decentralisation, 'micro-level accountability' to consumers and a role for non-governmental organisations.
3. *The legal framework for development*: there must be a set of rules known in advance, these must be enforced, conflicts must be resolved by independent judicial bodies and there must be mechanisms for amending rules when they no longer serve their purpose.
4. *Information and transparency*: there are three main areas for improvement, (a) information on economic efficiency; (b) transparency as a means of preventing corruption; and (c) publicly available information for policy analysis and debate.

Sources: ODA (Overseas Development Administration) (1993) 'Good Government', *Technical Note* no. 10 (London: ODA); World Bank (1992) *Governance and Development* (Washington D.C.: World Bank).

---

planned process, donors usually frame reform initiatives in developing countries as three to five-year projects.

Dunleavy and Hood (1994) identify two main 'shifts' in the move from public administration to the new public management. Moving 'down group', which means making the public sector less-distinctive from the private sector in terms of personnel practice, pay, procedures and other features: and moving 'down grid', which means reducing the density of general procedural rules governing public sector activity and increasing the discretionary power of senior and middle-level public servants, especially over staff, contracts and money (*ibid.*, p. 9). The main shifts in a switch to the new public management are summarized in Box 10.4.

Proponents of this new paradigm have been successful in disseminating its key features and persuading potential patients of its curative powers. Allied data have been mobilized to argue an empirical case that countries following this model have made

---

BOX 10.3

New Zealand: the new public management in action

The proponents of the New Public Management have often identified New Zealand as an exemplar of this contemporary mode of administrative reform. In the mid-1990s the New Zealand model embraces the following elements:

- A preference for retaining key governmental powers and responsibilities at the central government level with only limited devolution to sub-national government, despite considerable rhetoric about devolution in the 1980s.
- A strong emphasis on the use of incentives to enhance performance, at both the institutional and the individual level (e.g. short-term employment contracts, performance-based remuneration systems, promotion systems, etc.).
- An extensive use of explicit, generally written 'contracts' of various kinds, which specify the nature of the performance required and the respective obligations of agents and principals (e.g. performance agreements between ministers and departmental CEs, purchase agreements between ministers and departments, and contracts between funders and purchasers and between purchasers and providers). In addition to the emphasis on *ex ante* performance specification, more exacting monitoring and reporting systems have been introduced.
- The development of integrated and relatively sophisticated strategic planning and performance management systems throughout the public service. Key elements include the specification by ministers of strategic result areas and key result areas and the integration of these into CE's performance agreements and departmental purchase agreements.
- The removal, wherever possible, of dual or multiple accountability relationships within the public sector, and the avoidance of joint central and local democratic control of public services.
- The institutional separation of commercial and non-commercial functions: the separation of advisory, delivery, and regulatory functions; and the related separation of the roles of funder, purchaser, and provider.
- The maximum decentralization of production and management decision-making especially with respect to the selection and purchase of inputs and the management of human resources.

Source: Boston, J., Martin. J., Pallot, J. and Walsh, P. (1996) *Public Management: The New Zealand Model* (Auckland: Oxford University Press), p. 5.

BOX 10.4

From old public administration to new public management

- Reworking budgets to be transparent in accounting terms, with costs attributed to outputs not inputs, and outputs measured by quantitative performance indicators
- Viewing organizations as a chain of low-trust principal/agent relationships (rather than fiduciary or trustee-beneficiary ones), a network of contracts linking incentives to performance
- Disaggregating separable functions into quasi-contractual or quasi-market forms, particularly by introducing purchaser/provider distinctions, replacing previously unified functional planning-and-provision structures
- Opening up provider roles to competition between agencies or between public agencies, firms and not-for-profit bodies
- Deconcentrating provider roles to the minimum feasible sized agency, allowing users more scope to 'exit' from one provider to another, rather than relying on 'voice' options to influence how public service provision affects them.

Source: Dunleavy, P. and Hood, C. (1994) 'From Old Public Administration to New Public Management', *Public Money and Management* (July/Sept), pp. 9–16.

---

substantial savings in public expenditure and improved services (Osborne and Gaebler, 1992). Thus, few recipient governments have seriously challenged this prescription. Although policy-makers and senior administrators in many developing countries have grave reservations about the introduction of the new model these are usually presented in the form of it 'not being compatible with our culture'. Such vague statements are easily brushed aside by international agencies as the lament of those with vested interests in the maintenance of the status quo. Hood and Dunleavy's (1994, pp. 10–13) fourfold classification of the critiques of the new public management provides a framework for systematically examining the potential costs of introducing the model to specific developing countries. These can be weighed against the potential benefits.

The fatalist critique argues that the NPM cannot tackle the fundamental problems underlying public sector performance – human error, poorly designed programmes, corruption and patronage. This is a negative critique, in that it does not formulate an alternative, but it usefully points to the need to question whether NPM can change organizational culture or whether the approach will be rhetorically absorbed while pre-existing behaviours, such as centralization and an aversion to innovation, persist.

The individualist critique, usually associated with the right wing, argues that performance enhancement derives purely from 'entrepreneurial activity in response to market signals' (*ibid.*, p. 11). The NPM is not radical enough as it entails quasi-markets and quasi-contracts. Instead, all contracts should be market-based, purchaser–provider contracts should be open to litigation, no staff should have tenure and all staff should receive pay on a performance basis. Governments in developing countries have not adopted this extreme position to date although much diluted versions can be located in some of the dynamic Asian economies.

The hierarchist critique is concerned about the potential destabilizing effects of the NPM if the processes of change get out of hand and do irreversible damage to public sector provision. The NPM may encourage the pursuit of efficiency in flawed policies, a short-term focus on cost reduction and an erosion of state capacity to take a long-term perspective about technology, research capacity, education and the environment. The transaction costs of switching to contracts and quasi-contracts may be very high. This critique is the basis for much of the concern about NPM in developing countries. The bureaucracy may be inefficient, but it plays a key role in stabilizing the political economy of the nation. Rapid reform could have political consequences that raise the probability of unrest and civil strife. The social and economic costs of this could be enormous while political legitimacy and regime survival could be severely tested. Similarly, a short-term focus on efficiency might reduce the development of human resource potential in the long term. According to this critique, reform needs to be centrally steered, cautiously introduced and with the assurance that core public sector capacities are retained.

The egalitarian critique, which is associated with left-wing arguments, postulates that the NPM will promote self-interest and corruption. Policy-makers and senior civil servants will opt for privatization and marketization because of the increased opportunities for malfeasance. Welfare-reducing 'hiving off' of functions and agencies will occur as civil servants pursue both cost reductions and narrowly defined performance indicators. This will lower service quality and present citizens with a fragmented set of single-service providers of which they can make little sense. Accountability moves out of citizen hands and into those of a 'new magistracy'. From this perspective, it is argued that public servants must demonstrate the benefits of reform to citizens before large-scale change occurs; and, centrally controlled 'anti-corruption' units become important.

Observers of privatization in developing countries will find these arguments of great significance. The concerns of egalitarians are borne out by research in Sri Lanka about the selection of the owners of privatized public enterprises and the prices they paid (Kelegama and Dunham, 1993). Similar accounts have emerged from Pakistan, Eastern Europe and the former Soviet Union. These are not one-off problems, as in some cases public monopolies have been converted into private monopolies with weak regulatory frameworks. As economic theory confirms, there are few better investments than a private monopoly without regulation!

Problems and prospects of the new public management

The World Bank and powerful bilateral agencies (USAID and ODA) are keen to promote the NPM in developing countries. Responses are mixed but, interestingly, they are most likely to be supportive to NPM introduction when the egalitarian critique is valid: i.e. when the national élite recognizes the increased opportunities that marketization will provide for them.

Concerns about the NPM should not focus on an abstract notion of whether it is right or wrong. Rather, analysts and practitioners need to adopt the contingency approach that dominates contemporary thinking in organization theory (see Chapter 1) and ask in what contexts is the NPM likely to achieve performance improvements. In addition, they need to recognize the continuum from 'soft' to 'hard' approaches towards the NPM. In countries with pre-existing high levels of corruption, a key question will be whether the NPM will help reduce this or whether the NPM will permit malfeasance at higher levels than were previously possible. In fledgling democracies and contexts where political violence is common, the key question will be whether NPM reforms will strengthen or weaken national stability. As the former President of Sri Lanka, Julius Jayawardena, advised one of us when questioned about his failure to institute civil service reform – 'with an ethnic civil war in the North, a youth uprising in the South, my neighbour [India] rattling her sabre and plummeting commodity prices, do you think I needed to set the civil service on fire?'

Following along these lines, proponents of the NPM need to examine whether human resources and organizational capacities within a developing country are sufficiently developed to make market or quasi-market based competition feasible. In many smaller countries and poorer countries the likelihood of competing providers, or getting genuine second and third quotes for specialized services, which are the bulk of public services, is low.

Two further problems confront proponents of the NPM in developing countries, one conceptual and one empirical. The former relates to the broader notion of good governance: how can donors demand that governments are more democratic and more responsive to citizens needs and, at the same time, set conditions that require elements of the NPM to be adopted (that is deny citizens a full range of policy options). Our personal contacts with African and Asian policy-makers have revealed the cynicism that donors have created by good governance policies prescribing 'democratic decision-making as long as it coincides with their [the donor's] conditionalities' (quote from the former Minister of Finance of Bangladesh). The latter relates to the considerable empirical problem raised by the rapid development of East Asian and now Southeast Asian nations.

According to donors, good governance correlates closely with economic development. How then have Japan, Korea, Taiwan, Indonesia, Malaysia and Thailand experienced such rapid growth with public sectors based on the old public administration and/or indigenous models, featuring poor accountability (in terms of Western criteria), convoluted legal frameworks that do not foster adversarial legal action and low levels of transparency? Slowness, red tape and centralization have been common. Their 'democracy' has ranged from non-existent to 'guided' and/or 'corrupt'. Yet their economic performance and capacity to meet citizens' welfare needs have grown at unprecedented rates. Could it be that good governance and the NPM fail to recognize that there are many different paths to development? Or, conversely, as Dunleavy and Hood (1994) argue that 'inappropriate cloning' is a key feature of historical attempts at public sector reform: has NPM so rapidly advanced to this stage? Look at the the major components of New Zealand's version of NPM in Box 10.3 (often cited as an exemplar by NPM's proponents) and ask whether such arrangements are appropriate and/or feasible for particular developing countries.

Conclusion

The international environment has been of profound importance in shaping the nature of public administration and policy-making in developing countries. The effects of the colonial experience are still of fundamental significance for public sector activities in former colonies, and only relatively large countries (such as China and Indonesia) can try to ensure that internal, rather than external, ideas define the future role and nature of the administration.

The contemporary processes of globalization, in both their economic and socio-cultural dimensions, make international factors increasingly important. These operate indirectly, for example in terms of searching out localities for low-cost production; and directly in terms of the transmission of concepts about what governments and their agencies should do and how they should do it. While economic liberalization and the end of the Cold War promise benefits they also have demonstrated their downsides. There are questions about the capacity of organizations and individuals to cope with the constant changes of late twentieth century existence, while conflict and war seem to be escalating on all continents.

One element of the international scene which has not changed is the notion that 'advanced' nations should transfer finance and ideas to developing countries. In the 1950s and 1960s the ideas highlighted setting up clones of the Tennessee Valley Authority, establishing parastatals, national planning and big government. Ironically, in the 1990s they emphasize the closure or divestiture of parastatals, the abandonment of national planning and the downsizing of government. This propensity of donor nations, and the multilaterals they control, to transfer models for public policy-making, planning and administration to developing countries without adequately considering contextual differences seems set to continue: donors and development agencies have not yet learned how to cope with contingency. In the 1980s, the Training and Visit system for extension reform was not wrong (see Chapter 5): the main problems it encountered lay in its application to inappropriate contexts. Similarly, in the 1990s the new public management is not wrong, but it is presently being transferred to some developing country contexts in which it is likely to be dysfunctional.

11

Conclusion: What Future for the Public Sector?

Dominant ideas about the role of public sector organizations in development have changed dramatically. In the 1950s and 1960s, the public sector was awarded undisputed primacy as the creator and implementor of strategies for development. Its technical, and simultaneously altruistic, élites would guide economies and societies along the path of modernization. In the 1970s, critical self-reflection combined with assault from radical development theory saw the image of an efficacious public sector severely challenged. Could it generate and maintain the impetus for development? By the 1980s, the answer to this question was clearly and widely articulated. The public sector was a pariah, which actually hindered economic and social development. The time had come to roll back the state by privatizing the public enterprises so vigorously promoted in an earlier era and downsizing the ministries which had been encouraged to expand into ever more areas of social and economic life.

Such broad generalizations have frequently dominated debate on development policy and management over the past half century. But, as we have demonstrated in the preceding chapters, they fail to take account of the enormous diversity of administrative environments, organizational structures, policy processes and public sector performances that the empirical record reveals. Experience is not so neatly characterized when one's object of analysis comprises three-quarters of the world's population and more than 100 independent states. The common assumption that public sector organizations in developing countries have 'failed' is inaccurate. Admittedly, performances may often have been poor, particularly in relation to extravagant expectations associated with national independence, but they have not been uniform. While the bloated central bureaucracies of neo-patrimonial African governments and Bangladesh's sprawling civil service undoubtedly illustrate the weaknesses of public sector organizations, they must be contrasted with public services and public enterprises in South Korea, Taiwan, Malaysia, Indonesia and Thailand which have made significant contributions to national development and political stability. There are even islands of efficiency and effectiveness set in seas of indifferent and poor performance in some countries (such as the Local Government Engineering Board in Bangladesh).

Most public sector organizations, however, clearly have substantial opportunities to improve their performance and to deploy their resources more effectively. Earlier chapters have presented a variety of ideas about how this might be done: by maintaining greater awareness of the environment and its changing features (Chapter 2); by paying attention to the political feasibility of policy implementation (Chapters 2 and 3); by building capacity and investing in human resources (Chapter 5); by linking the mechanisms for accountability to performance (Chapter 5); by improving annual budgeting systems rather than emphasizing unrealistic long-term plans (Chapter 6); by moving away from blueprint planning to process approaches (Chapter 6); by reinvigorating local government and seeking to reduce its 'Cinderella' image (Chapter 7); by establishing the appropriate policy framework as a basis for public enterprises which provide quality services at the right price (Chapter 8); by utilizing performance contracts in public enterprises (Chapter 8); or by working more effectively in partnership with NGOs (Chapter 9).

These and other ideas which appear in the book are indicative of diversity and creativity. There is no 'one best way'. Rather, experience has provided us with a variety of organizational forms and local applications. What has been successful in one place may be inappropriate in another and the lessons of one country's reforms may be different for the various observers. However, there has been a recent trend towards convergence in public sector reform with the rise of the 'new public management' (NPM) or 'reinventing government'. The danger is that the variety of offerings on the reform menu may be greatly reduced and the propensity to experiment may be actively discouraged. In the USA and many OECD countries, the intellectual agenda has been seized by the NPM. Through offers of aid funding and threats of aid conditionality, the movement is being energetically promoted across developing countries by the World Bank, USAID, the UK's Overseas Development Administration and other bilateral donors.

Whatever the reasons – naivety, historical and environmental blindness, or ideology – a powerful international lobby is promoting a 'one size fits all' approach to public sector reform in spite of the evidence accumulated from organizational and management theory and from empirical study that the outcomes of planned changes in organizations are conditioned by many contingent factors, especially those in the organization's environment (Chapter 2). In some contexts, the NPM may yield its promised benefits, but in others the possibility of it contributing to reduced performance, and even political instability, must be recognized. As even the pro-reinventing government journal *The Economist* (20 May, 1995, p. 24) has observed, 'government and management are two different things'.

Political analysis and consideration of the circuits of power which link society and state have been persistently emphasized in this book. The configurations of power set limits both on the types of changes that can be promoted in the public sector and on the speed of change. Resistance is an ever-present feature of any organizational reform. Public bureaucracies can be powerful political interest groups in their own right. They must, therefore, be analysed not simply in technical or normative terms as the inanimate machinery of service delivery but also in political terms as major players in the political economies of most nations. The persistence of bureaucratic inefficiency and dysfunction, and the repeated disappointments of administrative reform efforts (Chapters 4 and 5) provide ample evidence of the capacity of these organizations and their members to resist or subvert reform efforts. Politicians have been far more aware of this than aid agencies which have frequently failed to appreciate the role bureaucracy can play, however inefficient, in holding states together. States can be extremely fragile creations as their collapse in Somalia, Liberia, the Lebanon, Yugoslavia and the former Soviet Union has demonstrated. Such experiences would appear to be far worse in human misery and economic cost than under-performance by the organizations of the state.

This is not to advocate state inefficiency but to further demonstrate the complexity of governance in developing nations. Deliberate intervention by the state to improve public sector performance is not simply a technical matter. Feasibility depends on far more than simple calculations of capacity, and even those are a notoriously difficult branch of mathematics! Furthermore, we have moved beyond the proposition that the state alone can centrally plan and then implement the strategies that will bring development. Firstly, precise knowledge of the future is a pipe-dream in the turbulent environments of developing countries. Secondly, there are participants other than the state which can make a major contribution to the development process. These include the private sector and NGOs. The idea is that development should be a partnership between the state and civil society, and that such a partnership harnesses the energies and creative abilities of individuals, communities, businesses and state organizations in a common cause. Development is too important simply to be left entirely at the discretion of the state's functionaries.

A final challenge for the state in its quest for public sector reform is the question of how to assist indigenously-based change measures. External agencies can force reforms on developing-country governments but the outcomes are just as likely to be negative as they might be positive. The bureaucratic organizations of developing countries have grown out of deep roots and have the legacies of pre-colonial, colonial and independence eras embedded within them. They are hybrids but they are distinctive with their own rationalities, operating structures and values. New grafts may be rejected especially when imposed on an unwilling host. Effective reforms must be indigenously owned if they are to be successful. But as we have stressed throughout this book, development is a multifaceted phenomena and ownership itself does not guarantee favourable outcomes. It could, however, give the participants a good start.

Bibliography

Abbott, J. (1992) *Politics and Poverty: A Critique of the Food and Agriculture Organisation of the United Nations* (London: Routledge).

Action Aid (1990) *The Effectiveness of British Aid for Training* (London: Action Aid).

Adamolekun, L. (1983) *Public Administration: A Nigerian and Comparative Perspective* (London: Longman).

Alavi, H. (1971) 'The Politics of Dependence: A Village in West Punjab', *South Asian Review*, vol. 4(2).

Alavi, H. (1982) 'State and Class under Peripheral Capitalism', in H. Alavi and T. Shanin (eds), *Introduction to the Sociology of 'Developing' Societies* (London: Macmillan), pp. 289–307.

Alderfer, H. F. (1964) *Local Government in Developing Countries* (New York: McGraw-Hill).

Allison, G. T. (1971) *Essence of Decision* (Boston: Little Brown).

Amin, S. (1976) *Unequal Development* (Hassocks, Sussex: Harvester).

Argyris, C. (1957) *Personality and Organization* (New York: Harper & Brothers).

Austin, J. E. (1990) *Managing in Developing Countries: Strategic Analysis and Operating Techniques* (New York: Free Press).

Baker, K. G. (1976) 'Public Choice Theory: Some Important Assumptions and Public Policy Implications', in R. T. Golembiewski *et al.* (eds), *Public Administration: Readings in Institutions, Processes, Behavior, Policy* (New York: Rand McNally).

Bates, R. H. (1981) *Markets and States in Tropical Africa: The Political Basis of Agricultural Policies* (Berkeley: University of California Press).

Bauer, P. T. (1981) *Equality, the Third World and Economic Delusion* (London: Methuen).

Bauer, P. T. (1984) 'Remembrance of Studies Past: Retracing First Steps', in G. M. Meier and D. Seers (eds), *Pioneers in Development* (New York: Oxford University Press), pp. 27–43.

Bayart, J.-F. (1991) 'Finishing with the Idea of the Third World: The Concept of the Political Trajectory', in J. Manor (ed.), *Rethinking Third World Politics* (London: Longman), pp. 51–71.

Beetham, D. (1987) *Bureaucracy* (Milton Keynes: Open University).

Bello, W. and Rosenfeld, S. (1992) *Dragons in Distress: Asia's Miracle Economies in Crisis* (London: Penguin).

Beneria, L. and Sen, G. (1979) 'Reproduction, Production and the Sexual Division of Labour', *Cambridge Journal of Economics*, vol. 3(3), pp. 203–25.

Bennis, W. G. (1966) *Changing Organizations* (New York: McGraw-Hill).

Benor, D. and Harrison, J. Q. (1977) *Agricultural Extension: The Training and Visit System* (Washington D.C.: World Bank).

Berg, E. (1993) *Rethinking Technical Assistance* (New York: UNDP).

Bickford, T. J. (1994) 'The Chinese Military and its Business Operations', *Asian Survey*, vol. 34(5), pp. 460–74.

Bienen, H., Kapur, D., Parks, J. and Riedinger, J. (1990) 'Decentralisation in Nepal', *World Development*, vol. 18(1), pp. 61–75.

Bird, R. M. (1990) 'Intergovernmental Finance and Local Taxation in Developing Countries: Some Basic Considerations for Reformers', *Public Administration and Development*, vol. 10(3), pp. 277–88.

Bjur, W. E. and Zomorrodian, A. (1986) 'Towards Indigenous Theories of Administration: An International Perspective', *International Review of Administrative Sciences*, vol. 52(4), pp. 397–420.

Blair, H. (1997) 'Donors, Democratization and Civil Society: Relating Theory to Practice', in D. Hulme and M. Edwards (eds), *NGOs, States and Donors: Too Close for Comfort?* (London: Macmillan; and New York: St Martin's Press).

Bratton, M. (1989) 'The Politics of Government–NGO Relations in Africa', *World Development*, vol. 17(4), pp. 569–97.

BRIVAS (Bureau of Research on Islamic Values of the Administrative System) (1992) 'The Position of Women in Public Administration in the Islamic Republic of Iran', *Asian Review of Public Administration*, vol.4(1), pp. 65–80.

Brown, D. (1989) 'Bureaucracy as an Issue in Third World Management: An African Case Study', *Public Administration and Development*, vol. 9(4), pp. 369–80.

Bruton, H. *et al.* (1992) *Political Economy of Poverty, Equity and Growth: Sri Lanka and Malaysia* (Oxford and New York: Oxford University Press).

Bryant, C. and White, L. (1982) *Managing Development in the Third World* (West Hartford: Kumarian Press).

Caiden, G. E. (1969) 'Development Administration and Administrative Reform', *International Social Science Journal*, vol. 21(1), pp. 9–22.

Caiden, G. E. and Kim, B. W. (1991) *A Dragon's Progress: Development Administration in Korea* (West Hartford: Kumarian Press)

Caiden, N. and Wildavsky, A. (1990) *Planning and Budgeting in Poor Countries* (New Brunswick: Transaction Publishers), originally published in 1974.

Cammack, P., Pool, D. and Tordoff, W. (1988) *Third World Politics: A Comparative Introduction* (London: Macmillan).

Cardoso, F. H. (1977) 'The Consumption of Dependency Theory in the United States', *Latin American Research Review*, vol. 12(3), pp. 7–24.

Cariño, L. V. (1991a) 'Regime Changes, the Bureaucracy and Political Development', in A. Farazmand (ed.), *Handbook of Comparative and Development Public Aministration* (New York: Marcel Dekker), pp. 731–43.

Cariño, L. V. (1992) *Bureaucracy for Democracy: The Dynamics of Executive–Bureaucracy Interaction During Governmental Transitions* (Quezon City: College of Public Administration, University of the Philippines).

Cariño, L. V. (ed.) (1991b) *Public Administration in Asia and the Pacific: Survey of Teaching and Research in Twelve Countries* (Bangkok: UNESCO).

Carroll, T. (1992) *Intermediary NGOs: The Supporting Link in Grassroots Development* (West Hartford: Kumarian Press).

Cassen, R. and associates (1994) *Does Aid Work?*, 2nd edition (Oxford: Oxford University Press), 1st edition 1986.

Cernea, M. (1991) *Putting People First: Sociological Variables in Rural Development* (New York: OUP).

Chambers, R. (1983) *Rural Development: Putting the Last First* (London: Longman).

Chambers, R. (1992) 'The Self-deceiving State', *IDS Bulletin*, vol 23(4), pp. 31–42.

Chambers, R. (1993) *Challenging the Professions: Frontiers for Rural Development* (London: IT Publishers).

Chambers, R. (1994) 'Participatory Rural Appraisal (PRA): Analysis of Experience', *World Development*, vol. 22(9), pp. 1253—68.

Chazan, N. (1989) 'Planning Democracy in Africa: A Comparative Perspective on Nigeria and Ghana', *Policy Sciences*, vol. 22(3–4), pp. 325–57.

Chazan, N., Mortimer, R., Ravenhill, J. and Rothchild, D. (1988) *Politics and Society in Contemporary Africa* (London: Macmillan).

Cheema, G. S. (1986) 'Reaching the Urban Poor: An Introduction', in G. S. Cheema (ed.), *Reaching the Urban Poor: Project Implementation in Developing Countries* (Boulder: Westview), pp. 1—18.

Chickering, A. L. and Salahdine, M. (1991) 'Introduction', in A. L. Chickering and M. Salahdine (eds), *The Silent Revolution: The Informal Sector in Five Asian and Near Eastern Countries* (San Francisco: ICS Press), pp. 1–14.

Child, J. (1972) 'Organizational Structures, Environment and Performance: The Role of Strategic Choice', *Sociology*, vol. 6(1), pp. 2–22.

Chitere, P. and Monya, J. (1989) 'Decentralisation of Rural Development: The Case of the Kenya District Focus Approach', *African Administrative Studies*, 32, pp. 31–51.

Choudhry, M. A. (1991) 'Promoting Productivity and Quality in Bureaucratic Performance in Pakistan', *Asian Review of Public Administration*, vol. 3(2), pp. 93–4.

Chowdhury, A. and Kirkpatrick, C. (1994) *Development Policy and Planning: an Introduction to Models and Techniques* (London: Routledge).

Chowdhury, A. M. R. and Cash, R. A. (1996) *A Simple Solution: Teaching Millions to Treat Diarrhoea at Home* (Dhaka: UPL).

Clapham, C. (1985) *Third World Politics: An Introduction* (London: Croom Helm).

Clark, J. (1991) *Democratising Development: The Role of Voluntary Organisations* (London: Earthscan).

Clay, E. J. and Schaffer, B. B. (1984) *Room for Manoeuvre: An Explanation of Public Policy in Agriculture and Rural Development* (London: Heinemann).

Cohen, J. M., Grindle, M. S. and Walker, T. (1985) 'Foreign Aid and Conditions Precedent: Political and Bureaucratic Dimensions', *World Development*, vol. 13(12), pp. 1211–30.

Cohen, M. D., March, J. G. and Olsen, J. P. (1972) 'A Garbage Can Model of Organizational Choice', *Administrative Science Quarterly*, vol. 17(1), pp. 1–25.

Col, J.-M. (1991) 'Women in Bureaucracies: Equity, Advancement, and Public Policy Strategies', in A. Farazmand (ed.), *Handbook of Comparative and Development Public Administration* (New York: Marcel Dekker), pp. 711–18.

Commonwealth Secretariat (1985) *Training for Decentralised Systems of Government Administration* (London: Commonwealth Secretariat).

Conaghan, C. M. (1990) 'Retreat to Democracy: Business and Political Transition in Bolivia and Ecuador', in D. Ethier (ed.), *Democratic Transition and Consolidation in Southern Europe, Latin America and Southeast Asia* (London: Macmillan), pp. 73–90.

Conyers, D. (1982) *An Introduction to Social Planning in the Third World* (Chichester: Wiley).

Conyers, D. (1986) 'Future Directions in Development Studies: The Case of Decentralisation', *World Development*, vol. 14(5), pp. 593—603.

Conyers, D. (1990) 'Centralisation and Development Planning: A Comparative Perspective', in P. de Valk and K. H. Wikwete (eds), *Decentralising for Participatory Planning?* (Aldershot: Gower), pp. 15–34.

Cook, P. and Hulme, D. (1988) 'The Compatibility of Market Liberalization and Local Economic Development Strategies', *Regional Studies*, vol. 22(3), pp. 221–31.

Cook, P. and Kirkpatrick, C. (eds) (1988) *Privatisation in Less Developed Countries* (London: Harvester Wheatsheaf).

Cook, P. and Minogue, M. (1990) 'Waiting for Privatization in Developing Countries: Towards the Integration of Economic and Non-economic Explanations', *Public Administration and Development*, vol. 10(4), pp. 389–403.

Cooper, R. and Fox, S. (1990) 'The "Texture" of Organizing', *Journal of Management Studies*, vol. 27(6), pp. 575–82.

Crook, R. and Manor, J. (1994) *Enhancing Participation and Institutional Performance: Democratic Decentralisation in South Asia and West Africa* (London: Overseas Development Administration).

Crouch, H., (1979). 'Patrimonialism and Military Rule in Indonesia', *World Politics*, vol. 31(4), pp. 571–87.

Crozier, M. (1964) *The Bureaucratic Phenomenon* (Chicago: University of Chicago Press).

Davis, D., Hulme, D. and Woodhouse, P (1994) 'Decentralisation by Default: Local Governance in The Gambia', *Public Administration and Development*, vol. 14(3), pp. 253—69.

De Guzman, R. P. and Reforma, M. A. (1992) 'Administrative Reform in the Asian Pacific Region: Issues and Prospects', in Z. Zhijian, R. P. de Guzman and M. A. Reforma (eds), *Administrative Reform Towards Promoting Productivity in Bureaucratic Performance* (Manila: EROPA), pp. 2—14.

De Soto, H. (1989) *The Other Path* (New York: Harper & Row).

Dessler, G. (1986) *Organization Theory: Integrating Structure and Behavior* (Englewood Cliffs: Prentice-Hall).

Dichter, T. W. (1989) 'NGOs and the Replication Trap', *Findings '89.* (Washington D.C.: Technoserve).

Domingo-Tapales, P. (1992) 'Women in Politics and Public Administration: The Case of the Philippines', *Asian Review of Public Administration*, vol.4 (1), pp. 1–8.

Drèze, J. and Sen, A. (1989) *Hunger and Public Action* (Oxford: Clarendon Press).

Dror, Y. (1986) *Policymaking Under Adversity*, (New Brunswick: Transaction Books).

Drucker, P. E. (1989) 'What Business can Learn from Nonprofits', *Harvard Business Review*, vol. 67(4), pp. 88–93.

Dube, S. (1992) 'An Ancient Foe Gains Ground in a Modern World', *Choices*, vol. 1(3), pp. 11–15.

Duffield, M. (1993) 'NGOs, Disaster Relief and Asset Transfer in the Horn: Political Survival in a Permanent Emergency', *Development and Change*, vol. 24(1), pp. 131–57.

Dunleavy, P. and Hood, C. (1994) 'From Old Public Administration to New Public Management', *Public Money and Management* (July/Sept), pp. 9–16.

Dwivedi, O. P. and Nef, J. (1982) 'Crises and Continuities in Development Theory and Administration: First and Third World Perspectives', *Public Administration and Development*, vol. 2(1), pp. 59–77.

EDI and ISAS (1992) 'Civil Service Reform: Its Role in the South Pacific', Report of the Seventh Conference of Heads of Public Service in the South Pacific (Fiji: Institute of Social and Administrative Studies (ISAS), University of the South Pacific).

Edwards, M. and Hulme, D. (1994) 'NGO Performance and Accountability in the New World Order', theme paper to the Second Manchester NGO Workshop, 27–29 June 1994, Institute for Development Policy and Management, University of Manchester.

Edwards, M. and Hulme, D. (1996) 'NGOs and Development: Performance and Accountability in the New World Order', *World Development*, vol. 24(6), pp. 961–73

Edwards, M. and Hulme, D. (eds) (1992) *Making a Difference: NGOs and Development in a Changing World* (London: Earthscan).

Edwards, M. and Hulme, D. (eds) (1995) *NGOs Performance and Accountability: Beyond the Magic Bullet* (London: Earthscan; and West Hartford: Kumarian Press).

Ekins, P. (1992) *A New World Order: Grassroots Movements for Global Change* (London: Routledge).

Emery, F. E. and Trist, E. C. (1965) 'The Causal Texture of Organizational Environments', *Human Relations*, vol. 18(1), pp. 21–32.

Esman, M. J. (1988) 'The Maturing of Development Administration', *Public Administration and Development*, vol. 8(2), pp. 125–34.

Esman, M. J. and Uphoff, N. (1984) *Local Organizations: Intermediaries in Rural Development* (New York: Cornell University Press).

Farrington, J. and Bebbington, A. (1993) *Non-Governmental Organizations, the State and Sustainable Agricultural Development* (London: Routledge).

Fayol, H. (1949) *General and Industrial Management* (London: Pitman).

Fesler, J. W. (1965) 'Approaches to the Understanding of Decentralisation', *Journal of Politics*, vol. 27(4), pp. 536–66.

Findlay, R. (1991) 'The New Political Economy: Its Explanatory Power for LDCs', in G. M. Meier (ed.), *Politics and Policy Making in Developing*

Countries: Perspectives on the New Political Economy (San Francisco: ICS Press), pp. 13–40.

Fowler, A. (1988) 'NGOs in Africa: Comparative Advantage in Relief and Micro-Development', *IDS Discussion Paper*, 249 (Brighton: IDS).

Frank, A. G. (1971) *Capitalism and Underdevelopment in Latin America* (Harmondsworth: Penguin).

Freire, P. (1972) *Pedagogy of the Oppressed* (London: Penguin).

Freire, P. and Shor, I. (1978) *A Pedagogy for Liberation* (London: Macmillan).

Friedman, H. J. (1983) 'Decentralised Development in Asia: Local Political Alternatives', in G S Cheema and D A Rondinelli (eds), *Decentralisation and Development: Policy Implementation in Developing Countries* (Beverly Hills: Sage), pp. 35–58.

Friedmann, J. (1992) *Empowerment: The Politics of Alternative Development* (Oxford: Blackwell).

Fuentes, M. and Frank, A. G. (1989) 'Ten Theses on Social Movements', *World Development* vol. 17(2), pp. 179–91.

Fukuyama, F. (1992) *The End of History and the Last Man* (London: Penguin).

George, S. and Sabelli, F. (1994) *Faith and Credit: The World Bank's Secular Empire* (London: Penguin).

German, T. and Randel, J. (1995) *The Reality of Aid 95* (London: Earthscan).

Gerth, H. H. and Mills, C. W. (eds) (1948) *From Max Weber: Essays in Sociology* (London: Routledge & Kegan Paul).

Giddens, A. (1989) *Sociology* (Cambridge: Polity Press).

Gillis, M., Perkins, D. H., Roemer, M. and Snodgrass, D. R. (1987) *Economics of Development*, 2nd edition (New York: W. W. Norton & Co.).

Gittinger, J. P. (1982) *Economic Appraisal of Agricultural Projects* (Baltimore: Johns Hopkins University Press).

Glaeser, B. and Vyasulu, V. (1984) 'The Obsolescence of Ecodevelopment?' in B. Glaeser (ed.), *Ecodevelopment: Concepts, Projects, Strategies* (Oxford: Pergamon), pp. 23–36.

Goetz, A. M. (1992) 'Gender and Administration', *IDS Bulletin*, vol. 23(4), pp. 6–17.

Goolsarran, S. A. (1994) 'A Welcomed Breakthrough in Public Accountability', *International Journal of Government Auditing*, vol. 21(2), p. 1.

Gosling, L. and Edwards, M. (1995) *Toolkits: A Practical Guide to Assessment, Monitoring, Review and Evaluation* (London: Save the Children).

Gould, D. J. (1991) 'Administrative Corruption: Incidence, Causes and Remedial Strategies', in A. Farazmand (ed.), *Handbook of Comparative and Development Public Aministration* (New York: Marcel Dekker), pp. 467–80.

Goulet, D. (1992) 'Development: Creator and Destroyer of Values', *World Development*, vol. 20(3), pp. 467–75.

Gow, D. D. and Morss, E. R. (1988) 'The Notorious Nine: Critical Problems in Project Implementation', *World Development*, vol. 16(1), pp. 1399–418.

Gran, G. (1983) *Development by People: Citizen Construction of a Just World* (New York: Praeger).

Griffin, K. (1981) 'Economic Development in a Changing World', *World Development*, vol. 9(3), pp. 221–6.

Grindle, M. S. (1980) 'Policy Content and Context in Implementation', in M. S. Grindle (ed.,) *Politics and Policy Implementation in the Third World* (Princeton: Princeton University Press), pp. 3–39.

Grindle, M. S. (1991) 'The New Political Economy: Positive Economics and Negative Politics', in G. M. Meier (ed.), *Politics and Policy Making in Developing Countries: Perspectives on the New Political Economy* (San Francisco: ICS Press), pp. 41–67.

Grindle, M. S. and Thomas, J. W. (1989) 'Policy Makers, Policy Choices and Policy Outcomes: The Political Economy of Reform in Developing Countries', *Policy Sciences*, vol. 22(3–4), pp. 213–48.

Gulhati, R. (1990). 'Who Makes Economic Policy in Africa and How?', *World Development*, vol. 18(8), pp. 1147–62.

Hage, J. and Finsterbusch, K. (1987) *Organizational Change as a Development Strategy: Models and Tactics for Improving Third World Organizations* (Boulder: Lynne Rienner).

Haile-Mariam, Y. and Mengistu, B. (1988) 'Public Enterprises and the Privatisation Thesis in the Third World', *Third World Quarterly*, vol. 10(4), pp. 1565–87.

Hanlon, J. (1991) *Mozambique: Who Calls the Shots?* (London: James Currey).

Harris, R. L. (1983) 'Centralisation and Decentralisation in Latin America', in G S Cheema and D A Rondinelli (eds), *Decentralisation and Development: Policy Implementation in Developing Countries* (Beverly Hills: Sage), pp. 183–202.

Harrison, D. (1988) *The Sociology of Modernization and Development* (London: Unwin Hyman).

Harrison, P. (1981) *Inside the Third World* (Harmondsworth: Penguin).

Hayllar, M. (1991) 'Accountability: Ends, Means and Resources', *Asian Review of Public Administration*, vol. 3(2), pp. 10–22.

Heady, F. (1984) *Public Administration: A Comparative Perspective*, 3rd edition (New York: Marcel Dekker).

Hicks, U. K. (1950) *Development from Below* (Oxford: Oxford University Press).

Hirschman, A. O. (1971) *A Bias for Hope: Essays on Development and Latin America* (New Haven & London: Yale University Press).

Hirschman, A. O. (1984) *Getting Ahead Collectively: Grassroots Experiences in Latin America* (Oxford: Pergaman Press)

Hirschmann, D. (1981) 'Development Administration? A Further Deadlock', *Development and Change*, vol. 12(3), pp. 459–79.

Hodson, R. (1992) 'Small, Medium or Large? The Rocky Road to NGO Growth', in M. Edwards and D. Hulme (eds), *Making a Difference: NGOs and Development in a Changing World* (London: Earthscan), pp. 127–36.

Hofstede, G. (1980), 'Motivation, Leadership and Organization: Do American Theories Apply Abroad', *Organizational Dynamics*, vol. 4(1), pp. 42–63.

Hogwood, B. W. and Gunn, L. A. (1984) *Policy Analysis for the Real World* (Oxford: Oxford University Press).

Honadle, G. H. and Rosengard, J. K. (1983) 'Politics versus Culture: An Assessment of 14 Mini-cases of Management Improvement in Developing

Countries', paper presented at the American Political Science Association National Conference, New York, 1983.

Horowitz, D. (1989), 'Is there a Third-World Policy Process?', *Policy Sciences*, vol. 22(3–4), pp. 197–212.

Hull, V.J. and Hull, T.H. (1992) 'Dimensions of Population and Development', *Briefing Paper* no. 26, Australian Development Studies Network, Australian National University.

Hulme, D. (1992) 'Enhancing Organizational Effectiveness in Developing Countries: The Training and Visit System Revisited', *Public Administration and Development*, vol. 12 (5), pp. 433–45.

Hulme, D. (1994a) 'Projects, Politics and Professionals: Alternative Approaches for Project Identification and Project Planning', *Agricultural Systems*, vol. 47(2), pp. 211–33.

Hulme, D. (1994b) 'Social Development Research and the Third Sector: NGOs as Users and Subjects of Social Enquiry', in D. Booth (ed.), *Rethinking Social Development* (London: Longman), pp. 251–75.

Hulme, D. and Edwards, M. (eds) (1997) *NGOs, States and Donors: Too Close for Comfort?* (London: Macmillan; and New York: St Martin's Press).

Hulme, D. and Sanderatne, N. (1995) 'Sri Lanka: Democracy and Accountability in Decline', in J. Healey and W. Tordoff (eds), *Votes and Budgets* (London: Macmillan).

Hulme, D. and Turner, M. (1990) *Sociology and Development: Theories Policies and Practices* (London: Harvester Wheatsheaf).

Hulme, D., Montgomery, R. and Bhattachrya, D. (1996) 'Mutual Finance and the Poor: the Federation of Thrift and Credit Cooperatives (SANASA) in Sri Lanka', in D. Hulme and P. Mosley (eds), *Finance for the Poor*, vol 2 (London: Routledge).

Huntington, S. (1968) *Political Order in Changing Societies* (New Haven: Yale University Press).

Huque, A.S. (1986) 'The Illusion of Decentralisation: Local Administration in Bangladesh', *International Review of Administrative Sciences*, vol. 52(1), pp. 79–95.

Hyden, G. (1983) *No Shortcuts to Progress: African Development Management in Perspective* (London: Heinemann).

IDS (Institute of Development Studies) (1993) *IDS Bulletin*, vol. 24(1).

IFC (International Finance Corporation) *Privatization: Principles and Practice* (Washington D.C.: World Bank).

Islam, N. (1993) 'Public Enterprise Reform: Managerial Autonomy, Accountability and Performance Contracts', *Public Administration and Development*, vol. 13(2), pp. 129–52.

Israel, A. (1987) *Institutional Development: Incentives to Development* (Baltimore: Johns Hopkins University Press).

Jackson, R.H. and Rosberg, C.G. (1982) *Personal Rule in Black Africa* (Berkeley: University of California Press).

Jacques, E. (1976) *A General Theory of Bureaucracy* (London: Heinemann).

Johnson, D.L. (ed.) (1985) *Middle Classes in Dependent Countries* (Beverly Hills: Sage).

Johnston, B.F. and Clark, W.C. (1982) *Redesigning Rural Development: A Strategic Perspective* (Baltimore: Johns Hopkins University Press).

Jones, M. (1992) 'Management Development: An African Perspective', in M. Jones and P. Mann (eds), *HRD: International Perspectives on Development and Learning* (West Hartford: Kumarian), pp. 108–21.

Jreisat, J. E. (1988) 'Administrative Reform in Developing Countries: A Comparative Perspective', *Public Administration and Development*, vol. 8(1), pp. 85–97.

Kasfir, N. (1976) *The Shrinking Political Arena* (Berkeley: University of California Press).

Kasfir, N. (1983) 'Designs and Dilemmas: An Overview', in P. Mawhood (ed.), *Local Government in the Third World* (Chichester: Wiley), pp. 25–47.

Kelegama, S. and Dunham, D. (1993) *Privatisation in Sri Lanka* (Colombo: Institute of Policy Studies).

Khan, M. (1981) *Administrative Reform and Theoretical Perspective* (Dacca: Centre for Administrative Studies).

Khan, M. M. and H. M. Zafrullah (1991) 'Politics of Bureaucracy in Bangladesh', in A. Farazmand (ed.), *Handbook of Comparative and Development Public Aministration* (New York: Marcel Dekker), pp. 651–61.

Khandwalla, P. N. (1987) *Effective Management of Public Enterprises* (Washington D.C.: World Bank).

Khanna, B. S. and Bhatnagar, S. (1980) 'India' in D. C. Rowat (ed.), *International Handbook of Local Government Reorganisation* (London: Aldwych Press), pp. 425–45.

Kiggundu, M. *et al.* (1983) 'Administrative Theory and Practice in Developing Countries: A Synthesis', *Administrative Science Quarterly*, vol. 28(1), pp. 66–84.

Killick, T. (1976) 'The Possibilities of Development Planning', *Oxford Economic Papers*, vol. 28(2), pp. 161–84.

Killick, T. (1989) *A Reaction Too Far: Economic Theory and the Role of the State in Developing Countries* (London: Overseas Development Institute).

Killick, T. (1994) 'East Asian Miracles and Development Ideology', *Development Policy Review*, vol. 12(1), pp. 69–73.

Kim, B. W. (1991) 'An Assessment of Government Intervention in Korean Economic Development', in G. F. Caiden and B. W. Kim (eds), *A Dragon's Progress: Development Administration in Korea* (West Hartford: Kumarian), pp. 135–43.

Kitchen, R. (1989) 'Administrative Reform in Jamaica: A Component of Structural Adjustment', *Public Administration and Development*, vol. 9(4), pp. 339–56.

Kitching, G. (1982) *Development and Underdevelopment in Historical Perspective* (London: Methuen).

Korten, D. C. (1980) 'Community Organization and Rural Development: A Learning Process Approach', *Public Administration Review*, vol. 40(5), pp. 480–511.

Korten, D. C. (1990) *Getting to the 21st Century: Voluntary Action and the Global Agenda* (West Hartford: Kumarian).

Korten, F. F. and Siy, R. Y. (eds) (1988) *Transforming a Bureaucracy: The Experience of the Philippine National Irrigation Authority* (Quezon City: Ateneo de Manila Press).

Kubr, M. and Wallace, J. (1983) 'Success and Failure in Meeting the Management Challenge: Strategies and Their Implications', *World Bank Staff Working Paper* No. 585 (Washington D.C.: World Bank).

Lane, J.-E. (1987) 'Introduction: The Concept of Bureaucracy', in J.-E. Lane (ed.), *Bureaucracy and Public Choice* (London: Sage), pp. 1–31.

Lane, J.-E. (1993) *The Public Sector* (London: Sage).

Larmour, P. (1990) 'Public Choice in Melanesia: Community, Bureaucracy and the Market in Land Management', *Public Administration and Development*, vol. 10(1), pp. 53–68.

Larmour, P. *et al.* (1985) *Decentralisation in the South Pacific* (Suva: University of the South Pacific).

Lawrence, P. R. and Lorsch, J. W. (1967) *Organization and Environment* (Cambridge, Mass.: Harvard University Press).

Leonard, D. K. (1982) 'Analysing the Organisational Requirements for Serving the Rural Poor', in D. K. Leonard and D. R. Marshall (eds), *Institutions of Rural Development for the Poor* (Berkeley: University of California Press), pp. 1–39.

Lewis, P. G. (1982) 'Obstacles to the Establishment of Political Legitimacy in Communist Poland', *British Journal of Political Science*, vol. 12(2), pp. 125–48.

Lindblom, C. E. (1959) 'The Science of Muddling Through', *Public Administration Review*, vol. 19(2), pp. 79–88.

Lindblom, C. E. (1979) 'Still Muddling, Not Yet Through', *Public Administration Review*, vol. 39(6), pp. 517–26.

Lindenberg, M. and Ramírez, N. (1989) *Managing Adjustment in Developing Countries* (San Francisco: ICS Press).

Lipton, M. (1977) *Why Poor People Stay Poor: A Study of Urban Bias in World Development* (London: Temple Smith).

Lorch, K. (1991) 'Privatization Through Sale: The Bangladeshi Textile Industry', in R. Ramamurti and R. Vernon (eds), *Privatization and Control of State-Owned Enterprises* (Washington D.C.: Economic Development Institute of the World Bank), pp. 126–52.

Mackintosh, M. (1992) 'Introduction', in M. Wuyts, M. Mackintosh and T. Hewitt (eds), *Development Policy and Public Action* (Oxford: Oxford University Press), pp. 1–12.

Maddick, H. (1963) *Democracy, Decentralisation and Development* (London: Asia Publishing House).

Maheshwari, S. (1990) 'Pruning Big Government: The Indian Experience', in M. Campbell and A. Hoyle (eds), *Government and People: Issues in Development* (Canberra: University of Canberra), pp. 58–74.

Manchester Papers on Development (1988) Special Issue on Integrated Rural Development, vol. 4(1).

March, J. G. (1984) 'Theories of Choice and Making Decisions', in R. Paton *et al.* (eds), *Organizations: Cases, Issues, Concepts* (London: Harper & Row), pp. 91–7.

March, J. G., Olsen, J. P. *et al.* (1976) *Ambiguity and Choice in Organizations* (Bergen: Universitetsforlaget).

Markowitz, I. L. (1977) *Power and Class in Africa: An Introduction to Change and Conflict in African Politics* (Englewood Cliffs: Prentice Hall).

Mascharenhas, J. *et al.* (1991) 'Participatory Rural Appraisal: Proceedings of the February 1991 Bangalore PRA Trainers' Workshop', *RRA Notes* 13 (London: International Institute for Environment and Development).

Mawhood, P. (1983) 'Decentralisation: The Concept and the Practice', in P. Mawhood (ed.), *Local Government in the Third World* (Chichester: Wiley), pp. 1–24.

Mawhood, P. (1987) 'Decentralisation and the Third World in the 1980s', *Planning and Administration*, vol. 14(1), pp. 10–22.

Max-Neef, M. A. (1991) *Human Scale Development* (London: Apex).

McCullogh, J. S. (1983) 'Financing Local Government Services in Developing Countries: Case Studies of Implementing Innovation', PhD thesis, University of North Carolina.

Meier, G. M. (ed.) (1991) *Politics and Policy Making in Developing Countries: Perspectives on the New Political Economy* (San Francisco: ICS Press).

Migdal, J. S. (1988) *Strong Societies and Weak States: State–Society Relations and State Capabilities in the Third World* (Princeton: Princeton University Press).

Miles, R. H. (1980) *Macro Organizational Behavior* (Santa Monica: Goodyear).

Mintzberg, H. (1979) *The Structuring of Organizations* (Englewood Cliffs: Prentice Hall).

Montgomery, J. D. (1972) 'Allocation of Authority in Land Reform Programs: A Comparative Study of Administrative Processes and Outputs', *Administrative Science Quarterly*, vol. 17(1), pp. 62–85.

Montgomery, J. D. (1988) *Bureaucrats and People: Grassroots Participation in Third World Development* (Baltimore: Johns Hopkins University Press).

Moore, M. (1993a) 'Introduction', *IDS Bulletin*, vol. 24(1), pp. 1–6.

Moore, M. (1993b) 'Declining to Learn from the East? The World Bank on "Governance and Development"', *IDS Bulletin*, vol. 24(1), pp. 39–50.

Moore, W. (1963) *Social Change* (Englewood Cliffs: Prentice Hall).

Moris, J. (1991) *Extension Alternatives for Tropical Africa* (London: Overseas Development Institute).

Morss, E. R. (1984) 'Institutional Destruction Resulting from Donor and Project Proliferation in sub-Saharan African Countries', *World Development*, vol. 12(4), pp. 465–70.

Moser, C. O. N. (1993) *Gender Planning and Development* (London: Routledge).

Mosley, P., Harrigan, J. and Toye, J. (1995) *Aid and Power: the World Bank and Policy-Based Lending*, 2nd edition (London: Routledge), 2 volumes, 1st edition 1991.

Mosse, D. (1994) 'Authority, Gender and Knowledge: Theoretical Reflections on the Practice of Participatory Rural Appraisal', *CDS Working Paper No. 2* (Swansea: Centre for Development Studies).

Munene, J. C. (1991) 'Organizational Environment in Africa: A Factor Analysis of Critical Incidents', *Human Relations*, vol. 44(5), pp. 439–58.

Murray, D. J. (1983) 'The World Bank's Perspective on How to Improve Administration', *Public Administration and Development*, vol. 3(4), pp. 291–8.

Myrdal, G. (1968) *Asian Drama: An Inquiry into the Poverty of Nations* (New York: Pantheon).

Narokobi, B. (1983) *Life and Leadership in Melanesia* (Suva and Port Moresby: Institute of Pacific Studies and University of Papua New Guinea).

Naya, S. (1990) *Private Sector Development and Enterprise Reforms in Growing Asian Economies* (San Francisco: International Center for Economic Growth).

Nellis, J. R. (1986) *Public Enterprises in Sub-Saharan Africa* (Washington D.C.: World Bank).

Nellis, M. and Kikeri, S. (1989) 'Public Enterprise Reform: Privatization and the World Bank', *World Development*, vol. 17(5), pp. 659–72.

Nerfin, M. (1986) 'Neither Prince nor Merchant: An Introduction to the Third System', *IFDA Dossier*, 56, pp. 3–29.

Nordlinger, E. A. (1987) 'Taking the State Seriously', in M. Weiner and S. P. Huntington (eds), *Understanding Political Development* (Boston: Little Brown), pp. 353–90.

Nunberg, B. and Ellis, J. (1990) 'Civil Service Reform and the World Bank', *Policy Research and External Affairs Working Papers*, no. 422, World Bank.

Nyerere, J. K. (1966) *Freedom and Unity: A Selection from Writings and Speeches, 1952–1965* (Dar es Salaam: Oxford University Press).

O'Brien, D. B. C. (1991) 'The Show of State in a Neo-colonial Twilight: Francophone Africa', in J. Manor (ed.), *Rethinking Third World Politics* (London: Longman), pp. 145–65.

Oakley, P. and Marsden, D. (1984) *Approaches to Participation in Rural Development* (Geneva: ILO).

Oberst, R. (1986) 'Administrative Conflict and Decentralisation: The Case of Sri Lanka', *Public Administration and Development*, vol. 6(2), pp. 163–74

ODA (Overseas Development Administration) (1993) 'Good Government', *Technical Note*, No. 10 (London: ODA).

ODA (Overseas Development Administration) (1995) *A Guide to Social Analysis for Projects in Developing Countries* (London: HMSO).

ODI (Overseas Development Institute) (1986) 'Privatisation: The Developing Country Experience', *Briefing Paper* (September).

OECD (1988) *Voluntary Aid for Development: The Role of NGOs* (Paris: OECD).

Oldenburg, P. (1987) 'Middlemen in Third World Corruption: Implications of an Indian Case', *World Politics*, vol. 39(4), pp. 508–35.

Osborne, D. and Gaebler, T. (1992) *Reinventing Government* (New York: Plume).

Ostrom, V. and Ostrom, E. (1971) 'Public Choice: A Different Approach to the Study of Public Administration', *Public Administration Review*, 31.

Ouma, S. O. A. (1991) 'Corruption in Public Policy and its Impact on Development: The Case of Uganda since 1979', *Public Administration and Development*, vol. 11(5), pp. 473–90.

OXFAM (1988) *Field Director's Handbook* (Oxford: OXFAM).

Pamudji, S. (1992) 'An Overview of Recent Administrative Reform in Indonesia', in Z. Zhijian, R. P. De Guzman and M. A. Reforma (eds), *Administrative Reform Towards Promoting Productivity in Bureaucratic Performance* (Manila: EROPA), pp. 93–6.

Paul, S. (1991) 'Accountability in Public Service: Exit, Voice and Capture', *Policy Research and External Affairs Working Papers* WPS 614, World Bank.

Pearce, J. (1997) 'Between Cooption and Irrelevance? Latin American NGOs in the 1990s', in D. Hulme and M. Edwards (eds), *NGOs, States and Donors:*

Too Close for Comfort? (London: Macmillan, and New York: St Martin's Press).

Peiqing, Y. (1992) 'Social Progress and Women's Participation in Politics: The role of Chinese women in Public Administration', *Asian Review of Public Administration*, vol.4(1), pp. 35–42.

Pereira, L. C. B. (1993) 'Economic Reforms and Cycles of State Intervention', *World Development*, vol. 21(8), pp. 1337–53.

Pfeffer, J. and Salancik, G. R. (1978) *The External Control of Organizations: a Resource Dependence Perspective* (New York: Harper & Row).

Pollitt, C. (1993) *Managerialism and the Public Services* (Oxford: Blackwell).

Porter, D. *et al.* (1991) *Development in Practice: Paved With Good Intentions* (London: Routledge).

Praxy, F. and Sicherl, P. (eds) (1981) *Seeking the Personality of Public Enterprise* (Ljubljana: International Centre for Public Enterprises in Developing Countries).

Quah, J. S. T. (1976) 'Administrative Reform: A Conceptual Analysis', *Philippine Journal of Public Administration*, vol. 20(1), pp. 50–67.

Rahman, A. B. A. (1995) 'Administrative Improvements in the Malaysian Civil Service: Implementation of the Client's Charter', *Asian Review of Public Administration*, vol. 7(2), pp. 53–66.

Randel, J. and German, T. (1993) *The Reality of Aid 93* (London: ICVA, Eurostep and ActionAid).

Ranis, G. and Stewart, F. (1993) *Government Decentralisation and Participation* (Geneva: UNDP).

Ray, A. and Kumptala, J. (1987) 'Zilla Parishad Presidents in Karnataka: Their Social Background and Implications for Development', *Economic and Political Weekly*, 17–24 Oct, pp. 1825–30.

Reilly, W. (1987) 'Management and training for development: the Hombe thesis', *Public Administration and Development*, vol. 7(1), pp. 25–42

Richter, L. (1990) 'Exploring Theories of Female Leadership in South and Southeast Asia', *Pacific Affairs*, vol. 63(4), pp. 524–40.

Riddell, R. (1987) *Foreign Aid Reconsidered* (London: Overseas Development Institute).

Riddell, R. and Robinson, M. (1995) *Non-Governmental Organizations and Rural Poverty Alteration* (Oxford: Clarendon Press).

Riggs, F. (1964) *Administration in Developing Countries: The Theory of Prismatic Society* (Boston: Houghton Mifflin).

Riggs, F. (1966) *Thailand: The Modernization of a Bureaucratic Polity* (Honolulu: East–West Center).

Robbins, S. P. and Barnwell, N. (1994) *Organisation Theory in Australia*, 2nd edition (Sydney: Prentice Hall).

Robinson, D. (1990) 'Civil Service Remuneration in Africa', *International Labour Review*, vol. 129(3), pp. 371–465.

Robinson, M. (1992) 'NGOs and Rural Poverty Alleviation: Implications for Scaling-up', in M. Edwards and D. Hulme (eds), *Making a Difference: NGOs and Development in a Changing World* (London: Earthscan), pp. 28–39.

Robinson, M. (1993) 'Will Political Conditionality Work?', *IDS Bulletin*, vol. 24(1), pp. 58–66.

Robison, R. (1986) *Indonesia: The Rise of Capital* (Sydney: Allen & Unwin).

Rondinelli, D. A. (1981) 'Government Decentralisation in Comparative Perspective', *International Review of Administrative Sciences*, vol. 47(2), pp. 133–45.

Rondinelli, D. A. (1983) *Development Projects as Policy Experiments: An Adaptive Approach to Development Administration*, 1st edition (London: Methuen).

Rondinelli, D. A. (1992) 'UNDP Assistance for Urban Development: An Assessment of Institution-building Efforts in Developing Countries', *International Review of Administrative Sciences*, vol. 58(4), pp. 519–37.

Rondinelli, D. A. (1993) *Development Projects as Policy Experiments: An Adaptive Approach to Development Administration*, 2nd edition (London: Routledge).

Rondinelli, D. A. and Minis, H. P. Jr (1990) 'Administrative Restructuring for Economic Adjustment: Decentralisation Policy in Senegal', *International Review of Administrative Sciences*, vol. 56(3), pp. 447–66.

Rondinelli, D. A. and Nellis, J. R. (1986) 'Assessing Decentralisation Policies in Developing Countries: A Case for Cautious Optimism', *Development Policy Review*, vol. 4(1), pp. 3–23.

Rondinelli, D. A., McCullogh, J. S. and Johnson, R. W. (1989) 'Analysing Decentralisation Policies in Developing Countries: A Political-economy Framework', *Development and Change*, vol. 20(1), pp. 57–87.

Rowat, D. C. (1990) 'Comparing Bureaucracies in Developed and Developing Countries: A Statistical Analysis', *International Review of Administrative Sciences*, vol. 56(2), pp. 211–36.

Ruffing-Hilliard, K. (1991) 'Merit Reform in Latin America: A Comparative Perspective', in A. Farazmand (ed.), *Handbook of Comparative and Development Public Aministration* (New York: Marcel Dekker), pp. 301–12.

Saasa, O. S., (1985) 'Public Policy-making in Developing Countries; The Utility of Contemporary Decision-making Models', *Public Administration and Development*, vol. 5(4), pp. 309–22.

Sachs, W. (1992) 'Development: A Guide to the Ruins', *New Internationalist*, June, pp. 4–6.

Sagasti, F. R. (1988) 'National Development Planning in Turbulent Times: New Approaches and Criteria for Institutional Design', *World Development*, vol. 16(4), pp. 431–48.

Salamon, L. (1993) 'The Global Associational Revolution: The Rise of the Third Sector on the World scene', *Institute for Policy Studies Occasional Paper no.15* (Baltimore: Johns Hopkins University).

Samonte, A. G. (1970) 'Patterns and Trends in Administrative Reform', in H-B. Lee and A. G. Samonte (eds), *Administrative Reforms in Asia* (Manila: EROPA), pp. 287–302.

Sandbrook, R. (1985) *The Politics of Africa's Economic Stagnation* (Cambridge: Cambridge University Press).

Schaffer, B. B. (1969) 'The Deadlock in Development Administration', in C. Leys (ed.), *Politics and Change in Developing Countries* (Cambridge: Cambridge University Press), pp. 177–211.

Schaffer, B. B. (1974) 'Introduction: The Ideas and Institutions of Training', in B. Schaffer (ed.), *Administrative Training and Development: A Comparative Study of East Africa, Zambia, Pakistan and India* (New York: Praeger), pp. 1–68.

Schaffer, B. B. (1984) 'Towards Responsibility: Public Policy in Concept and Practice', in E. J. Clay and B. B. Schaffer (eds), *Room for Manoeuvre: An Exploration of Public Policy in Agricultural and Rural Development* (London: Methuen), pp. 142–90.

Schumacher, E. F. (1973) *Small is Beautiful: Economics as if People Mattered* (New York: Harper & Row).

Seers, D. (1977) 'The Meaning of Development', *International Development Review*, vol. 19(22), pp. 2–7.

Shih, C-Y. (1994) 'A Research Note on School Enterprise in China', *Asian Profile*, vol. 22(3), pp. 177–87.

Shirley, M. and Nellis, J. (1991) *Public Enterprise Reform: The Lessons of Experience* (Washington D.C.: World Bank).

Shivji, I. G. (1976) *Class Struggles in Tanzania* (London: Heinemann).

Siddiquee, N. A. and Hulme, D. (1994) 'Decentralization and Development in Bangladesh: Theory and Practice', *IDPM Discussion Paper* No. 37 (Manchester: IDPM).

Siffin, W. J. (1976) 'Two Decades of Public Administration in Developing Countries', *Public Administration Review*, vol. 36(1), pp. 61–71.

Simon, H. A. (1957) *Administrative Behaviour*, 2nd edition (Macmillan: London).

Sklar, R. L. (1979) 'The Nature of Class Domination in Africa', *Journal of Modern African Studies*, vol. 17(4), pp. 531–52.

Slater, D. (1989) 'Territorial Power and the Peripheral State: The Issue of Decentralisation', *Development and Change*, vol. 20(3), pp. 501–31.

Smith, A. (1980) *How Western Culture Dominates the World* (Oxford: Oxford University Press).

Smith, B. C. (1985) *Decentralisation: The Territorial Dimension of the State* (London: George Allen & Unwin).

Smith, W. E., Lethem, F. J. and Thoolen, B. A. (1981) 'The Design of Organizations for Rural Development Projects – A Progress Report', *World Bank Staff Working Paper*, no. 375.

Standish, B. (1983) 'Power to the People? Decentralisation in Papua New Guinea', *Public Administration and Development*, vol. 3(3), pp. 223–38.

Sto Tomas, P. A. (1995) 'Client Satisfaction as a Performance Measure in the Philippine Civil Service', *Asian Review of Public Administration*, vol. 7(2), pp. 100–7.

Stone, D. C. (1965) 'Government Machinery Necessary for Development', in M. Kriesberg (ed.), *Public Administration in Developing Countries* (Washington D.C.: The Brookings Institution), pp. 49–67.

Streeten, P. (1993) 'Markets and States: Against Minimalism', *World Development*, vol. 21(8), pp. 1281–98.

Sweezy, P. M. (1982) 'Center, Periphery and the Crisis of the System', in H. Alavi and T. Shanin (eds), *Introduction to the Sociology of 'Developing' Societies* (London: Macmillan), pp. 210-17.

Swerdlow, I. (1975) *The Public Administration of Economic Development* (New York: Praeger).

Tang, M. and Thant, M. (1994) 'Growth Triangles: Conceptual Issues and Operational Problems', *Economic Staff Paper*, no. 54, Asian Development Bank.

Taylor, F. W. (1911) *The Principles of Scientific Management* (New York: Harper & Row).

Teka, T. (1994) 'International NGOs in Ethiopia: A Case Study of Wolaita', Ph.D thesis, University of Cambridge.

Tendler, J. (1987) 'Livelihood, Employment and Income-generating Activities' (New York: Ford Foundation).

Terray, E. (1986) 'Le climatiseur et la veranda', in *Afrique Plurielle: Hommage a George Balandier* (Paris) *The Pacific Review* (1992) vol. 5(4), special issue on the New Rich in Asia.

Thomas, J. W. and Grindle, M. S. (1990) 'After the Decision: Implementing Policy Reforms in Developing Countries', *World Development*, vol. 18(8), pp. 1163–81.

Thompson, J. D. (1967) *Organizations in Action* (New York: McGraw-Hill).

Tinker, I. (1990) 'A Context for the Field and for the Book', in I. Tinker (ed.), *Persistent Inequalities: Women and World Development* (New York: Oxford University Press), pp. 3–13.

Todaro, M. P. (1994) *Economic Development*, 5th edition (London: Longman).

Toulabor, C. M. (1986) *Le Togo sous Eyadema* (Paris: Karthala).

Toye, J. (1987) *Dilemmas of Development* (Oxford: Basil Blackwell).

Turner, M. (1989) '"Trainingism" revisited in Papua New Guinea', *Public Administration and Development*, vol. 9(1), pp. 17–28.

Turner, M. (1990a) 'Authoritarian Rule and the Dilemma of Legitimacy: The Case of President Marcos of the Philippines', *The Pacific Review*, vol. 3(4), pp. 349–62.

Turner, M. (1990b) *Papua New Guinea: The Challenge of Independence* (Ringwood: Penguin).

Turner, M. (1991) 'Issues and Reforms in the Papua New Guinea Public Service Since Independence', *Journal de la Societe des Oceanistes*, vol. 92–93 (1&2), pp. 97–104.

Turner, M. (1995) 'Subregional Economic Zones, Politics and Development: The Philippine Involvement in the East ASEAN Growth Area (EAGA)', *The Pacific Review*, vol. 8(4), pp. 637–48.

Umeh, O. J. (1992) 'Capacity Building and Development Administration in Southern African Countries', *International Review of Administrative Sciences*, vol. 58(1), pp. 57–70.

UNDP (United Nations Development Programme) (1992) *Human Development Report 1992* (New York: Oxford University Press).

UNDP (United Nations Development Programme) (1996) *Human Development Report 1996* (New York: Oxford University Press).

Uphoff, N. (1992) *Learning from Gal Oya: Possibilities for Participatory Development and Post-Newtonian Social Science* (New York: Cornell University Press).

Uphoff, N. (1995) 'Why NGOs are not a Third Sector', in M. Edwards and D. Hulme (eds), *Non-Governmental Organizations - Performance and Accountability: Beyond the Magic Bullet* (London: Earthscan) pp. 17–30.

Van de Walle, N. (1989) 'Privatization in Developing Countries: A Review of the Issues', *World Development*, vol. 17(5), pp. 601–15.

Van der Gaag, J. (1995) *Private and Public Initiatives: Working Together for Health and Education* (Washington D.C.: World Bank), pp. 35–7.

Van Ufford, P. Q. (1988) 'The Hidden Crisis in Development: Development Bureaucracies in between Intentions and Outcomes', in P. Q. van Ufford, D. Krujit and T. Downing (eds), *The Hidden Crisis in Development Bureaucracies* (Tokyo and Amsterdam: The UN University and Free University Press), pp. 9–38.

Wallerstein, I. (1979) *The Capitalist World-Economy* (Cambridge: Cambridge University Press).

Wallis, M. (1990a) *Bureaucracy: Its Role in Third World Development* (London: Macmillan).

Wallis, M. (1990b) 'District Planning and Local Government in Kenya', *Public Administration and Development*, vol. 10(4), pp. 437–54.

Waterston, A. (1965) *Development Planning: Lessons of Experience* (Baltimore: Johns Hopkins University Press).

Weick, K. E. (1977) 'Enactment Processes in Organizations', in B. M. Staw and G. Salancik (eds), *New Directions in Organizational Behavior* (Chicago: St Clair Press), pp. 267–300.

Wilson, E. (1986) 'The Public–Private Debate', *Africa Report*, July-August.

Wongtrangan, K. (1988) 'Thai Bureaucratic Behaviour: The Impact of Dual Values on Public Policies', in T. G. Lim (ed.), *Reflections on Development in Southeast Asia* (Singapore: Institute of Southeast Asian Studies), pp. 49–79.

Woon, T. K. (1991) 'The Role of the State in Southeast Asia', in N.C. Yuen and N. Wagner (eds), *Marketization in ASEAN* (Singapore: Institute of Southeast Asian Studies), pp. 11–24.

World Bank (1983) *World Development Report 1983* (New York: Oxford University Press).

World Bank (1987) *The Jengka Triangle Projects in Malaysia: Impact Evaluation Report* (Washington D.C.: World Bank).

World Bank (1988) *Rural Development: World Bank Experience 1965–86* (Washington D.C.: World Bank).

World Bank (1989) *Sub-Saharan Africa: From Crisis to Sustainable Growth* (Washington D.C.: World Bank).

World Bank (1990) *World Development Report 1990* (New York: Oxford University Press).

World Bank (1991) *World Development Report 1991* (New York: Oxford University Press).

World Bank (1992a) *World Development Report 1992* (New York: Oxford University Press).

World Bank (1992b) *Governance and Development* (Washington D.C.: World Bank).

World Bank (1993) *The East Asian Miracle: Economic Growth and Public Policy* (New York: Oxford University Press).

World Bank (1994) *World Development Report 1994* (New York: Oxford University Press).

World Bank (1995a) *World Development Report 1995* (New York: Oxford University Press).

World Bank (1995b) *Bureaucrats in Business: The Economics and Politics of Government Ownership* (New York: World Bank).

World Bank (1996) *World Development Report 1996* (New York: Oxford University Press).

Wraith, R. (1972) *Local Administration in West Africa* (New York: Africana Publishing Corporation).

Wynia, G. W. (1990) *The Politics of Latin American Development*, 3rd edition (Cambridge: Cambridge University Press).

Zifcak, S. (1994) *New Managerialism: Administrative Reform in Whitehall and Canberra* (Buckingham: Open University Press).

Zinkin, M. (1953) *Asia and the West* (London: Chatto & Windus).

Index